UNDER DEVIL'S PEAK

The life and times of Wilfrid Cooper,
an advocate in the age of apartheid

GAVIN COOPER

Published by Mercury
an imprint of Burnet Media

•

Burnet Media is the publisher of Mercury and Two Dogs books
info@burnetmedia.co.za   www.burnetmedia.co.za
PO Box 53557, Kenilworth, 7745, South Africa

•

First published 2016
1 3 5 7 9 8 6 4 2

•

Distributed by Jacana Media
www.jacana.co.za

•

Printed and bound by Paarl Media
www.paarlmedia.co.za

•

ISBN 9781928230366

Set in Adobe Caslon Pro 12pt

UNDER DEVIL'S PEAK

'I would say that the whole life of any thinking African in this country is driven continuously to a conflict between his conscience on the one hand and the law on the other ... The law as it is applied, the law as it has been developed over a long period of history, and especially the law as it is written by the Nationalist government is a law which in our view is immoral, unjust and intolerable. Our consciences dictate that we must protest against it, that we must oppose it and that we must attempt to alter it.'

– NELSON MANDELA, 1962

To Wilfrid and Gertrude,
who from humble beginnings achieved much in their lives
and did as much as they could for others

CONTENTS

FOREWORD
by Amanda Botha

As a student I was fascinated by the law profession and enthusiastically read reports of court cases in *Die Burger*. My first memory of a significant case dates back to 1961, when Marthinus Rossouw was accused of the sensational murder of Baron von Schauroth. The Von Schauroths lived in a block of flats in Gardens, the part of Cape Town where I grew up – one of many references in the case to places and people I was familiar with. And so I became acquainted with the name of Wilfrid Cooper in this roundabout manner – through newspaper reports of the trial in which he argued in defence that Rossouw had been contracted as a hired killer by the person killed. I followed the case, and Wilfrid's role in it, closely.

Five years later, as a junior reporter at *Die Burger*, I became involved in covering the hearing of Demitrio Tsafendas, who had assassinated the Prime Minister, HF Verwoerd, in the House of Assembly. I had learnt that Wilfrid Cooper would be the defence advocate and, with youthful impetuosity, introduced myself to him. It was the most important case of the day, and Wilfrid played a starring role in it.

A few years later I met Wilfrid again in the company of his wife, Gertrude, then a social reporter with the *Cape Times*. A special working relationship and friendship started, continuing until 2001, shortly before Gertrude's death. We mostly met at social gatherings and always shared a chat, often about court cases. Wilfrid also often spoke about his interest in writing –

not only law publications, but creative writing, which he worked at unbeknown to others. When speaking about his favourite author, James Joyce, he would become animated and enthusiastic.

One day in their garden in Newlands after a Sunday lunch, Wilfrid told me that Verwoerd's death in 1966 could have been the death knell for apartheid. It was an unconscious motivation, he also said, that by defending those who were accused of opposing apartheid, he could make his own contribution to its dismantling. He knew that he would pay a high price for defending them and would be denied advancement in the judicial system or profitable government appointments. As an advocate, Wilfrid would sometimes have no work at all, earning an income only by lecturing at the University of Cape Town. He also knew that he had the attention of the Security Police, especially for taking on inquests into the deaths of political detainees that no-one else would touch. I always admired the fact that, however precarious Wilfrid's position, he fearlessly stood by his convictions, doing what he knew he should without compromise.

Wilfrid enthusiastically collected newspaper reports of the cases in which he acted. This allowed me my first 'collaboration' with him: I made sure he received enough Afrikaans newspapers to make up a complete set of clippings. When he had filed his clippings after a case, he would send me a letter of thanks in his spidery handwriting. That is who he was: an empathetic, endearing, humble man who never lost the simple decency of gratitude and acknowledgement.

Wilfrid and I had several friends in common, such as former Judge President Helm van Zijl, politician Japie Basson and writers Elsa Joubert and Klaas Steytler. We often discussed the fact that he was time and again overlooked for an appointment to the Bench, the consensus being that it was because he had defended 'terrorists'. When he was eventually offered a position, it was in the Eastern Cape. He was grateful but also disappointed, because he had to leave his family behind in Cape Town. Thankfully, he was later transferred to the Cape Supreme Court, where he served until his retirement in 1998.

A few months before he retired, Wilfrid invited me to dinner and told me that he had to step down for health reasons. He wanted to spend the time writing his memoirs while he was still able to and invited me to work with him. After his retirement we met at his and Gertrude's Constantia townhouse. He had gathered many files with notes he'd made on his various court cases. We started reading them in his study, where he told me what he intended with his memoirs and what role he wanted me to play. Sadly, our efforts did not proceed as hoped because of his and Gertrude's declining health. It was a great sadness of his that he lost the opportunity to account for his life and career.

Subsequently, Wilfrid invited me to walk with him in the vineyards at Groot Constantia. I remember a frail man who for the first time revealed to me his disappointment in certain people in positions of power whom he had once defended and who now barely acknowledged him. Now, years later, I remember him for his brilliant insights and the way he expressed them – a man who was prepared to pay a high price to remain true to his conscience. He was not a man of compromises and he was prepared to give things up as long as his humanity remained intact. I also remember him as a man of compassion, an honest man who served his profession with dignity and honour. For me he signified what it meant to be a friend – a friend of value – someone on whom you could always rely.

I hope this overdue account serves as a marker of a proud man who did the right thing in difficult times, and of his remarkable and honourable career.

INTRODUCTION

J ust after lunch on the afternoon of Tuesday, 6 September 1966, a relaxed atmosphere prevailed in the Houses of Parliament in Cape Town. By all accounts it was a lovely early spring day and members of Parliament, back from enjoying a long weekend, milled around, exchanging pleasantries and talking in the lobby outside the House of Assembly as they prepared to enter for the afternoon session. There was a sense of expectation that the Prime Minister, Dr Verwoerd, who had not attended Parliament for some time, was going to deliver an important speech.

In the normality of the occasion little attention was paid to a thickset, swarthy man in the blue uniform of a messenger, who was also waiting in the lobby outside the door to the chamber. Back from lunch at his official residence, Groote Schuur, in Rondebosch, a jovial Verwoerd arrived with his wife, Betsie. He kissed her goodbye as she went to the upstairs visitors' gallery from where she could watch him deliver his much anticipated speech. Just before entering the House, he took leave of his secretary and personal bodyguard, who also went upstairs to the gallery. Verwoerd walked through the chamber and had just seated himself at his bench when the messenger entered and, as though delivering a message, bustled towards him, fiddling with his clothes. When a few feet away, he drew a dagger, removed its sheath, dived across the bench and plunged it into the Prime Minister's chest. Such was the force of the blow that the dagger was buried to the hilt. After a brief pause the messenger pulled the dagger out and stabbed Verwoerd a further three times before he was tackled by members of Parliament and forcibly dragged away from the mortally wounded Prime Minister, who now lay slumped in his seat.

All this took place when I was seven and in Sub B. I have little recollection of what exactly happened at the time but I do recall that I became a minor celebrity in the playground when the local newspapers reported that my father would defend the assassin, Demitrio Tsafendas. As I got older, I came to realise how different my father was from my friends' fathers, who appeared to lead less public lives. My parents were also active on the Cape Town social scene and entertained regularly at home. Their 25th wedding anniversary was almost a who's who of Cape Town's rich and famous.

In time I started to pay more attention to the newspapers and read about the inquest into the death of Imam Abdullah Haron while in police detention; and about the trial of Robert Kemp for demonstrating with other University of Cape Town students on the steps of St George's Cathedral. Wilfrid and I discussed the sensational Marlene Lehnberg trial, especially his reasons for appealing against the initial judgment, and I recall his sense of achievement at having her death sentence reduced to a jail term. The Swakopmund SWAPO trial, in which he was involved, became quite real for me, as it was I who took the original call from the Windhoek attorneys asking Wilfrid to represent the six SWAPO accused; and, after the trial, we travelled together on holiday to Swakopmund and saw the court. There were many other well-known people whom he chose to defend, then mostly on the political fringes but now big names in the history of the liberation struggle. Among them were Steve Biko, Mapetla Mohapi, David Rabkin and Jeremy Cronin.

When I turned 18, I obtained a driver's licence and soon took over from my mother the task of driving my father back and forth to the airport when he flew to cases around the country. His battered briefcase was festooned with luggage tags like winning rosettes. In April 1978, on a pass from the army when

I was stationed as a conscript at Voortrekkerhoogte, I spent a weekend with him at the Sunnyside Park hotel in Johannesburg, which was his base for the Bethal treason trial. In 1989, when he was on the Bench in the Eastern Cape, I again spent time with him while on leave from my work. He was enjoying the challenges of the Bench but missed home and Gertrude. Soon thereafter, he was back in Cape Town and making the most of his time on the Cape Bench and his walks in Newlands Forest.

When Gertrude died in April 2002 and Wilfrid in March 2004, I realised I had only a patchwork of memories of my father and knew little detail of what he had done and the contribution he had made to help bring about the momentous changes in South Africa that occurred in the early 1990s. Time was moving on and memories were blurring fast. All this spurred me on to embark on the project of writing a book to record his and Gertrude's achievements. It was the least I could do for both of them. They had come from simple beginnings, being the children of railway employees, but with hard work they had established themselves in their respective professions and at the same time been wonderful parents to my two sisters and me.

Gertrude worked for the *Cape Times* for just over forty years, latterly as the social editor, and after retirement she took a job with a public relations company, which she held for another ten years. Wilfrid started his working career as a clerk in the Senate and then rose to become a Senior Counsel at the Cape Bar, a respected writer of books on South African law, an academic with two doctorates, and finally, and belatedly, a judge of the Supreme Court.

Gertrude was the rock of the family, always active (for eight months of the year she swam forty lengths of the swimming pool almost every day), always on the go right until the end. With Wilfrid away so often on cases, she took on the full responsibility of attending to the wellbeing of the family and home – and this while working full-time at the *Cape Times*, which would often require her to attend functions five nights of the week. She fiercely believed in all of us and was the family goad to achieve more or better. While often critical of Wilfrid, she would champion him at every turn. She always believed he could do things better – such as improve his writing style, for she had a great command of English – and would spend hours with him polishing sections of his books. She would not defer to him if she believed she was right. This often led to quite heated squabbles, as Wilfrid could be equally stubborn.

Despite having written a number of books on law, the book Wilfrid never succeeded in writing was that of his life. Work was his life: his cases, his teaching and examining duties at the University of Cape Town, and his writing of legal books. His recreation was confined to reading (much of it James Joyce), a little overseas travel and occasional forays into the veld to shoot a buck or game bird, or to fly-fish one of the rivers of the Western Cape. He would also restlessly walk the lower slopes of Table Mountain.

After ill health forced him to retire from the Bench, he set out to write his memoirs, but as his mind lost its sharpness and his mobility declined, the project slipped further and further away from realisation. Gertrude endeavoured to assist him, but they had divergent ideas, sometimes quite argumentatively expressed, as to what form the book should take. She was a sharp journalist and he was an advocate and academic, so it was a case of oil and water when it came to approach and style. He wanted to follow his literary hero, James Joyce, and produce a definitive work called *The Quest for Mimis*, which would centre on Demitrio Tsafendas and his assassination of Hendrik Verwoerd. She wanted something down to earth that could be read easily by all.

The death knell of the project came in early 2002, when Wilfrid left his study door unlocked one night and the computer on which everything had been typed was stolen. Sadly, there were no backups, and only bits and pieces of his memoirs remained in hard copy. Gertrude died a few months after this and, with her gone, there was no one to cajole and push him, as she had done for all their married life. The project came to a halt.

After Wilfrid's death I took up the challenge of writing his book. Though its production has been drawn out over the subsequent years, the time I have spent on it has been stimulating for me, not only in learning about my father but also in weaving what he did into the fabric of South African history. It is my hope that it will serve as a worthy record of his life and that of his beloved 'Skattie', and that it walks the line between the two rather different books that each wanted.

CHAPTER 1

EARLY YEARS: KLAWER, MALMESBURY AND WYNBERG

Wilfrid's formative years, spent at first in the small country towns of the platteland, where he developed an independence of mind and spirit and an awareness of the deep divisions in society

'He has been regular and punctual in his attendance, his conduct has been excellent and he has been a conscientious and painstaking pupil who has made very satisfactory progress in his work. He has shown himself trustworthy and reliable and he leaves with an unblemished record.'

– EXTRACT FROM WILFRID'S
HIGH SCHOOL LEAVING TESTIMONIAL

I have always felt a strong connection with the southern suburbs of Cape Town. This no doubt can be attributed to the fact that four generations of Cooper men have all lived at the foot of Devil's Peak. My father, Wilfrid Edward Cooper, was born in Scott Road, Observatory, on 22 May 1926. He was named after his father's best friend and Edward, Prince of Wales, who had visited South Africa in May of the previous year.

Wilfrid was one of three children: the first-born, John, died in infancy, and his younger sister, Nancy, was born in November 1930. Their father, Victor Norman Cooper, who had been born in Woodstock, was, like his own father, William Henry, an engine driver for the South African Railways. William, in fact, was one of the men who drove the funeral train of Cecil John Rhodes from Cape Town in April 1902, carrying the body of the arch imperialist to its burial place in the Matopos in what is now Zimbabwe, for which William was presented with a commemorative medal.

In 1933, when Wilfrid was six, his father secured a promotion and was transferred to the small town of Klawer on the banks of the Olifants River, some 300 kilometres from Cape Town. Here the family lived for three years in one of the *sinkhokke* – the wood-and-corrugated iron railway cottages – along the line near Klawer station. The railway served as the conduit for supplies to the district, whose agricultural products – grapes and lucerne – were then sent by train to Cape Town and other markets. The district is sparsely vegetated, with low rainfall, and in summer the temperatures can be very high. Wilfrid's mother, Rose, would then make him stay indoors and order him to rest under his bed until it cooled down, whereupon he could venture outdoors again.

The railway line linking Klawer to Cape Town runs over a bridge spanning the Olifants River. Along the river there are numerous vineyards and green lucerne fields irrigated by a network of canals. In winter the river usually flows strongly, being fed by melted snow from the catchment areas in the Cederberg mountains; but in summer it is dry and largely waterless except for stagnant pools of brown-green water. Around the pools are dense reeds where swarms of raucous green, yellow and red weaver birds spend hours making their intricate, upside-down nests, as well as small reed warblers, usually unseen but identifiable by their call of *cheerup-chee-trrrree*.

While still young, Wilfrid was given a Diana air rifle by his father for Christmas, an expensive gift for a boy in a poor country town. Wilfrid treasured it and years later passed it on to me. With the air rifle, either alone or sometimes with his friend Koos Geldenhuys, he would trek across the countryside hunting birds. The love of the veld and of hunting that he acquired stayed with him for the rest of his life. He was at his happiest in the veld, learning about the animal and bird life and the plants, as well as appreciating the solitude of the vast landscape.

Growing up in Klawer imbued Wilfrid with a love for the life of small country communities. In later life he strove to recapture some of this feeling by regularly taking up legal cases in *platteland* towns, which were often disdained by many of his colleagues. A lot of the social life of Klawer took place in the general dealers' stores. His mother patronised Brewer's store, which was situated near the railway station, and would visit it most days to buy odds and ends, accompanied by Wilfrid. Sometimes a commercial traveller's motor car would be parked outside the shop – a sure sign for customers that they should come in and investigate what new wares were on offer. With the flurry of activity in his shop, a jovial Mr Brewer would comment: 'Mrs Cooper, Klawer is getting more like London by the day.'

From time to time Wilfrid would be allowed onto the footplate of his father's steam locomotive. Initially he found it a frightening experience, what with the heat from the furnace, the noise and the violent hissing of steam. Then the fear subsided and it became exciting for him to be in the cab as the locomotive rumbled along the tracks. At night an element of mystery would be added: the darkened countryside would rush past the locomotive, while inside Wilfrid was conscious of the contrast offered by the red and orange flickering light emanating from the furnace. As a student Wilfrid recalled this vivid experience when reading the priest's description of hell in James Joyce's *A Portrait of the Artist as a Young Man*: 'the fire of hell, while retaining the intensity of its heat, burns eternally in darkness. It is a never ending storm of darkness, dark flames and dark smoke of burning brimstone, amid which the bodies are heaped one upon another without even a glimpse of air.'

Wilfrid's father left him very much to his own devices. With the confident feeling that his father trusted his judgement, Wilfrid developed an independence in thought and spirit and a sense of responsibility that would stand him well in life. Even before he went to school, Victor put him by himself on the passenger train to Bitterfontein to visit the family of a fellow railwayman there. While it was a relatively short trip, he had to converse en route with people he did not know, and in this and other ways he gained the self-confidence that stood him in good stead in later years. Wilfrid's ability to interact with strangers left us amazed when my sisters and I grew up and travelled with him. Wherever we went, it appeared that he knew someone. We came to think that we could leave him in any *dorp* in South Africa and he would know someone, or know of someone, who lived there.

In Klawer, Wilfrid was also exposed to the economic harshness of life in the district. As an engine driver his father was relatively well-off, and the family had a comfortable house and an acceptable standard of living. While Wilfrid wore sandals, many of his friends, whose fathers were mostly mere labourers, went barefoot and only wore shoes for special occasions such as church or funerals. He recalled the funeral of a young girl by the name of Margarethe du Plessis, who had died unexpectedly, which was attended by the school children dressed in their best. It was a hot day and the cemetery was about three miles outside the town along a dirt road. Not used to walking this distance in shoes, most of the boys' feet soon started hurting, so they took them off and walked barefoot, the hard soles of their feet impervious to the stones.

If the whites were mostly poor, the local 'coloured' people were impoverished and largely unemployed. A few of the women had jobs as domestic workers in houses in the town, but casual work for the men was scarce and they survived by their wits. From this Wilfrid developed both an awareness of social and economic inequalities and injustice, and a sense of fairness towards those less fortunate than he was.

At the beginning of 1933, when Wilfrid was six-and-a-half, he began to attend the small co-educational white junior school in Klawer. By the time he started school he was already comfortable speaking both English and Afrikaans and could think and express himself equally well in both languages. Then in 1935 his father was notified that he would be transferred to Malmesbury. This delighted his mother, Rose, as Malmesbury was not only bigger than Klawer, but was much closer to Cape Town and therefore to her family and the people she knew. The furniture was packed into wooden crates and placed in a railway truck, their house was emptied of its belongings and they embarked on the train, which soon rumbled past the *sinkhokke* that had been his home, and crossed the high bridge over the Olifants River. Wilfrid felt a great wrench leaving his friends, but he took with him an accumulation of memories and experiences and a connection with the *platteland* that would remain with him, and influence him, for the rest of his life.

*

The town of Malmesbury was much bigger than Klawer and had grown to be the largest town in the Swartland. The main road north to Moorreesburg and Piketberg ran through its centre, past the Dutch Reformed and Anglican churches and the important businesses of the town. The Dutch Reformed Church, as in most South African *platteland* towns, was very active in the area and emphasised the devout Calvinist persuasions of the population. The town was dominated by the handsome white Dutch Reformed church, with its imposing spire, situated on the hill. Lower down, the Coopers settled into a semi-detached house in Arnaud Street near the synagogue. Shortly after being transferred, Victor was able to afford a car, a blue Plymouth sedan, and the family started to travel the national road regularly to visit his mother's family in Mowbray in Cape Town. They regularly passed the lonely spot near Vissershoek where decades later the body of Baron Dieter von Schauroth would be found. Wilfrid, who appeared at the trial of the alleged murderer, would be reminded of these journeys at the inspection *in loco* of the crime scene.

The immediate effect of the move on Wilfrid was that he had much further to walk to school. In Klawer it took him a mere ten minutes, but he now had a thirty-minute walk to the Hoër Jongenskool, which he attended from 1935 to 1940 for standards 1 to 5. He was to find that most of the boys at the school were older than he was and he had to exert himself to keep up with them.

His independence continued to be encouraged. In 1938 he caught the steam train to return to Klawer where he stayed with his friend Koos Geldenhuys and visited his old haunts. Later in the year he travelled to Cape Town to see the final test between the touring British Lions and the Springboks at the Newlands rugby grounds. The train also enabled Wilfrid to explore further afield and he went to visit family in Springs and Durban. On one of these trips, when travelling through the Karoo he saw 'coloured' urchins running barefoot alongside the slow-moving train as it left one of the stops, passengers throwing pennies into their outstretched hands. The scene reminded him of the poverty he had first encountered at Klawer, and it unsettled him. He came to realise both that there was a gulf between rich and poor and that being non-white was an indicator of poverty, disadvantage and exploitation.

One evening when Wilfrid was in the bath, his father noticed marks on his buttocks from a caning he had received at school that day from one of the teachers, a Mr Potgieter. Victor abhorred corporal punishment. As a boy himself, he had been threatened with a beating by a teacher, but being a big, strapping fellow, he grabbed the cane and thrashed the teacher instead. As a result he was expelled from school and then ran away to join the army and fight in the Great War. Victor never raised his hand to Wilfrid, and Wilfrid, despite a few provocations on my part, would certainly never raise his hand in any earnestness to me. It would be left to my mother to physically discipline me when necessary.

On seeing his weals, Victor was immediately angered that Wilfrid had been beaten. The following morning his father informed him that he would be taking him to school by car so that he could deal with Mr Potgieter. Dressed in his best jacket, he set off with Wilfrid. Arriving at the headmaster's office, Victor demanded to see Mr Potgieter, who was duly summoned. At this juncture Wilfrid was told to leave the room, but through the door he heard his father in a loud voice threatening to knock Mr Potgieter's head off if he ever touched Wilfrid again. From then on he was never caned.

After the Potgieter episode, Victor decided it was opportune that Wilfrid should go to a good school in Cape Town. In the end Wynberg Boys' High School was chosen. From its beginnings in 1841, Wynberg Boys had grown into an institution with a fine sporting and academic reputation. So, on a Sunday afternoon in January 1941, aged fourteen-and-a-half and wearing a pair of grey shorts, a grey blazer, a grey hat with blue-and-white band, white shirt and blue-and-white school tie, Wilfrid left Malmesbury in his father's Plymouth for the journey to Wynberg Boys, where he was to be a boarder. It was a proud moment for all, but especially for his father, who was providing Wilfrid with the education he had been denied.

For Wilfrid the excitement ended the next morning at breakfast in the boarding house, when the matron, Mrs Clegg, a large, domineering woman, who was the wife of the headmaster, noticed that he was not eating his porridge and questioned him about this. Wilfrid replied that he did not like porridge and that it had salt in it, which he was not used to. He was sternly berated for his fussiness and consequently disliked porridge even more from then onwards. From that moment he also hated boarding school and looked forward to the day when he would no longer have to board.

As was Wilfrid's way, he was soon meeting people and making friends. Michael Lloyd Mitchell was one of the first boys he came to know in boarding school. Later, after studying law at Cambridge, Mitchell was admitted to the Natal Bar and in 1961 elected as the United Party MP for Durban North. He subsequently left politics and was appointed to the Natal Bench. Another of Wilfrid's friends was Trevor Baskin, a weekly boarder, whose father, David Baskin, was a well-known attorney with a criminal practice in Cape Town. In October and November 1940 the community was shocked when four women were raped and murdered in the southern suburbs. Ultimately, one Gamal Salie Lineveldt was arrested and went on trial in June 1941. Trevor Baskin proudly told his school friends that Lineveldt was his father's client. Lineveldt was found guilty of his crimes and executed by hanging in Pretoria in 1942.

At Wynberg Boys sport formed an important part of school life. In Malmesbury Wilfrid had developed a keen interest in rugby. He played in the under-13 team and, after seeing the Springboks in action against the British Lions in 1938, he had the ambition to play one day at the famous Newlands rugby grounds. But after fracturing his right arm in a match at Wynberg, which required an operation, he was told by the orthopaedic surgeon that it was inadvisable to play rugby again. His goal of appearing at Newlands was thus never to be realised. But this did not stop Wilfrid from taking part in middle-distance and cross-country running, as well as playing cricket. In 1944, his final year at school, he came third in the 880 yards and won the open one mile at the school's annual athletic meeting. He also played cricket for the school until he left.

Wilfrid was active in the school's debating society, arguing such topics as 'That trial by jury should be abolished' and 'That school traditions serve no purpose and should be abolished'. It was noted at the time how 'fluent and confident' he was in his presentations. In September 1944 he won a second prize of £15 in an essay-writing competition on the subject 'The African and How to Promote His Welfare'. He also took part in a number of school plays, in which he played mainly minor roles.

Wilfrid stayed in the boarding house at the school for only a year, and for the three years thereafter he lived with his grandmother Rose in her single-storey tenement house in Mowbray. This arrangement enabled him to concentrate on his studies, away from the distractions of the boarding house. It also helped to reinforce and extend the independence that his parents had already fostered in Klawer and Malmesbury. From his second year at school he developed an active mind with a critical approach to most matters and was always ready to argue a point should the occasion arise. So with these traits and ambitions, he made the decision at an early stage to take up law when he left school.

In his testimonial, written in October 1944, the headmaster of Wynberg Boys said this of Wilfrid: 'He has been regular and punctual in his attendance, his conduct has been excellent and he has been a conscientious and painstaking pupil who has made very satisfactory progress in his work. He has shown himself trustworthy and reliable and he leaves with an unblemished record. From my knowledge of his character, abilities, and attainments I have the greatest pleasure and the fullest confidence in recommending him.'

Wilfrid thus left Wynberg Boys' High School with a promising future ahead of him. Years later he would discover that he had left it having walked the same halls as a man he would encounter at formative stages of his career and who would ultimately prove the subject of his most high-profile case: Hendrik Frensch Verwoerd. Verwoerd's family had immigrated to South Africa from Amsterdam in 1903 after the Boer War – a show of sympathy for the Afrikaner people – and Verwoerd had attended Wynberg Boys from 1904 to 1912, until the age of 11. Though he then completed his schooling at Milton High School in Bulawayo, Southern Rhodesia, their paths would intersect once again when Wilfrid moved on to university.

CHAPTER 2

STELLENBOSCH UNIVERSITY AND NUSAS

Wilfrid's Stellenbosch University years, where he acquired his training in the law and where he also showed his mettle in setting up a branch of NUSAS at a time when Afrikaner nationalism was in full flood

'In Stellenbosch Julian realised all the different aspects which were slowly making him. His career was like his heart and his heart was everything he did. And his career was his head too and his head watched over everything he did. Julian tried to understand himself and what was happening round him.'

– WILFRID COOPER, EMULATING JAMES JOYCE

Wilfrid believed his legal career began when he enrolled in 1945 as a law student at the University of Stellenbosch. He saw his application for admission as effectively a tacit election based on his experiences over the course of the first 18 years of his life. With its excellent academic record of producing legal practitioners and jurists, Stellenbosch was an obvious and logical choice for his studies. That the lectures would be in Afrikaans meant little to him in view of his knowledge of the language.

For his first year at Stellenbosch, Wilfrid chose to live in the men's residence of Dagbreek. Huis Dagbreek was the second-oldest residence on the campus, having been established in 1911 and called initially John Murray House after the founder of the theology school. It has been the alma mater of many national sportsmen, writers, artists and politicians – the cream of the Afrikaner establishment. Here, Wilfrid would follow once again, as he had done at Wynberg Boys, in the footsteps of Hendrik Verwoerd, South Africa's prime minister from 1958 to 1966. Later, while studying for his undergraduate and master's degrees and finally for his doctorate in psychology (interestingly, on the blunting of the emotions), Verwoerd had been a resident of Dagbreek. Another Dagbreker who would have a major effect on Wilfrid's future career was Balthazar John Vorster, who also studied law at Stellenbosch. Later, as minister of justice, and then as prime minister from 1966 to 1978 after Verwoerd's assassination, he would vigorously pursue the opponents of apartheid, using the Terrorism Act to detain people without trial and deliver them into the hands of the ruthless Security Police.

Late one evening in early 1945, two days before the official start of his first academic year, Wilfrid and another fresher arrived at Stellenbosch station and took a taxi together to Dagbreek. The building, which consisted of various sections, was lit up like a white castle. They entered with some trepidation to enquire where their rooms were and came across a room full of seniors. They were immediately told, with little formality, that from now on they were to be known as '*sotte*' (freshers) and were led away up seemingly endless steps to a room where a group of other *sotte* were wrestling, for the amusement of the seniors. The event seemed quite well organised, with one *sot* timing the rounds, which were sounded on the lid of a biscuit tin. Wilfrid and his fellow *sot* were told to strip and given filthy athletic supporters to wear. Fortunately, another senior came into the room where they were changing and, after a brief conversation, took a liking to Wilfrid for some reason and hauled him off to his room to talk.

Wilfrid's year at boarding school had by then become a distant memory and Dagbreek, which was home to about 300 students, took some getting used to. His preceding four years at the English-medium Wynberg Boys had dulled his memory of Afrikaans, in which he had been fluent while growing up in the country. But as all his lectures were in Afrikaans, he was soon up to speed in the language. His command of Afrikaans improved so greatly that he found himself thinking in the language, and could speak his mind and express himself fluently on most topics and issues with his fellow students. In later years, Wilfrid's ability in speaking the language was often better than those for whom Afrikaans was their mother tongue. This familiarity with the language gave him the confidence, manner and a style that would later earn him the nickname 'Tiger' when he came to the Bar and started to examine witnesses.

On his arrival at Stellenbosch, Wilfrid was delighted to meet up with an old school mate from Klawer, Kowie Adriaanse. He soon found that their friendship was not as close as it had been, for they now differed in their political views. Indeed, Wilfrid's ideas about society and politics set him apart from the mainstream of the Afrikaner student community. Within a few months of starting at university, Wilfrid joined the Union Youth Front of the United Party, whose executive chief was Japie Basson, who later entered Parliament and was subsequently expelled by Verwoerd from the National Party for his independent views. With his liberal ideas Wilfrid attracted the antagonism of many Stellenbosch students, though in time they would develop grudging respect towards him.

In October 1945, towards the end of his first year, he became involved in establishing a branch of NUSAS, the National Union of South African Students, with the assistance of University of Cape Town (UCT) NUSAS executive members and some mainly English-speaking students at Stellenbosch. The idea of having a branch had been mooted a few years before but rejected because the organisation was considered to be too liberal. NUSAS stood for being 'open to all studying at institutions of higher learning in this country. The sole criterion of association is studenthood, without regard to race, colour, creed, language or opinion.' With the rise of Afrikaner nationalism in the 1930s, this stance had come under increasing opposition from the Afrikaans campuses. In 1933 a more politicised student organisation called the Afrikaanse Nationale Studentebond was established and students from the universities of Bloemfontein, Potchefstroom and Pretoria withdrew from NUSAS. Stellenbosch followed in 1936.

Within NUSAS itself, two groups jostled for control and dominance. The first championed the idea of a broad white student national body and worked for the return of the Afrikaans-speaking universities; while the other, predominantly left-wing and radical in orientation and based primarily at the University of the Witwatersrand (Wits), called for NUSAS to become a racially more inclusive organisation and admit the University College of Fort Hare, which was predominantly 'African' in student composition, to membership. This conflict was decisively resolved in 1946 when returning ex-servicemen, imbued with democratic ideals, were instrumental in opening the doors of NUSAS to all students.[1]

In Wilfrid's day, the majority of students at Stellenbosch were against the re-establishment of a NUSAS branch. The students' representative council (SRC) went as far as to decree that the new branch could not use any of the university's facilities. This meant that Wilfrid had to make regular trips to the UCT campus in order to conduct the day-to-day affairs of the Stellenbosch branch. This was in many ways a blessing in disguise, as it enabled him to meet a much wider circle of NUSAS members. The anti-NUSAS feeling at Stellenbosch reached a level of personal antagonism when one evening Wilfrid was forcibly thrown out of his seat in the dining hall at Dagbreek by some of his fellow students. When he complained to the house committee, which was in charge of disciplinary matters in the residence, they did nothing about it. Undeterred, he took the matter to the rector of the university, Professor RW Wilcocks, who said he would look into it. Nothing happened, and when Wilfrid approached him a second time, Wilcocks told him in a few carefully chosen words that he could not waste his time on personal matters and that it was, in any case, something for the house committee to deal with.

The ethos of the men's residence of Dagbreek had a certain crude robustness about it that Wilfrid sometimes found amusing; but at times he was taken aback by the degree of racial animosity and aggression he witnessed there. One day at lunch the students at a table in the dining hall were waiting impatiently for the waiter to take their dishes away and bring more pudding, which was being served with custard. A theology student grabbed the waiter by the collar of his white jacket as he bent to pick up his plate. Startled, the waiter broke loose and in pained anger flung the jug and dish in his hands at the student, sending the custard and pudding all over his trousers. After a moment of shocked silence, a howl of protest erupted and the students took off en masse like a pack of hyenas in pursuit of a hapless wildebeest calf, the waiter dashing in great haste for the sanctuary of the kitchen. Despite baying for justice for their fellow student's custard covering, the pack was prevented from entering. For a few days subsequently, the waiter was absent from the dining hall.

In the quad afterwards, Wilfrid remonstrated with the students about their conduct and pointed out their lack of respect for the hard-pressed waiter, but there was no sympathy. Similar incidents continued to occur, and Wilfrid became known as a *kafferboetie*[2] in certain quarters. This concern for defending the interests of those less privileged in society became a marked feature of his conduct and career.

In 1946, after the summer holidays, Wilfrid went back to Stellenbosch to resume his studies and his NUSAS activities. His tolerance of Dagbreek had reached its limits, and he took a room in a house in quiet Noordwal-Oos, from whose window he could see the mountains surrounding the town. He also indulged himself and bought a radio, which he would own and use for more than twenty years. As a second-year student he had more status than the *sotte* and more freedom. He continued to spend a lot of time on his NUSAS work, almost to the detriment of his studies. Given the animosity from his fellow students on the campus, he feared that if he did not make an effort the NUSAS branch might fail.

In June he went to Johannesburg for his first NUSAS conference. Here his energy and efficiency were recognised, and he found himself being elected chairman of a sub-working group and also onto the executive. The conference was a great success in his view, for he enjoyed interacting with like-minded people and became known and admired among his NUSAS colleagues for his perseverance at Stellenbosch and the progress he had made there. This camaraderie continued when he returned. On most Saturday mornings he would meet NUSAS members and supporters at a tearoom in Cape Town and discuss important matters of the day.

One of the projects on which he expended a great deal of energy in 1946 was organising a fundraising event for the Nederlandse Studente-Noodleningsfonds (the Dutch Students' Emergency Fund). NUSAS had been requested by the Geneva-based World Student Relief[3] to contribute towards the rebuilding of Dutch universities that had been damaged during the war by German occupying forces. In view of the historical ties of many South Africans and in order to attract the widest support from students at South African universities, the Netherlands was chosen as the country to benefit from the project. The project was supported by the SRC at Stellenbosch. At a mass meeting of students in May 1946 a committee of nine students was elected to organise the campaign, with Wilfrid as chairman. The chief fundraising event was a concert in the Stellenbosch town hall with the Cape Town Municipal Orchestra and the soprano Cecilia Wessels, who donated her services as soloist to the event. The concert raised £273.92.

Wilfrid had hoped that the participation of the Stellenbosch SRC in the relief project as well as NUSAS's policy of bilingualism would soften the SRC's stance against the NUSAS branch on the campus, but this was not to be. Indeed, in 1947 Stellenbosch, like the universities of Potchefstroom and Pretoria, refused to send delegates to a meeting of SRCs held in Cape Town under the auspices of NUSAS in July of that year. In a letter to the vice-president of NUSAS, the Stellenbosch SRC stated that it would not recognise NUSAS, it could not work with it and that attending the meeting would endanger Stellenbosch's principles relating to the colour bar.

Nonetheless, the conference went ahead. At UCT at this time there was a restriction in place on socialising across the colour line. This meant that student delegates would be allowed to mix socially only at tea times. Even this innocuous contact was contrary to the ideology of the National Party, then in opposition, which was against social interaction of this nature at both UCT and Wits.

On the first day of a plenary session of the NUSAS conference Wilfrid, as chairman, was asked why invitations to the mayor of Cape Town's reception and dance had only been sent to white delegates. As a student newspaper reported, 'The chairman pointed out that the invitations to the mayor's dance had been issued by the national executive and that in accordance with NUSAS policy and precedent of observing a social colour bar while recognising the academic equality of European and non-European students, invitations had not been sent to non-European delegates.'[4] This was the start of four days of heated debate and controversy. In the thick of the fray was the head of the UCT SRC, Harold Berman, who would later be a friend and colleague of Wilfrid's at the Cape Bar and on the Bench. On the morning of the second day Berman tabled a motion 'that NUSAS reaffirms its policy with regard to complete academic equality among all students, but acknowledges that for all practical purposes there must be a social colour bar in South Africa, which NUSAS will neither circumvent nor shrink from enforcing'. The motion was passed by 11 votes to 8.

This did not conclude the matter, as that afternoon Wilfrid announced to the student assembly that the mayor had been placed in an embarrassing position by a misleading newspaper report that it was he who had insisted on a colour bar at the dance. 'The onus of clearing the mayor', Wilfrid said, 'rested on NUSAS.' The Wits delegation tried to reopen the matter, but it was agreed that the mayor would be informed of the resolution passed that morning, and it would be made known in the press that it was NUSAS who had insisted that the dance should have a colour bar and not the mayor. The dance went ahead and was attended by most of the delegates, though the more radical members attended a racially open dance at an off-campus venue organised by the UCT Students' Socialist Society.

Such issues did not deter Wilfrid from remaining an active member of NUSAS and becoming extensively involved in the organisation. In a student newspaper of June 1947, it was written of him: 'W.E. Cooper. New Vice-President of NUSAS is dynamic, restless Wilfred [*sic*] Cooper, 21 years old, a third-year BA LLB student at Stellenbosch, he is the mainstay of NUSAS there, and founded the branch.

'NUSAS positions: National Secretary for Economics and Politics,'45–'46, National Director of Research and Studies, '46–'47. Helped evolve the new Research program.

'When in Cape Town can always be found using the NUSAS office phone.

'Chief obsession: that James Joyce's works are just too wonderful.'

During his visits to the NUSAS office at UCT, Wilfrid came to know a number of students there, one of whom was Clive Small. Small, who would later become a correspondent for the BBC, mentioned to Wilfrid that he knew a girl who was 'quite a thing' and was graced with beautiful long legs; she played tennis and was a very active swimmer. An introduction was duly made to the outgoing Gertrude Posthumus. Small was correct, as she did have lovely legs and was a good few inches taller than Wilfrid, but they started seeing each other on a regular basis.

As the student report on Wilfrid made clear, James Joyce was one of Wilfrid's great passions from the time he was a student, and he devoured Joyce's books whenever he could. In 1970 he would make a pilgrimage to Ireland to walk the streets and breathe the air of his literary hero. In some of his early writing Wilfrid tried to emulate Joyce in describing his life as a student in Stellenbosch, giving himself the persona of Julian.

'In Stellenbosch Julian realised all the different aspects which were slowly making him. His career was like his heart and his heart was everything he did. And his career was his head too and his head watched over everything he did. Julian tried to understand himself and what was happening round him.

'Stellenbosch was the town with the water running down the millstreams in the middle of the town under the oaks and into the furrows of the large gardens in front of the large white houses. And the blue mountains that went pale pink at sunset. It was also a place of loneliness and occasional friction with his fellow students. Women who rode bicycles and the Calvinists who went to church in hideous suits of brown and black on Sunday mornings and Sunday evenings with their girls.'

Wilfrid's years at Stellenbosch are best summarised in the testimonial he received at the end of his time there from the great jurist Professor JC de Wet. 'I hereby declare that I have known Mr W.E. Cooper from the beginning of 1946. Mr Cooper was a student for the BA degree with legal subjects, with which he should graduate at the end of this year.

'He is shrewd and industrious, and has always delivered work of a high quality.

'Mr Cooper has broader interests than the average student. He had a keen interest in social issues and relationships, and in this regard took the lead in student circles and in the public life of our town. I can confidently recommend him for any job he can do and I am convinced that he will be an asset to any employer.' [My translation]

Wilfrid graduated with a BA (Law) on 11 December 1947. But in October he had already applied for and been appointed to the position of temporary messenger in the Senate, the upper House of Parliament. He commenced work on 1 December 1947 at a salary of £25 a month, with a probationary period of one year.

NOTES:

[1] *Becoming Liberal: A History of the National Union of South African Students, 1945–1955* by Clare Larkin (UCT, 2001)

[2] An abusive reference to a person considered to be friendly to black people.

[3] The World Student Relief was formed in 1943 to assist students during the war, and this was then extended in the post-war reconstruction period.

[4] *Varsity*, 10, 4, Friday 1 August 1947

CHAPTER 3

THE YOUNG ADVOCATE

Wilfrid's first criminal case: not only the first time he would appear for the Crown in the Supreme Court, but also his first appearance as prosecutor where a jury was present

'For the first time I heard Verwoerd speak in the Senate. He was an impressive figure – heavily built, over six feet tall, the self-appointed oracle of Afrikaner white supremacy. He expressed himself with self-righteous conviction, in a never-ending concatenation of disingenuous arguments. Listening to him was like listening to a mad man.'

– WILFRID COOPER

The year 1948 would not only mark the start of Wilfrid's working career as a clerk in the Senate but was also the year of a general election that would herald great changes in South Africa. Contrary to the predictions of most political experts, the ruling United Party of Jan Smuts was defeated by the Reunited National Party of Dr DF Malan, which came to power on the platform of apartheid. In the elections Hendrik Verwoerd, then editor of *Die Transvaler* newspaper, narrowly lost in the constituency of Alberton, but as compensation he was elected a senator for the Transvaal and resigned from the newspaper to devote himself to politics. This was the start of a parliamentary and political career that would be cut short by his assassination in the House of Assembly in 1966.

From the outset Verwoerd dominated the Senate and the parliamentary scene, taking a lead in the debates about the great question in white politics, that of race relations. On 3 September 1948 Verwoerd outlined the policy of apartheid, which would determine the direction of the country for the next forty years. As a roadmap for the implementation of his idea of 'separate development', the speech was remarkably prescient and clear in outlining the plans which the government would pursue under his direction. Verwoerd declared, 'The [National] Party believes that a determined policy of separation between the European race and the non-European racial groups, and the application of the principle of separation between non-European racial groups as well, is the only basis on which the character and the future of each race can be protected and made secure and enabled to develop in accordance with its own national character, abilities and destiny.

'In their own areas the non-European racial groups will be afforded a full opportunity of development and they will be able to develop their own institutions and social services, and in that way the abilities of the more progressive non-Europeans will be enlisted in the advancement of their own people.'

'The policy will aim at concentrating in so far as it is possible the main ethnical groups and sub-groups of the Bantu in their own separate territories, where each group will be able to develop into a self-sufficient unit.'[1]

Wilfrid later recalled his first encounter with Verwoerd in the Senate: 'Being a member of staff I was on duty when the Senate was in session. For the first time I heard Verwoerd speak in the Senate. He was an impressive figure – heavily built, over six feet tall, the self-appointed oracle of Afrikaner white supremacy. He expressed himself with self-righteous conviction, in a never-ending concatenation of disingenuous arguments. Listening to him was like listening to a mad man.'

Verwoerd's intellectual dominance within the party and his unshakeable belief in his own ideas soon saw him elevated to positions of increasing power. In 1951 he was appointed to the Cabinet as minister of native affairs. This had traditionally been something of a Cinderella department, but under Verwoerd's iron control and through his overweening ambition it was to grow into one of the most powerful state departments in the country. His visionary leadership was recognised by the National Party when in 1958 he was chosen to become prime minister. In 1966 this 'man of granite' was toppled by an assassin's blow, and it was Wilfrid Cooper who would represent the assassin. But all this was in the future.

In 1948, the year the National Party took power, Wilfrid enrolled for his LLB as a part-time student at the University of South Africa. While still studying, in January 1950 he was appointed as a clerical assistant (grade II) at the Wynberg Magistrate's Court and remained there until August 1952, when he received his LLB degree. He then immediately applied for admission to the Cape Bar and was enrolled on 3 October 1952.

Without much delay Wilfrid was allocated his first criminal case. As *pro deo* defence counsel, he appeared on 13 October for Frans George, who had been charged with the murder of a city council nightwatchman, Jacob 'Kombuis' Hoffman. According to the charge sheet, at about 11pm on Friday, 30 May 1952, Hoffman was on duty and smoking his pipe in his watch hut behind the Dock Road power station in Cape Town when George and two accomplices, John 'Whitey' Patrick and Martin Claassen, approached him with the intention of robbing him of his purse. They did not attack him immediately, but after drinking some wine, which George had with him, Patrick picked up an iron bar lying near the hut and hit Hoffman in the face. George then hit him with a spade, while Claassen struck him with a wooden pole and a bottle, which left Hoffman badly mutilated. He died outside his watch hut. The robbers took his purse, but as they ran away into the night Hoffman's small dog, clearly loyal to his now dead master, bit Claassen's left foot.

After investigations by the police, the men were arrested in July. When confronted with the evidence, Patrick confessed to the murder. Together with the evidence of a fourth man, Norman Matthews, against whom there was insufficient proof of involvement in the crime, George and Claassen were found guilty of murder and condemned to death.

The death sentences handed down brought home to Wilfrid, very early in his career, the burden that an advocate had to bear when defending a client and the consequences if he was unsuccessful in his efforts. From an early age Wilfrid had been opposed to the death penalty and saw its application as a reflection of the social and political power relations of South Africa, as it was mainly poor whites, Indians, coloureds and blacks who were executed in the country. In 1917 the death penalty had been made mandatory for offences such as murder, rape and treason. After 1958 the list of capital offences would be expanded to include robbery, aggravated house breaking and terrorism. All in all, between 1911 and 1968 2,323 people were hanged in South Africa, of whom only 85 were white. In December 1971 Wilfrid chaired a symposium on capital punishment held by the Jaycees, at which both Professor Chris Barnard and Advocate Harry Snitcher QC argued against the death penalty. At the symposium Wilfrid called for a commission of inquiry to investigate the abolition of capital punishment or, alternatively, a restriction on the number of capital crimes. Eventually, in February 1990, executions were suspended by President FW de Klerk, and one of the first rulings by the newly established Constitutional Court in 1995 declared the death penalty unconstitutional.

The 1950s were formative years in Wilfrid's career, during which he built his reputation at the Bar and honed his skills as a criminal advocate. In view of the paucity of work, most advocates undertook other work to supplement their erratic income and many wrote books on law. In 1955 Wilfrid produced, with colleague, Brian Bamford, his first book, *Handbook on the Criminal Procedure Act*. Its appearance marked the start of a relationship with the publisher Juta that would span forty years and involve the publication of thirteen books, the last being *Delictual Liability in Motor Law*, produced in 1997, just before he retired. Perhaps they were not titles of Joycean appeal, but over the years they began to be a worthy alternative source of income for a career that sometimes found Wilfrid without court work, partly because of his unpopular defence of political activists. Wilfrid also lectured on the law of evidence at the University of Cape Town in 1956, 1957 and 1959 and continued to lecture regularly on various law subjects from then until 1988. In later years he became at various times an external examiner for the law faculties of both the University of Cape Town and the University of the Western Cape.

As his family grew, Wilfrid sought additional work and in early 1954 was appointed as a part-time translator for Hansard. This would include the translation of many of Hendrik Verwoerd's speeches in the Senate. Verwoerd invariably spoke in Afrikaans, but as all proceedings in Parliament had to be recorded in Hansard in both official languages, his speeches had to be translated. The usual procedure was for the original translation to be sent to the MP or senator for correction, which was understood to involve only simple typographical errors or changes that would not alter the meaning of a passage. Wilfrid was to note, however, that Verwoerd did not confine his corrections to this accepted protocol, but often made extensive changes that materially affected the meaning of passages. At home Wilfrid and Gertrude would work on the translations into the early hours of the morning, between attending to their first-born, Susan-Ann, with Gertrude typing each of the lengthy speeches on her Underwood typewriter. The money they earned from this would help them buy their first car, which made a great change in their working and social lives.

In 1955, three years after his admission to the Bar and much to his surprise, Wilfrid was approached by the Attorney General of the Cape to appear for the Crown in a prosecution in the Supreme Court. When Wilfrid received the papers, he learned that the accused was a medical doctor, Dr Arthur Val-Davies, who practised in the Namaqualand town of Springbok. The case arose from the death on 10 July 1955 of a 19-year-old woman, Engela de Waal, in the doctor's house. Dr Val-Davies, 38, and his unqualified assistant and nurse, Elizabeth Aletta Coetzee, were charged with culpable homicide and two counts of abortion. The trial was to be heard by Judge JT (Theo) van Wyk and a jury.[2] Wilfrid knew that the judge had grown up in the town of Vredendal, where his older brother Hennie was practising as an attorney, and had gone to school in nearby Vanrhynsdorp. Van Wyk was a member of the National Party and a recent political appointment to the Bench. It was said by one of his colleagues in later years that he brought to the Bench the same defining characteristic he had had at the Bar: he tried to find a smart, unorthodox solution to every case he tried.[3]

Van Wyk disliked Wilfrid, perhaps because he knew he had helped found the first post-war branch of NUSAS at

Stellenbosch University. Van Wyk would later hear an appeal by the Afrikaans author André Brink against the banning of his first book, *Kennis van die Aand*. Of Van Wyk, Brink noted: 'Known as an arch conservative, narrow-minded rightist with a number of axes to grind with liberals in general…' In 1966 Van Wyk was chosen to head the commission of inquiry into the circumstances surrounding the assassination of Hendrik Verwoerd.

The trial of Val-Davies was an important one for Wilfrid. Not only was this the first time he would appear for the Crown in the Supreme Court but it would be his first appearance as prosecutor where a jury was present. There were also some 'big guns' whom he would have to face up to in the trial. The leading silk Advocate Bobby Bloch QC appeared for the doctor, with Hannes Fagan acting as his junior and also appearing for the nurse. The instructing attorney was Arnold Galombik, who also came from Vanrhynsdorp, and was a senior partner in one of Cape Town's biggest firms of attorneys. The accused pleaded not guilty.

Before the trial started, the investigating officer told Wilfrid what the police knew about the people whom he would defend. The two accused were living together. Val-Davies was the medical doctor at the mine hospital at the O'Kiep Copper Company in Nababiep; he was an alcoholic and was estranged from his third wife. To obtain money for alcohol, he performed illegal abortions at night on the kitchen table, assisted by Coetzee, whom he had met at the mine. When searching his house, the police found a foetus in a carton addressed to him.

The trial, which lasted for seven days, was held in the second-largest courtroom in the Supreme Court in Keerom Street. In those years abortions could only be legally performed by doctors and then only for very specific reasons. The alleged death of a young woman from a 'backstreet abortion' attracted much public interest from the outset. For Judge Van Wyk the trial was his first opportunity to enact his new role, and he revelled in the interest shown by the press and the public. His family was also present and sat at the back of the court behind the accused from where they had a clear view of the new judge.

Mrs Joyce Val-Davies, the doctor's third wife, attended the trial in support of her husband. During an adjournment Wilfrid got to know her when they met in the Café Royal in Church Street, a few blocks away from the Supreme Court. Wilfrid later recalled that she was an attractive woman who accepted that her husband was an alcoholic and displayed no hostility to him, her only concern being for his health. She told Wilfrid how on one occasion, after consulting with his counsel in Temple Chambers, her husband had had an epileptic attack as he was leaving, which required medical attention.

As prosecutor, Wilfrid tendered the evidence of the witnesses to the court who directly implicated both accused. The facts of the case were straightforward. In March 1955 Miss Engela de Waal discovered she was pregnant, and at the end of June the man responsible for her condition, a Mr Olivier, arranged with Val-Davies to procure an abortion for a fee of £50. At the beginning of July, De Waal visited Val-Davies two or three times and was given injections to abort the pregnancy. On 8 July Olivier again took De Waal to Val-Davies's house where she remained until her death on Sunday, 10 July of septicaemia caused by a septic foetus. A post-mortem examination revealed the presence in her vagina of a broken stick two-and-a-half to three inches long. The report concluded that the foetus had probably been dead for a week or more before Miss De Waal died, and the stick could not have contributed to her death. Other witnesses testified that Val-Davies had on two other occasions performed abortions and had each time been paid £50.

Trials, especially ones where the death of a young woman is concerned, are serious affairs, but the Val-Davies trial, as Wilfrid recalled, was conducted in a somewhat relaxed manner and there were even moments of levity. When Wilfrid led evidence to prove that De Waal had been pregnant and that the man who was responsible had been a local rugby player, it amused those listening to hear that he played in the position of hooker. From then on, Advocate Bloch would humorously refer to him as 'the hooker of the north-west'.

After hearing the evidence, argument by counsel and the judge's summing up, the jury adjourned to consider their verdict. While the jury was out, counsel spent their time playing cards in an adjacent waiting room. After what seemed an eternity the jury filed back into court. The foreman announced their verdict: the accused were found guilty on two counts of attempted abortion but not guilty on the count of culpable homicide. After hearing pleas in mitigation, Judge Van Wyk passed sentence. Val-Davies received six months' imprisonment on the two counts plus a fine of £50, while Coetzee was sentenced to six months' imprisonment on one count and a fine of £50 on the other. The verdict of attempted abortion was a compromise to avoid a conviction of culpable homicide, which would have carried a heavier penalty. This no doubt influenced the jury to return their verdict.

On advice of their counsel, both accused appealed to the Appellate Division in Bloemfontein against their convictions. Wilfrid was briefed to appear for the Crown, another first in his legal career. After hearing arguments, the court dismissed the appeals against the convictions and on the count of attempted abortion it approved the instruction given to the jury by Judge Van Wyk that 'Where an attempt is made to commit an abortion and that attempt does not succeed merely because there is no foetus to remove or the foetus is dead, the crime committed is attempted abortion; attempted abortion is accordingly a competent verdict in this case.' On the count of culpable homicide the Appellate Division could not interfere because the verdict was based on the jury's finding on the facts.

His appeal having failed, Val-Davies had to surrender himself to the authorities to serve his sentence in prison. Upon doing so, he explained to the warder that he was an alcoholic and asked that he should not be immediately deprived of alcohol as he would experience withdrawal symptoms. His request was ignored and he suffered severe withdrawal symptoms in his first weeks in prison but by the time he was released he was no longer dependent on alcohol.

When he was freed, Dr Val-Davies visited Wilfrid in his chambers. He thanked him for being responsible for sending him to prison, thereby forcing him to break his dependency on alcohol and enabling him to start his new life free of it. After his release his wife took their two small children back to Britain, from where she came. They would never see their father again.

While the Val-Davies trial was not of any significance in legal terms, it was of great importance to Wilfrid. It had been his debut as a leading participant in a prominent trial that captured the public interest – the first of a series of notable trials in which he appeared throughout his career. He had also faced up against one of the 'big guns' of the Bar, and had held his head high in front of not only the trial judge, whose personal dislike of him might well have affected the outcome, but also the three appeal judges in Bloemfontein, who concurred with the trial proceedings. In his personal files Wilfrid noted that the Val-Davies trial and the subsequent murder trial of Marthinus Rossouw were key in preparing him for the hearing of Dr Verwoerd's assassin in 1966. The trial also appealed to his inner self, as the eventual outcome was the rehabilitation of a man who had hit rock bottom in his life.

While Val-Davies was in prison, his name was struck off the roll of medical practitioners. Fortunately, this did not disqualify him from being employed by a pharmaceutical company when he returned to society and started putting his life back together. Sadly, Arthur Val-Davies could not shake his past. In researching this case, I learnt from his niece Pamela Lewin that, contrary to Wilfrid's hopes, Val-Davies eventually went on to start drinking again and taking drugs. Though he initially attempted to avoid contact with his former nurse and co-defendant, Elizabeth Coetzee, she pursued him, abandoning two of her children in the process. She eventually became his fourth wife. Astonishingly, he managed to have his name restored to the medical roll, apparently through force of charm and charisma, and even secured a job as a medical officer in Port Elizabeth. He died there in 1970 at the age of 53.

NOTES:

[1] Hansard, 3 September 1948, p. 241

[2] In those days the accused could elect in terms of the Criminal Procedure Act 56 of 1956 to be tried either by a judge or a jury. The general feeling was that those who were guilty chose to face a jury and those who were not guilty would place their fate in the hands of a judge, who could elect to be assisted by two assessors.

[3] *Bar, Bench and Bullshifters: Cape Tales 1950–1990* by Gerald Friedman and Jeremy Gauntlett (Cape Town, Syberink, 2013)

CHAPTER 4

MARTHINUS ROSSOUW AND THE MURDER OF A BARON

The scandalous criminal case that captured the imagination of the South African public in the early 1960s and would prove to be, in many ways, a forerunner of an equally famous case more than four decades later

'When in fact a person wants to die and somebody else is asked to kill him and he does it, however much you disapprove of it – I disapprove of it; one must disapprove of it – it nevertheless is a mitigating and extenuating circumstance.'
– WILFRID COOPER

A prominent businessman lies shot to death on the side of a South African road, the victim of an apparent hit. At first his murder makes the headlines for these bare facts alone, but soon the rumours emerge that there is more to the case than meets the eye. The man was having money problems, it seems. He knew the gunman, they say. The newspapers are abuzz and dinner-party conversation is fuelled by conjecture and conspiracy. The case becomes a national sensation. Could it be that the man arranged his own murder?

Today this scenario is inevitably associated with one person: Brett Kebble.

On the night of 27 September 2005 the larger-than-life mining magnate was shot seven times on a lonely road in Melrose, Johannesburg, as he drove to meet a business associate for dinner. He was just 41 when he died.

At first, it appeared to be a botched hijacking. Then, when an autopsy revealed that low-velocity bullets had been used, as favoured by those in the personal security industry, the talk was of a contract killing – and, indeed, this proved to be the case. The assassins were three local bouncer-types, Mikey Schultz, Nigel McGurk and Faizel 'Kappie' Smith. But there was a shocking twist: Kebble, it turned out, had contracted them himself.

The death of Brett Kebble preoccupied the South African media and public for years, spawning several bestselling books, a somewhat obscene documentary re-enactment and a court case of far-reaching political consequences. Kebble had been a figure of much public fascination, a politically well-connected businessman with links to then Deputy President Jacob Zuma. Kebble lived the high life, partied with members of the ANC Youth League and was said to have owned a hundred cars at one time – and yet he was also vilified as a con artist and corrupter, allegedly involved in the multibillion-rand fraud of two mining houses he controlled, JCI and Randgold & Exploration.

Before his murder Kebble had heavily insured his life and in the aftermath the insurance companies in question paid out R10 million to his wife. Ingrid Kebble went on to receive from his executors a bond-free property and an extensive art collection said to be worth millions, thereby ensuring that she and her four children could continue their lives in comfortable fashion.

Meanwhile, the killers received indemnity for testifying against the alleged mafia boss Glenn Agliotti in a farcical case that saw them present evidence of their bumbling ineptitude – they needed three separate attempts to do the deed – before they walked free without consequences. Agliotti followed suit as the prosecution's case fell apart.

Many observers were left aghast that something like this could happen: that a man could hire someone to shoot himself in order to escape the realities of his life while still claiming the insurance money for his family. But, as the saying goes, history repeats itself; this was not the first time such an 'assisted suicide' had made headlines in the land. Almost half a century before the death of Brett Kebble an incident with many similarities took place near Cape Town and Wilfrid Cooper was the man called in to defend the murderer.

*

Baron Dieter von Schauroth, 36, was originally from South West Africa, now Namibia, and as the eldest son had inherited the family title. His father, Baron Erich Friedrich Maximilian von Schauroth, born in Danzig on 8 June 1874, came from a noble German lineage that could trace its roots back to 1287. Erich arrived in South West Africa in 1904 as a young lieutenant, part of a force to fight a Herero-Nama group under Captain Jacob Morenga, who was known as the Black Napoleon. Stationed in the arid Karasburg area, Von Schauroth came across a valley with a spring of good, fresh water while on patrol one day.

It was known by the local people as Blinkoog because of the way the clean water sparkled in the sunlight.

Erich returned to Germany in 1907 and was posted to Berlin, but the memory of South West Africa lingered with him. The family fortunes in Germany having declined, he saw an opportunity to rebuild them in the arid vastness of South West Africa, so he applied to buy Holding no. 30, as Blinkoog was officially known. In 1913, after finishing his service in the army, he moved to Blinkoog where he would spend the next 45 years building up a farm, erecting a castle on it and creating a future for his family. Blinkoog would later be divided with the northern section of 23,000 acres including the castle retaining the name, and the southern section of approximately 27,000 acres being called Panorama.

In February 1917 Erich von Schauroth married Talita Cumi Le Riche, eldest daughter of Peter Le Riche, who owned the farm Stinkboom, also near Karasburg. They had two daughters, Thekla (b. 1918) and Hildegard (b. 1919), before Erich's first son, Dietrich Joachim Gunther, Dieter for short, was born on 30 November 1924. A second son, Udo Erik Friedrich, was born three years later. Erich had high hopes that Dieter would grow up to be the salvation of the Von Schauroth name and Blinkoog, but he was to be sadly disappointed. As Dieter grew older, he failed with each opportunity presented to him, his only success being the breeding of karakul sheep.

Erich died in March 1958. In terms of the will, Udo inherited Blinkoog and the castle, and Dieter Panorama. The farms were not debt-free; Erich had mortgaged them and the sons also had to pay their mother £50 each per month for the rest of her life. There was also a restriction in the will on the sale of the farms; they had first to be offered to family members before being put on the open market.

With the inheritance Dieter von Schauroth found himself asset-rich but cash-poor. Though he now considered himself a wealthy farmer, he was soon leading a lifestyle that belied his true financial status. He didn't spend much time on the farm and was away regularly in pursuit of fanciful ways to make his fortune, including illicit diamond dealing, possibly as a result of an intriguing story he heard of a man who had died in the nearby desert with a packet of diamonds worth £50,000.

On a whim in January 1959 he drove his car, a large and powerful Ford Galaxie of which he was very fond, down to Cape Town for a holiday. As a carefree bachelor, Von Schauroth soon gravitated towards a seedy club called Darryl's in the lower end of the city, where the owner introduced him to the 17-year-old Colleen Priscilla Cairns, who was there in the company of her mother. Colleen came from a poor background, the fourth child of a family of nine. She had left school at sixteen with a school-leaver's certificate and worked as a shop assistant at Faulkner's Jewellers, earning £10 per month.

Von Schauroth wined and dined Colleen the night they met and she was seduced by his title, charm and apparent wealth. He too was clearly taken with her. The following morning he picked her up from her shabby home and took her shopping for clothes before driving north back to Karasburg. Despite Von Schauroth's family, especially his brother Udo, not being enamoured of his new paramour, they were married in the Cape Town Magistrate's Court in May 1959 before returning to live on the farm. Colleen gave birth to a son, Friedrich, on 21 January 1960.

Von Schauroth's exuberant spending, combined with a drought on the farm, quickly eroded the couple's cash reserves. It wasn't long before he was forced to sell off his karakul sheep and equipment and leave the farm. He told those who would listen that he intended to return one day when the rains had come and the grazing improved.

In May 1960 he moved back to Cape Town with his wife and infant son, taking up residence in a well-appointed flat in Upper

Mill Street in Gardens. After spending £1,000 on, among other things, new furniture from a store in Bellville, Von Schauroth had sufficient funds for his immediate needs. But with no regular income and a certain lifestyle to uphold, it was apparent to him that this would not last long. By this time he had taken out insurance policies on his life totalling £201,000, with premiums of £2,458 due in the first half of 1961 it is likely he had only £2,755 left in cash. His financial situation was precarious, to say the least, and he was therefore on the lookout for business opportunities, be they fair or foul. Eventually he succumbed to the lure of the illicit diamond-broking trade, the solution, he believed, to his financial problems.

*

Marthinus (Martiens) Rossouw was 24, had passed standard 7 and was married with two children. He and his family were lodgers in Hatfield House Residential Hotel at 124 Hatfield Street, Cape Town. Though located not far from the Von Schauroth's residence, the hotel was by contrast rudimentary: the Rossouw family lived, slept and cooked in a single room. Since 1954 Rossouw had been employed by the South African Railways, first as an apprentice in Pretoria for a year and then at the Salt River workshops in Cape Town as an electro-technical fitter. He had been transferred temporarily to Bitterfontein in Namaqualand and, while drinking with the locals, was told of the diamonds in the area. He learned that it was difficult to find reliable buyers and there was the ever-present risk of police traps. Having spent a year there, he was transferred back to the Salt River workshops.

Rossouw's background and record were far from illustrious. In 1956 he had been sentenced to five strokes for theft, he had maliciously damaged railway property, he drank heavily, he dressed like a ducktail, and his arms were emblazoned with tattoos, including one reading JOHANNA DYNAMITE in honour of a woman he had won in a fight.

Baron Dieter von Schauroth and Marthinus Rossouw were introduced in January 1961, one a blue blood with an inherited title dating back to 1804, the other a blue-collar railway worker who came from nothing. Notwithstanding their divergent backgrounds, they had one thing in common: each was in pursuit of solving his financial problems. From the start, it was a friendship based on illusion. Rossouw sold himself as someone with diamond contacts in Namaqualand and Von Schauroth, always immaculately turned out, presented himself as a big-shot dealer in the market to buy diamonds. They soon struck up a friendship. Rossouw accepted Von Schauroth as a man of means and professed to him to have a purchasing contact in Bitterfontein.

With little delay, the two of them drove the 400 kilometres north in Von Schauroth's Ford Galaxie on what was to be an abortive search for the gemstones. Von Schauroth maintained the illusion of his means and paid all the expenses from a roll of banknotes he kept in his pocket. On the return journey Rossouw took over the driving for a while, but at one stage drove so recklessly that Von Schauroth accused him of being a cowboy. As Rossouw later testified, Von Schauroth said to him, 'It looks to me you are a cowboy; one day I must ask you to shoot someone for me.' Von Schauroth, he repeated to the court, was suggesting he shoot someone for him, but as he had said it with some laughter Rossouw took it as a joke. Still, it struck him as a curious comment, and it was one that Von Schauroth repeated in the coming months.

*

Dieter von Schauroth's neatly dressed body was found a short distance from some trees alongside the Old Malmesbury Road, just outside Cape Town, on the morning of Saturday, 25 March 1961. The 36-year-old had been shot twice in the back of the neck, and the empty bullet casings had fallen alongside his body not far from several uncut diamonds. It appeared to have been a diamond deal gone wrong. Within a few days Rossouw was arrested for the murder and after intense interrogation he confessed to being the shooter. But had he committed a crime? And, if so, what was it? Rossouw was charged with murder and the trial date set for 12 September 1961.

The trial judge in the case was the Judge President, Andries Beyers, a man of immense personality and formidable intellect, an intimidating minder of proceedings. Rossouw's counsel was originally Advocate Jan Steyn, who had been admitted to the Bar two years before Wilfrid, and he was to be assisted by Advocate Roger Whiting. However, on the morning of the second day of the trial Steyn fell seriously ill and Wilfrid took over as lead defence counsel. The judge adjourned proceedings for a week to give him time to familiarise himself with the case and prepare for the trial.

Living up to his nickname of 'Tiger', Wilfrid vigorously cross-examined the string of State witnesses in an attempt to support Rossouw's story that Von Schauroth was unhappily married, in financial difficulty and had recently taken out a number of insurance policies on his life and, most critically, that he had established a plan for Rossouw to end his life, thereby ensuring that his family was well provided for. Throughout the trial Rossouw insisted that his friend had asked him to shoot him and had promised that he would be paid a fee of £5,000 by his bank over and above the £1,150 he had given him in the form of a post-dated cheque from Von Schauroth's brother, Udo, for the balance of the inheritance Udo owed to him. Dieter had written a note dated 28 February 1961, presented as Exhibit W at the trial, which read: 'I, the undersigned, hereby give to Marthinus Rossouw cheque No. CA11358158 posted dated [*sic*] to 3 July 1962, signed by U. von Schauroth, for the sum of R2,300. Which my brother owes me. I give it to him for service rendered.'

It is apparent from the court record that Judge Beyers disliked the line of questioning Wilfrid followed in attempting to describe to the jury the circumstances leading up to the shooting. Beyers was particularly dismissive of evidence that supported Von Schauroth's spree of buying extensive life insurance, making comments such as 'I am not at all sure that this is relevant to the present enquiry before this Court', 'if you want to make an insurance case out of a murder trial, by all means let us have it then' and 'I shall later on draw the attention of the jury to the same fact that this is a murder trial and not an insurance case'.

Beyers would also not allow evidence to be introduced by the receiver of revenue as to the precarious nature of Von Schauroth's financial state of affairs. 'I have no intention of ordering their disclosure,' he said. 'They are, if at all, most obliquely relevant to the case. I have allowed this case to travel into spheres where the relevancy of the case in relation to the charge of murder has become almost too vague to see it any longer.' Testimony from the receiver, had it been permitted, would have confirmed that Von Schauroth was broke.

Once all the evidence had been led, Wilfrid made his final address to the jury on the points raised by the prosecution. Probably the most succinct are those he made for extenuating circumstance. He asked the jury to accept the fact that the victim had asked Rossouw to shoot him, and described it as 'a curious story of two rather unbalanced people, the one in dire financial and other distress, but not wishing to let his family down, in the last resort using a pawn, which I submit the accused was at all material times in this case, and persuading him to kill him.'

He concluded as follows: 'Gentlemen, in mitigation I ask you first of all to accept the accused's explanation of what led up to it – that this is the most probable explanation of what happened.

On that basis I ask you to return a verdict of guilty of murder with extenuating circumstances. I ask you to find and to hold that the extenuating circumstances are the fact that the deceased asked the accused to shoot him. I put it to you on this basis that a different situation arises when a person dearly wants to live and is deprived of his life. When in fact a person wants to die and somebody else is asked to kill him and he does it, however much you disapprove of it – I disapprove of it; one must disapprove of it – it nevertheless is a mitigating and extenuating circumstance. I ask you further to find the fact that the accused was under the influence of the deceased, that in fact the shooting was the result of the influence operating on the mind of the accused, and I ask you further to find that the circumstances which operated on the night in question and the immediately preceding three days – the generosity of the deceased in giving him the £20 towards the car, in giving him the post-dated cheque, and combined with the manner, the subtle manner in which the accused was drawn to the final place, exposed place next to the road – that the accused in those circumstances genuinely believed and accepted in that frame of mind, in the light of these circumstances which operated in his mind, that the deceased genuinely wanted him to shoot him.

'I ask you, gentlemen, to find that in fact the accused never derived any monetary benefit from the shooting, and in fact the suggestion of a monetary benefit contained in his confession was a rationalisation, an attempt to rationalise "Why did I do it? Why did I shoot this man? Was it really worth the £5,000 for my wife?" and he says "Yes, it was for the £5,000 for my wife". I would submit, gentlemen, that that in fact was subsidiary, ancillary, to the main motive, and that is that he shot the deceased because of the influence, because of the deep friendship that existed between them, a friendship which resulted in this tragic situation, that is that the accused shot the best friend he ever had.'

Despite Wilfrid's best efforts, the jury did not believe Rossouw's story and he was found guilty of murder with no extenuating circumstances. He was sentenced to death. Wilfrid immediately filed papers for leave to appeal, but Judge Beyers, who heard the application, maintained his intransigence. Despite a man's life being at stake, all aspects of the appeal were rejected, as was any notion of the judge himself being, as Wilfrid had contended, biased in his handling of the trial.

'The specific points raised in the application have been opposed by the State on the grounds they are frivolous,' Beyers reasoned. 'I am refusing to exercise the right to make any special entries, and I would base it rather on the ground that I can find nothing which in my mind could by any Court be regarded as an irregularity of something not in accordance with law.'

The state president was also petitioned for clemency, but this too failed.

In an unusual turn of events the date of Rossouw's execution was deferred to allow him to testify at a hearing brought by Von Schauroth's wife and sister, the executors of his estate, to compel the South African National Life Assurance Company (SANLAM) to pay out one of the policies that Von Schauroth had taken out on his life. Notwithstanding that the jury had found Rossouw guilty of murder, SANLAM declined to settle the claim for a number of reasons. The primary one was the contention that Von Schauroth had committed suicide by having Rossouw shoot him. In doing so, they argued, Von Schauroth had died as the result of an illegal act and thus the estate should not benefit. Five other insurance companies that had insured Von Schauroth's life also rejected the estate's claims and joined SANLAM at the hearing, which commenced in December 1961. The total claimed by the estate was £190,000, a substantial sum of money at that time.

Wilfrid and Roger Whiting represented the insurance companies, while the estate for Von Schauroth took on the services of the Johannesburg advocate Aaron Mendelow QC, a seasoned and formidable cross-examiner who had been called to the Johannesburg Bar in 1945 and took silk in 1959. Mendelow cross-examined Rossouw for 35 hours, which translated into 1,000 pages of transcript. Though the author Benjamin Bennett would later write in his book *The Amazing Case of the Baron von Schauroth* that 'nothing remained of Rossouw's version of events or defence but the ashes of the lies on which he based them', the commission did not find for the estate and the insurance companies continued their repudiation of the estate's claims. The matter dragged on until June 1963, at which point the estate ran out of money to pursue the legal action any further, and a settlement was reached: the claim of £190,000 was withdrawn and the insurers made an *ex gratia* payment of £10,000, plus the estate's costs.

On being wound up, Von Schauroth's estate was found to have a surplus of £3,522, of which his wife Colleen received £1,006, with the balance going to his mother, sister and brother. Colleen also received the proceeds of a 1944 policy of £1,518. The farm Panorama went to Von Schauroth's young son, now bond-free.

Rossouw was executed in Pretoria Central Prison on 20 June 1962. His estate consisted only of the post-dated cheque for £1,150, which Von Schauroth had given him for 'service rendered'. The cheque was never cashed.

*

A number of books were written on this prominent case. The author of one, Henry John May, a QC who practised in Johannesburg and Durban, confidentially approached Wilfrid in October 1965 to read his draft manuscript for comment on its accuracy. Describing Wilfrid's address to the jury as 'remarkable and brilliant', he wanted to be sure that he did not 'misrepresent or prejudice' Wilfrid in his paraphrasing of events. 'My conclusion on the Rossouw case', he wrote, 'is that it was a miscarriage of justice. Not only should he have been believed, in his main story, but the psychiatrists' reports leave no room for doubt that he was wrongfully hanged.'[1]

Nearly five decades later, after the 'suicide' of Brett Kebble, it is interesting to note how the relevant insurance company paid the claim on Kebble's life policy almost immediately and without demur, despite the curious circumstances that would seem to have given them legitimate claim to object. Even after August 2010, when various witnesses, under immunity from prosecution by the State, testified in the South Gauteng High Court as to the planning that had taken place to ensure that Kebble's death would look like a 'hit', the insurer still did nothing to try to recover what had been paid out to Kebble's widow.

In the case of the prominent murder-suicide of 2005, it was the killers who walked free and the insurance company that took the knock, which led to speculation that Kebble's political influence reached beyond the grave. In the parallel case from 44 years before, the results were reversed. Wilfrid had in effect won the insurance case, but lost the criminal proceedings using the same defence. And his client, the coerced killer Marthinus Rossouw, paid the ultimate price.

It was an injustice that rankled Wilfrid. The legal system had failed a weak, less-fortunate member of society despite the fact that it had been put in place, Wilfrid believed, to look after precisely such people. It was anathema to him that Judge Beyers had not allowed the jury to consider the broader issues of the crime: the truth as to why it had been committed; that a man so desperate to help his family survive could take the life of his friend, possibly his only true friend, to appease him in his equally desperate attempt to have his family financially secure after his death.

The execution of Marthinus Rossouw was the sad end to Wilfrid's most high-profile case to date and it was a personal landmark that would only encourage his search for the truth –

an ongoing quest that would reveal further injustices to come in the political trials of his future.

NOTES:

[1] For readers wanting the full and accurate account of this tragic story, I suggest the book *Murder by Consent* by Henry John May QC (London, Hutchinson, 1968).

CHAPTER 5

AT HOME AT RIVERSIDE

The Coopers set up home in Newlands,
where Gertrude created a small Eden
for their family and friends

The patio under the syringa tree was also the venue for many
happy braais, drinks parties and dinners with Wilfrid and
Gertrude's numerous friends. On these occasions many bottles
of wine were consumed – 'libations', as Wilfrid called them –
from his cellar in the garage.

I n October 1949 Wilfrid married Gertrude Posthumus, whom he met through his NUSAS friend at the University of Cape Town. Gertrude had grown up in the small town of Worcester, the daughter of an engineer on the South African Railways. On graduating from UCT in 1944 with a BA degree, she became a junior reporter at the *Cape Times*. During the royal visit in February 1947, she had a scoop when she managed to interview HRH Princess Elizabeth. In 1949, at the age of 25, she was appointed to the position of women's editor and over the years she expanded her role and became an influential social arbiter. She was much in demand on the diplomatic social scene during parliamentary sessions and many of the diplomats became personal friends with whom she stayed in contact long after they left their postings in South Africa. In the latter part of her career she started 'Gertrude Cooper's People's Page', into which she poured much of her time and energy. This became a social page that everyone who was anyone sought to appear in and it enhanced her status as a truly professional journalist. Years later, the journalist Tony Weaver recalled 'the wonderful, incredibly glamorous Gertrude Cooper'. 'It was Gertie the subversive who rallied the secretaries, the high-speed dictation typists and the men from the presses to threaten downing tools when a hostile takeover loomed. The night Madiba died, I walked into the *Cape Times* just before midnight and into controlled chaos. Gertie would have loved it.'[1]

As they loved the leafy suburbs nestled below Table Mountain and Devils Peak, Wilfrid and Gertrude chose to live in rented accommodation in the Fernwood and Newlands areas after they were married. With their first daughter, Susan-Ann, born in 1954, and with a second child on the way, Gertrude began to look around for a house of their own. In 1956, shortly before the birth of Megan in October, she found a property that they could afford, tucked away down a gravel panhandle off Palmboom

Road in Newlands. Located on the banks of the Cannon Stream, which flows off Table Mountain, the house would be called Riverside.

The area had a long history of colonial occupation stretching back to the late seventeenth century. With the availability of clean water from the Liesbeek River and the presence of several springs in the area, it has been particularly associated with beer brewing. Already in 1695, the man who held the concession for brewing beer at the Dutch Cape, Willem Menssink, whose amorous liaison with the slave girl Trijntje has been entertainingly related by the historian Nigel Penn,[2] was granted the farm Papenboom in the area. The first batch of beer was produced in 1696 and was sold mainly to the Dutch East India Company for consumption by its sailors. By the turn of the nineteenth century Newlands was the centre of beer brewing in the Cape Colony, with the industry dominated by Ohlsson's Cape Brewery and the Mariendahl Brewery on the Papenboom estate. What is now known as Newlands Village was at one stage called Irish Town because of the community of Irish beer makers who lived here. Kildare Road bears witness to this era. In the early 1960s I recall that the Mariendahl Brewery, which had stopped operating years before, was a derelict shell with a ghostly appearance: I would rush past it when returning home from walking the dogs late in the afternoon. It was subsequently demolished and the ground was developed into tennis courts and playing fields for the South African College School (SACS).

When Gertrude came across Riverside, which sat on two-thirds of an acre, Wilfrid initially saw no need to buy such a big property, particularly as they could barely afford it. Gertrude, however, was of the firm opinion that this was what she wanted and that it would also be a practical and prudent acquisition. She saw the potential in what was a slightly rundown house on a rambling property, as a place where the family could live and grow. The house had started off life as the potting shed of a flower nursery and there had been a number of additions made to it; some ramshackle outbuildings of corrugated iron would later serve us as garages and a garden shed. These structures had numerous leaks and no drainage, and so, in winter, with the heavy Newlands rains, the insides turned into mud baths. Over the years, as money became available, they were demolished and a new building was erected. With this and with renovations to the main house, the property grew to accommodate the Cooper family comfortably and to produce over the next three decades a trove of memories. Sadly, when the time came to downsize and move elsewhere, despite an assurance by the new owner that the property would remain intact, it was subdivided and three townhouses built on it, thereby destroying the small Eden that Gertrude had created.

At the time of moving in, the Coopers were the only white family in the road. Our neighbour was Richard Dudley, who taught at Livingstone High School. He himself had been schooled at Livingstone, thereafter studying at UCT, where he gained a BSc, an MSc and a teacher's diploma. Just before his death in 2009 the university would confer on him an honorary doctorate in education. After graduating, he returned to Livingstone High, where he became a highly respected teacher for 39 years. His influence on countless students during that time is legendary. A prominent member of the Unity Movement, which maintained a policy of strict non-collaboration with apartheid structures, he was banned in the early 1960s and prohibited from participating in political activities. But, in grudging acknowledgement of his superb teaching abilities, he was never banned from the classroom.

Sadly, in 1961 his parents were forcibly removed under the Group Areas Act from the home their family had owned for more than a century and in which his parents had lived since they were married. It was the house in which both Richard and his father had grown up. In recognition of this, Gertrude fought tooth and nail with the city council to have the small passage that serviced the houses in the street to be named Dudley Lane in his memory. Long after the Dudley family had been forced to move, and not many years before Wilfrid and Gertrude 'downsized' and moved away to Constantia, Gertrude finally succeeded in having the name established. It stands in recognition of their efforts: Richard's against apartheid and Gertrude's against bureaucracy.

With a stream at the bottom of the garden and an open wild field beyond that demanded exploring, Riverside was a wonderful place for a small boy to grow up. I played there for many happy hours in what was my equivalent of Klawer during Wilfrid's youth. In winter the Cannon Stream would be a raging torrent and in summer, while the volume of water was much reduced, it was still sufficient in those days for the local boys from up the road to swim in its pools. As soon as I was old enough Wilfrid gave me the Diana air rifle that his father had presented to him at about the same age and in this semi-rural environment I too would hunt for birds. I also caught Cape galaxias, an indigenous mountain minnow, in the stream with bait of earthworms dug from the rich soil of the garden.

Later, when I was older, I was allowed to go off on my own to fish the Liesbeek River, into which the Cannon Stream flowed. This was stocked annually by the Cape Piscatorial Society with rainbow trout from the Jonkershoek hatchery in Stellenbosch. Sadly, SA Breweries, which owned the land around the Cannon Stream, sold it in the late 1960s. It was developed into a housing estate and the paradise was lost. The road through the estate was called Ohlsson Way, in honour of Anders Ohlsson, who had founded the commercial brewing industry in South Africa, the cornerstone of what is now the second-largest brewer of beer in the world, SAB Miller.

One of our other neighbours was an Englishwoman, Meg Allan, who took a liking to me. I used to visit her almost daily after I got back home from kindergarten. What impressed me about her was that she had her own toolbox, something Wilfrid did not own. When she decided to return to England she gave me the toolbox as a present, and with this and some guidance from our handyman, Bert Hankey, the small repairs in the house became my responsibility. This, I think, was a great relief to Wilfrid, as he was all thumbs when it came to practical matters and my new-found skills enabled him to concentrate on matters of the mind.

Meg Allan used to go on fly-fishing holidays in the Underberg, in what was then Natal. When she moved back to the UK, she also gave me her fly-fishing equipment. Armed with my newly acquired rod and accessories, I was taken by Wilfrid to visit his old friend, the writer Elsa Joubert, who had a house in Stellenbosch on the banks of the Eerste River. Naught came of my efforts in the river, but on the return trip we stopped at the wine farm Meerlust to visit Wilfrid's friend and the owner, Nico Myburgh. On the farm there was an old quarry full of water, which had been stocked with rainbow trout. It was there that I caught my first rainbow of about ten inches. Wilfrid was immensely proud of this achievement and on the basis of this success he introduced me to Judge Jack Watermeyer, who was then president of the Cape Piscatorial Society (CPS) and who later became Judge President of the Cape from 1979 to 1981. I became a junior member of the CPS. This was the start of many forays with Wilfrid into the hinterland to visit various rivers in the Western Cape. From these trips – in hindsight, all too few – I gained an insight into him and some of the people he encountered in his legal escapades.

Gertrude was a keen swimmer and gardener. She saved up to build one of the first private swimming pools in Cape Town and landscaped the garden around it. For eight months of the year she swam every morning; and most weekends in summer were spent mowing the lawn, digging, planting and pruning. Out of the many hours she laboured and the money she spent on plants, compost and fertiliser, she created a small Eden, which the whole family loved. Wilfrid, though never a gardener, would come home from chambers on summer evenings and sit on the patio in the centre of the garden under a magnificent syringa tree, reading the newspaper or a book or listening to his radio, and there seek solitude from whatever was preoccupying him 'at work'.

The patio under the syringa tree was also the venue for many happy braais, drinks parties and dinners with Wilfrid and Gertrude's numerous friends. On these occasions many bottles of wine were consumed – 'libations', as Wilfrid called them – from his cellar in the garage. The word 'cellar' is used very loosely, as some of the wine was kept in a long cupboard he had built or in an empty coal bin, or else boxes were stacked wherever there was space. These were not ideal conditions for maturing wine. Together with wine – not all of it fine, unfortunately – went good food. Gertrude was a wonderful cook and she prepared many memorable dishes. The empty wine bottles – 'dead soldiers', according to Wilfrid – were thrown onto the lawn to be collected at a later stage. Wilfrid was an inveterate recycler of bottles and would hoard them in the garage until the boxes were overflowing and it became time to take them down to the local bottle store.

As I grew older I would be pressed into looking after the braai or helping in some way. While at times I found it irksome, it also drew me into the company, where I was able to listen to the interesting conversation. From a young age the three of us children were treated as adults and involved where practicable with the entertainment of Wilfrid and Gertrude's friends, with the result that we became comfortable in the company of adults.

One of the regular visitors in the summer who helped empty many of the wine bottles was the celebrated English chef John Tovey, who ran Miller Howe Hotel in the Lake District.

Gertrude, who had a great interest in and knowledge of food, met John on one of his cooking demonstration tours of South Africa and they became the best of friends. He would flee the gloom of the English winter to enjoy the Cape Town summer and spend hours around our pool. Then, when Wilfrid and Gertrude returned from a day's work – they seldom took holidays at that time of year; in fact they seldom took holidays – they would join him in the garden and the food, wine and conversation would flow. Gertrude and John would disappear into the kitchen to create wonderful things and were often heard bickering about how to make some dish or other. In many instances John learned more from Gertrude, who was an excellent, practical cook.

While much of the joy of Riverside was taken outside, the inside was as important a space for us children. In all parts of the house there were books and Wilfrid and Gertrude encouraged us to read from an early age. Wilfrid was an avid reader on a wide variety of topics, but his true passion was James Joyce. In the main passage of the house there were bookshelves reaching to the ceiling that were stuffed with all manner of 'important' books, including a set of *Encyclopaedia Britannica* – the Google of our time – and extending to books on nature, history and politics, as well as a vast range of other subjects. In the passage outside my sisters' bedrooms was a long, low set of shelves that contained our books. These started off with works by Enid Blyton and the like, but as we got older we graduated to novels by Ed McBain, Zane Grey and Alistair MacLean, interspersed with many other genres and topics. In the dining room, later changed to a TV room, was a smaller row of shelves full of Penguin paperbacks; and in the lounge, in a closed-off doorway, was part of Gertrude's collection of cookery books; the rest were housed in the kitchen on a shelf above the stove, which literally groaned under their weight. Finally we each had our own collection in our bedrooms. All this was on top of Wilfrid's working library at his chambers, consisting of law reports and other law books, which he donated to the University of the Western Cape when he retired. As the shelves at home filled beyond capacity, piles started growing in all sorts of other places around the house.

Thinking back now, the number and diversity of books were staggering. Sadly, a great many of them would be culled when Wilfrid and Gertrude moved to Constantia in 1994. The move from Riverside would also be the end of the lunches and dinners we had enjoyed with friends outside, and there would be no more dead soldiers tossed onto the lawn.

NOTES:

[1] *Cape Times*, December 2013

[2] *Rogues, Rebels and Runaways* by Nigel Penn (Cape Town, David Philip, 1999)

CHAPTER 6

THE TRIAL OF STEPHANIE KEMP AND THE A.R.M. SABOTEURS

Wilfrid's first major political trial in which he defended three young white saboteurs

> '*The wind of change is blowing through the continent and whether we like it or not, this growth of national consciousness is a political fact. We must accept it as a fact and national policies must take account of it.*'
> – HAROLD MACMILLAN, 3 FEBRUARY 1960

The year 1960 was a dramatic one for South Africa, a 'turning point at which South Africa did not turn'.[1] The stage was set by the visit of British Prime Minister Harold Macmillan, who in a prophetic address in Parliament on 3 February announced to South African MPs that they could no longer ignore the 'wind of change' that was sweeping through Africa. It was not long before the turbulence was felt in South Africa. In March, police fired on unarmed people in the township of Sharpeville outside Vereeniging who had come to the police station to protest about the hated pass laws in a campaign organised by the Pan Africanist Congress (PAC). Rioting broke out in other cities and the government, facing its biggest crisis to date, declared a state of emergency, arrested thousands of people and then banned both the ANC and PAC.

Three weeks later South African Prime Minister Hendrik Verwoerd appeared at a fifty-year anniversary celebration of the 1910 Union of South Africa at the Rand Easter Show at Milner Park. In his speech there was no mention of Sharpeville or the ensuing countrywide violence. Afterwards he strolled around the grounds looking at prize livestock before returning to his seat in the VIP area. Seated nearby was a wealthy businessman, David Pratt, with farming interests in the Magaliesburg. Soon after Verwoerd was seated, Pratt rose, walked across to him and shot him twice in the face with a .22 calibre pistol. Pratt was immediately taken into custody.

Having been afflicted by epilepsy as a young boy, Pratt had gone on to receive psychiatric treatment throughout most of his adult life. After his first divorce, he suffered acute depression and underwent electric shock treatment in the United States. Between 1956 and 1958 he was repeatedly hospitalised, and his second wife left him to return to her native Holland with their two children. It was therefore of little surprise that even before the trial, his counsel, Advocate Issy Maisels QC, lodged an application to the court that Pratt was insane and would not be fit to stand trial. The Judge President of the Transvaal, Judge FLH Rumpff, presided over the trial and ordered that Pratt be sent for two weeks' observation at Weskoppies Mental Hospital. The head physician's report to the court concluded that Pratt was indeed insane and he was committed to a mental hospital in Bloemfontein, where he committed suicide in October 1961, aged 53.

Meanwhile, though seriously wounded by the assassination attempt, Verwoerd recovered. Moreover, he drew the lesson that his being spared was a mark of divine approbation and this filled him with the conviction that he should pursue his political path with renewed vigour. A showdown with the opponents of apartheid seemed inevitable.

Even before Sharpeville, leading figures in the ANC had been debating the question whether, in the face of the government's implacable refusal to countenance black demands, the resort to armed struggle and violence was not perhaps justified and inevitable. This question acquired greater urgency after the events surrounding Sharpeville. Finally, on 16 December 1961 the formation of Umkhonto we Sizwe (MK, or Spear of the Nation), the ANC's armed wing, was announced with the aim of being 'a fighting arm of the people against the government and its policies of racial oppression'. In its first years MK would confine itself to acts of sabotage without endangering human life. It conducted more than 200 operations to damage public installations and infrastructure, but this only spurred on police efforts to apprehend the perpetrators. A tip-off from an informant eventually led to the arrest of a number of senior ANC and MK leaders in July 1963 at the farm Liliesleaf outside Johannesburg. On 9 October 1963 the Rivonia Trial commenced at the Palace of Justice in Pretoria and it ended with the accused, including Nelson Mandela, Govan Mbeki and Walter Sisulu, being sentenced to life imprisonment on Robben Island.

But the turn to 'armed struggle' was not only confined to black opponents of apartheid. In 1960 some disaffected white members of the Liberal Party and like-minded others, who now believed that a strategy of non-violence could no longer be sustained, set up the small and obscure National Committee for Liberation (NCL), which never had more than 60 members in both Johannesburg and Cape Town. Two years later, in an attempt to rejuvenate itself, it would change its name to the African Resistance Movement (ARM). The ARM, according to a contemporary newspaper report, 'had as its aim the overthrow of the South African Government, or the coercion thereof to change its policies of apartheid and limited franchise for non-whites'.[2]

In the second half of 1963, the ARM began a campaign of sabotage of government installations and services, explicitly eschewing violence against people. In the Cape Peninsula, attempts were made to blow up a number of signal cables for railway lines, power pylons outside Cape Town and the Constantiaberg radio mast, with varying degrees of success. The climax of the campaign came in June 1964 with the sabotaging of five pylons, two in Johannesburg and three in Cape Town. On 4 July 1964, as part of a week-long series of raids, the police visited the flat of Adrian Leftwich, a lecturer at the University of Cape Town and former president of NUSAS, who was then a member of the planning committee of the ARM. While searching his premises in Lemon Lane, Newlands – close to where Wilfrid and Gertrude lived – they found by chance a training document on the use of explosives hidden in a book.

The police allowed Lynette van der Riet, Leftwich's girlfriend and another member of the planning committee, who was present at the time of the raid, to leave. She rushed to her home in Rosebank to dispose of equipment, explosives and incriminating documents that, contrary to ARM rules, had been stored in her flat and garage. But she was followed by the police and arrested, as was Leftwich shortly thereafter. Soon after being detained, she was beaten by the police and within a few days was 'broken' and started divulging the names of members of the ARM. During the ensuing police dragnet, explosives, detonators and more training material were found in the garage of another ARM member, student Michael Schneider, in Sea Point, as well as in other garages around the Peninsula.

As chief organiser, Leftwich had been deeply involved with the ARM and knew a great deal about the organisation. He was detained under the General Law Amendment Act, commonly known as the 90-day law, for it allowed the detention of people for up to 90 days without charge. From an early stage in his interrogation, certainly before he was subjected to serious physical abuse, Leftwich started to divulge information damaging to the organisation. Slowly he revealed the names of his ARM colleagues and friends in Johannesburg, including his close friend, Hugh Lewin. The tipping point in the interrogation came with the planting of a bomb by ARM member John Harris at the Johannesburg railway station[3] on 24 July 1964, which killed a 77-year-old woman and injured 23 others, five of whom suffered terrible burns. The bombing enraged the police and, faced with their obvious anger, the imminent threat of violent interrogation and the knowledge that he could be sentenced to death for his involvement in acts of sabotage, Leftwich capitulated and divulged everything he knew about the organisation. Given the amount of incriminating evidence he revealed, the judge at his trial, Andries Beyers, would in his wry manner say of Leftwich that to call him a rat would be unfair to rats.

The news of Leftwich's detention spread rapidly among his friends. While some members of the ARM fled across the borders to Botswana and Swaziland or to the United Kingdom, 29 were arrested and taken into detention by the police. Among those arrested was Stephanie Kemp, then 23, who came from a strong Afrikaner background. Born in 1941 in the small Eastern Cape town of Steynsburg on the edge of the Great Karoo, Kemp moved when her father was transferred to the same *platteland* town in which Wilfrid had grown up, Malmesbury. And as Wilfrid had, she too observed how the Dutch Reformed Church dominated the town. In the early 1950s her father was transferred once more, this time to Port Elizabeth where she attended Collegiate Girls' High and where she became aware of the poverty and injustice around her. In 1960 she began studying physiotherapy at UCT where she came to realise that 'Sharpeville and detention without trial were ways in which my people [Afrikaners] were trying to claw their way into white privilege in our country'. On campus she met and became involved with Adrian Leftwich. According to him, she was recruited into the ARM around March 1963. She was arrested on 12 July 1964, detained under the 90-day law and held at Maitland police station for three weeks. She was then moved to Caledon Square police station in central Cape Town, all the time being held in solitary confinement and subjected to regular interrogations by the Security Police two or three times a day. Though at first they were not severe, this changed with the Harris bombing. The police then began to intensify their interrogation of her and she received the full attention of the notorious Sergeant 'Spyker' van Wyk.[4]

On 1 August she was taken to a small room in Caledon Square and made to stand through the day and into the night. Then in the early hours of 2 August, Van Wyk and Captain Rossouw, his superior, entered her cell and after a brief lecture from Rossouw that she should confess everything she knew he left the room, leaving Van Wyk to live up to his reputation. He brutally assaulted her until she lost consciousness.[5] She would be the first woman in South Africa to be assaulted in detention. This incident signalled a general change in the degree of violence the police would use in their interrogations in the years to come, regardless of race or gender. After he finished with Kemp, Van Wyk and his sidekick, Detective Constable Theo Zandberg, then went to her co-accused, the student Alan Brooks, who had also been detained and was also in solitary confinement. They beat him, with Zandberg sitting on Brooks's back and twisting his ankle with such force that he fractured it.[6]

While they were still in detention, the parents of Alan Leftwich, Alan Brooks and Stephanie Kemp approached Himan Bernadt, a senior partner in the firm of attorneys Frank, Bernadt & Joffe, which was known for taking on anti-apartheid clients.[7] A quiet-spoken and fatherly man who always appeared composed, Bernadt had a lot in common with Wilfrid Cooper. Not only were he and Wilfrid involved in a number of politically related trials and inquests, but Himie and his wife Jean were good friends of the Coopers and they would often see each other socially either at the Coopers' home in Newlands or the Bernadt home in Kenilworth. After the Rivonia trial, Himie would look after the affairs of Nelson Mandela and other members of the ANC on Robben Island. It was Himie whose help and legal representation the Leftwich, Kemp and Brooks families sought when their children were eventually charged and free to consult with a lawyer.

Through messages smuggled out of prison, Bernadt knew that Brooks and Kemp had been assaulted by Spyker van Wyk and his cohorts.[8] He contacted Albie Sachs, a junior advocate at the Cape Bar and activist who also represented people arrested for their opposition to apartheid. Sachs himself was on the authorities' radar, having been detained twice and held in solitary confinement, as it would turn out, in the same cells in which Brooks and Kemp found themselves. Over lunch Sachs and Bernadt discussed the matter without reaching a conclusion about how to proceed in view of the fact that the three were being detained under the 90-day law and were unavailable to them. A short while later local newspapers published accounts of their treatment in jail under the headline 'Smuggled messages told of assault' and informed readers that the British consul had visited Alan Brooks as he was a British citizen and that his attorney would be taking steps to have the ill-treatment investigated. The Security Police declined to comment.

A few weeks later Bernadt contacted Sachs again, this time to inform him that the detainees were finally going to be charged and that he had written instructions from the parents of the three to represent them. Bernadt was duly present in court for the hearing, but Leftwich was notably absent from the proceedings and only Brooks and Kemp were there to be charged. While he was technically still his client, the police refused to let Bernadt see Leftwich. This seemed to confirm, as had been speculated, that he was being held by the police to leach him of information and use him as a witness against his former ARM colleagues.

At an interview at Roeland Street jail with their clients, now only two in number, Bernadt and Sachs saw for themselves the results of the beatings administered by the police and heard in detail what had happened while their clients had been detained. On the assumption that Leftwich was going to act as a witness for the State, they knew that defending their clients in court would not be easy and it was uppermost in Bernadt's mind that he had to choose his lead counsel well. Many advocates at that time were not keen to handle political cases and preferred to focus on ordinary commercial and criminal matters to earn a living. He knew, however, that Wilfrid would be unafraid to act in a trial of this nature.

In his book *Stephanie on Trial* (1968), Sachs wrote: 'The leader of the team responsible for Alan [Brooks] and Stephanie's defence was Wilfred [*sic*], a lithe, ambitious advocate regarded as one of the leading trial lawyers at the Cape Bar. Before starting to practise he had been a public prosecutor and had developed a fierce cross-examining style which had led many of his colleagues to call him by the nickname "Tiger". His court manner had lost none of its attack, and his lively temperament, which he always harnessed fully to his client's cause, drew many people to watch him in action. Yet the main basis of his successes was less spectacular: the fanatical thoroughness with which he always prepared his cases and his flair for adjusting rapidly and sensibly to the shifting fortunes of trial. His appearance was strikingly youthful, but he had a penetrating caustic voice and verbal facility of a much older man. The wide interests of his earlier years – he was now approaching forty – had given way to a passion to be a respected advocate and, one day possibly, a judge. The pending sabotage trial threatened to raise many tricky issues for the defence, but if well-handled could materially enhance counsel's reputation. Many of our colleagues would have found a way out of accepting such a brief, but Himie was confident that even if he disagreed profoundly with their views, Wilfred [sic] would do wholehearted and intelligent battle for his clients.'[9]

Bernadt asked Sachs to act as Wilfrid's junior. He agreed, albeit with some reluctance, as he himself was then receiving much attention from the authorities and was planning to leave the country in the next few months because of the political climate. But from the first time Sachs had read in the newspapers of Stephanie Kemp's arrest and detention, he had become intrigued with and enamoured of her and this was no doubt a significant reason for his decision to remain in Cape Town and see the trial to its conclusion.

The trial attracted significant interest in the press. It was clear that this was not going to be a low-key event. Four legal teams had been assembled to represent the five accused: accused no. 1 was a 30-year-old 'coloured' photographer, Edward (Eddie) Daniels; accused no. 2 the student David 'Spike' de Keller; accused no. 3 the student Anthony Trew; accused no. 4 Alan Brooks; and accused no. 5 Stephanie Kemp. The trial was to commence on 2 November 1964 and had been set down for six weeks in Court 1. The defence team speculated that the trial judge would be the Judge President, Andries Beyers. Sachs, who had not appeared before him, initially thought that having Judge Beyers preside could be a possible advantage to them as in his youth Beyers had been, he was told, a bit of a firebrand and thus might be sympathetic to their clients. But Wilfrid knew from his encounter with the judge at the Rossouw trial three years before that Beyers was unpredictable and would not hesitate to impose the death penalty if he saw reason to do so. Judge Beyers could be charming at times and then scathing in his handling of counsel. It was said that a day in court with Judge Beyers was like a week with any other judge on the Bench – a gruelling experience.

The defence team met in Wilfrid's chambers in Dorp Street, where they studied the charge sheet and started working through a mountain of papers related to their clients' activities. The main charge was conspiracy to commit acts of sabotage over a period of ten months – this carried a sentence of no less than five years in jail, with the maximum being the death penalty. They were also charged with being members of an unlawful organisation and, as an alternative, furthering the aims of communism in terms of the Suppression of Communism Act. As they sifted through the paperwork, they discovered that Brooks had allegedly received training in how to handle explosives and had been involved in attempts to blow up signal cables; his situation was serious. Kemp's position was less so, as her active involvement was confined to her hiring a garage in Oranjezicht for use as a workshop and twice driving a car used by saboteurs. As the documents that the prosecution had given the defence team did not reflect the names of the accused, it was apparent that the prosecutor would be relying on the testimony of witnesses, which no doubt included Leftwich, to implicate the accused and bolster the State's case at the trial.

Wilfrid's instructions were that his clients would plead not guilty to the charges they were facing. Consequently, the defence team decided to focus on Leftwich and build up as much information as they could to use against him in Wilfrid's cross-examination. From the papers they gauged that Leftwich had crumbled early on in his interrogation by the Security Police[10] and they surmised that, even if not told by the police, it would have dawned on him that he faced the death penalty for his leading role in the ARM. Wilfrid therefore knew he would probably be a motivated, credible and crucial witness for the State, so it was essential that he try to deflect his testimony from Brooks and Kemp. As Leftwich was still being held by the police, Wilfrid would only know what he would divulge to the court and how it would affect the defence of his clients when Leftwich was on the witness stand.

While the defence team was united in its opposition to apartheid and wholeheartedly dedicated to rendering the best defence they could for their clients, it became apparent during their time together that Sachs and Wilfrid were not necessarily of the same mind on politics in general. After studying the documents that the State had seized, Wilfrid voiced the opinion that the ARM was really a self-styled group of unknown idealists, mainly white, and rank amateurs in what they were trying to do. Van der Riet had led the police to her flat where most of the incriminating papers had been stored right next to the explosives, all easily found by the police when they conducted their search. When the police started their arrests, many of the main members fled the country, while Leftwich, one of their leaders, had almost immediately confessed everything he knew to the police. The cumulative effect of all this was that the organisation collapsed in just a few weeks. Their underground activities, Wilfrid told Sachs, were almost treated like some game. Sachs disagreed with his evaluation and said he believed they were brave young people, suggesting that from a technical point of view they had actually been quite successful in their efforts and at the same time – John Harris apart – had not injured anyone when conducting their sabotage. Sachs felt they could be compared with the untrained, ill-equipped but motivated resistance fighters in France in the Second World War, who at the war's end came to be regarded as heroes by their countrymen. Wilfrid did not share this sentiment and retorted that time would not show any of the ARM members to have been heroes; in the end they would be lost in historical obscurity.

At the Rivonia trial a few months earlier, the accused had disputed the legitimacy of the courts and condemned the laws under which they were being charged. Nelson Mandela's profound speech from the dock, in which he expressed such sentiments, would reverberate around the world. But given the ARM's minor role in the liberation struggle, the defence team did not believe this would be a prudent approach for their clients. Sachs therefore suggested that their clients should be presented to the court not as criminals but as idealists, who were responsible for their actions in the context of what was happening in the country at the time.

As the date of the trial approached the team met with Stephanie Kemp at Roeland Street jail. Both Bernadt and Sachs had seen her on a number of occasions – Sachs had visited her so regularly that the warders started to call him her boyfriend. In some ways this was not far from the truth, for on one occasion he breached legal etiquette with a client and brought her a rose. Wilfrid, as the defence team leader, had not yet met her. At that time he was 38, had been at the Bar for 12 years, had established name as an academic and writer on law and was planning the next important step in his career the following year, that of taking silk. His approach with Kemp was professional and his voice carried the strength of his convictions as her defence advocate. Talking quietly and distinctly, he methodically explained the reason for the meeting and proceeded to outline what she could expect in her coming court appearance – it all came down to what the State could prove, he told her, about the extent of her involvement in the ARM's sabotage activities. He also told her that he had discussed with the prosecutor, Mr M Beukes, the statement she made while in detention and had pointed out to him that it was made under duress and not, as required by the law, committed to writing before a magistrate. Beukes had therefore agreed that he would not refer to the document in the trial proceedings. Wilfrid also touched on the matter of her assault by Spyker van Wyk and said that this would be a matter for a civil action at a later stage.

With weeks of preparatory work behind them, the trial was now imminent and they knew for certain that Andries Beyers would be the presiding judge. Wilfrid told his team that this would have an important effect on how the trial would unfold. While the trial had been set down on the court roll for six weeks, he could not see Beyers wanting to take so long on the matter and the judge would therefore look for ways to truncate proceedings. This, Wilfrid feared, would affect the time he would be allowed for cross-examination of witnesses and ultimately the direction of his defence. The risk was that he would again have to parry with the judge, as he had done in the Rossouw trial. What is more, his experience of State witnesses had given him cause to think that guilt for betraying their former friends and colleagues might make them venomous on the stand. If Leftwich were like this, he could adversely affect the defence strategy. Wilfrid therefore worked tirelessly on his list of questions that he believed would counter Leftwich's testimony and expose him for what he was.

On the Sunday before the trial started, the team met at Wilfrid's chambers. While deliberating on how to handle the various hurdles that faced them, Wilfrid had a phone call from the defence team for Anthony Trew. Headed by Johannesburg advocate Sydney Kentridge,[11] they had just arrived in Cape Town and wanted to meet later that morning and compare notes on the trial. Not much came of the meeting but in the late afternoon Wilfrid was again called and this time he was informed that Trew's team had been in some delicate discussions with the prosecutor. The latter was now prepared to accept that Trew could plead guilty to the alternative charge of furthering the aims of communism and, in consideration of this, the charge of sabotage would be dropped. This meant that the death sentence would no longer be a factor and Trew would merely face a term of imprisonment.

Wilfrid immediately discussed this with Sachs and Bernadt. They agreed that the same option would be a great advantage to their clients as their involvement in ARM had been less than Trew's. The stance that the prosecutor had taken until that time was such that the team had seen little opportunity to negotiate a plea, but now a precedent had been set. They needed to initiate discussions with the prosecutor as soon as possible; but it was too late then, and there would be little time the following morning as the trial was set down to commence at ten o'clock. They agreed that first thing in the morning Wilfrid would go alone and see the prosecutor in his chambers to establish if there was room for similar negotiations for Brooks and Kemp.

On the Monday morning Sachs and Bernadt arrived early at Wilfrid's chambers and he set off to see the prosecutor. After a wait longer than they would have liked, he returned with the good news that after conferring with the police, the prosecutor agreed to drop the charge of sabotage against Brooks and Kemp and for them to plead guilty to the lesser charge. With the court about to commence, they gathered their papers and briefcases and set off to see their clients in the holding cells to tell them the good news – it was barely a quarter of an hour before Judge Beyers would walk into Court 1. Immediately upon being informed by the prosecutor of the guilty pleas to the alternative charge, Beyers ordered that the trials of Brooks, Trew and Kemp be separated from that of Daniels and De Keller, and their hearing was set for the following week on 9 November.

The new trial judge would be BFJ Banks, who had a more benign reputation.

After the separation of the trial and the agreement with the prosecutor, Wilfrid now also took over the defence of Trew, with Advocate Roger Whiting as his junior. The team met on the Sunday before the trial to finalise how they would proceed in court the following day. After some debate it was agreed that they would follow the unusual approach of not asking any questions of the prosecution witnesses unless circumstances required it. Their clients would make admissions only to the extent that it would be necessary for the prosecution to lead their evidence. The three accused would then make statements to the court about their actions and would be followed by their fathers, who would give evidence in mitigation as to the good character of their children. With this strategy and with guilty pleas agreed upon with the prosecutor, the trial would be a short affair, probably no more than a day. To Wilfrid's chagrin this meant that while Leftwich would give evidence for the prosecution, he would now not have the opportunity to ask the questions he had spent so long preparing for the cross-examination – there would be no opportunity for him to expose Leftwich for the turncoat that he was. The court record shows that Leftwich's evidence was ultimately largely banal.

The proceedings moved along smoothly. By lunch time Leftwich and the three policemen who had found the explosives and investigated the bombings had all testified. In the afternoon, it was left to the three accused to make their statements to the court. Trew was the first up. He described how in March 1964 he had come to meet Michael Schneider and learned of his involvement in an organisation that was collecting 'political intelligence'. At the end of May Schneider, as a matter of great secrecy, had informed him of plans to sabotage electrical pylons, away from buildings and people, in order to 'bring pressure to bear on public opinion'. In June his involvement in the organisation, whose name he still didn't know, escalated and he helped blow up an electricity pylon near Durbanville. Later he felt that it was a futile gesture and severed ties with Schneider and the organisation. In July, when he read of Leftwich's arrest, Schneider called to warn him that he was in danger of being arrested too, but he could not bring himself to leave the country and would rather 'face what was coming'. He concluded that 'Schneider never told me of any long-term aims, or any political programmes. I gathered that he was anti-communist and that his group's policy was simply opposition to apartheid. I no longer think that it was right for me to have helped him.'

Brooks then read a very brief statement to the court on how in the latter half of 1962 he joined the ARM 'because of a feeling of frustration' about the current situation in South Africa. Leftwich was his only contact, but he never got to know anything of the organisation and its activities. By June 1963, despite attempts to obtain a clear statement of the organisation's aims, nothing satisfactory was ever shown to him and he left.

Kemp was the last to read her statement to the court. This expressed a surprising level of naivety about the NCL/ARM and clearly tried, as with her admissions to the court, to place the blame for her involvement at the feet of Leftwich. 'I joined this organisation, the National Committee for Liberation, almost entirely because of Adrian Leftwich. He was a persuasive and dynamic person and when he approached me to join the organisation I felt flattered by his interest in me. Adrian to me personified the spirit of idealism and integrity. We developed a friendship that grew into a very intimate and personal association. I wanted to help humanity and I wanted to help Adrian – that was why I agreed to join the organisation.' She would claim that beyond 'brief discussions' she knew little about the ARM and its activities and saw no documents, that Leftwich had asked her to hire the garage in Oranjezicht and that she did so without asking any questions. 'My feelings for

Adrian were extremely deep, and the whole experience has been shattering to me.'

As a matter of procedure Judge Banks then found the three guilty of the charges and Wilfrid was allowed to introduce evidence in mitigation from Trew's and Brooks's fathers. For Kemp he called her father and also Dr Hymie Gordon, a lecturer in medicine at UCT and medical officer at SHAWCO, the students' outreach health service, where she had worked with him. From the testimony it was clear that all of them were shocked at their children being arrested, detained and tried in terms of the draconian apartheid legislation. After Wilfrid addressed the court in mitigation, the judge concluded the proceedings and postponed sentencing.

In his address in mitigation to the court, Wilfrid tried to deflect the personal responsibility of the three. In the case of Trew he was preoccupied with philosophy and personal issues and felt strongly about the injustices suffered by black people in South Africa. Schneider must therefore have had a strong influence over him, which led him to join the organisation. Brooks, he said, had been disillusioned with the organisation and left it of his own volition in June 1963 before any of the acts of sabotage had been committed. As for Kemp, he stressed that her young, warm and sympathetic nature, allied to a social conscience, left her 'susceptible to Leftwich's influence'. She was flattered by the approach of this leading personality, her involvement was primarily a personal one and 'not only has the organisation been destroyed, her feelings and attachment to Leftwich have been crushed'.

On being informed that the judge was ready to pronounce sentence on 11 November, Wilfrid, Bernadt and Sachs met in Wilfrid's chambers and speculated on the sentence the judge would hand down to their clients. The conversation turned to how Leftwich would fare. Again, the different views of Sachs and Wilfrid came to the fore. Wilfrid believed that from the start there had been little altruism in Leftwich, that people were basically selfish and that most people would want to avoid a lengthy term in jail and so would do whatever they could to save themselves from this fate. Leftwich's words from the witness box, that 'the common denominator was that we hoped a more fluent [sic] situation would arise in the country which would give opportunity for the changes we want', lacked substance and were only expressed to impart some importance to his actions and those of the ARM. At the end of the day Wilfrid believed that all Leftwich had really been interested in was himself and 'playing around with power and impressing a couple of silly starry-eyed girls, whose knowledge of politics hadn't extended beyond what they learned between the sheets'.[12]

In Sachs's account of the trial, he noted that the bluntness of Wilfrid's sentiments had challenged his own beliefs and caused him to reflect on the success of his own actions against apartheid up to that time. Sachs knew of Wilfrid's history in establishing NUSAS at Stellenbosch University and that he was politically aware and abhorred what the National Party government was doing to the country and its people. He knew him to be ambitious; his career as a successful advocate was on the rise and, in time, he had no doubt that he would be appointed to the Bench. He recognised that being prepared to act for political clients such as Brooks, Trew and Kemp took courage on Wilfrid's part and did not endear him to the government. It was his 'dogged sense of right'[13] that led him, despite having a family, to discard any self-interest that might have curtailed him from acting in such cases.

The sentencing was as anti-climactic as the trial. After reviewing the evidence presented, the role of the three accused and the evidence offered in mitigation, Judge Banks found that it was difficult to distinguish between Brooks and Trew and the roles they played. With Kemp, he accepted that she was under the influence of Leftwich, which to some extent mitigated her actions, but he could not ignore that she had been a member of the ARM for a considerable time, which included the period in which the acts of sabotage were committed. In concluding, he said that there must have been some objective consistent with their beliefs, but found it difficult to understand why they did not appreciate the utter futility of their actions and the consequences for themselves and their families. He sentenced Trew and Brooks to four years' imprisonment with two years suspended for three years, and Kemp to five years' imprisonment with three years suspended, provided she was not convicted again in terms of the Sabotage Act and the Suppression of Communism Act.

After her release from jail in December 1965, Kemp and Sachs's relationship blossomed. In July 1966, after being detained again and coerced by the Security Police to make a statement involving his political friends who had been arrested, Sachs left South Africa and went into exile in England, where he continued with his law studies and his work for the ANC. Kemp followed shortly after and they married later that year. They would have two children together, Alan and Michael, before divorcing in 1980. Sachs would later lose his arm to a car bomb when targeted by the apartheid government while in Mozambique. He would go on to play a major role in drawing up the constitution of the new South Africa and become one of the first judges appointed to the Constitutional Court.

The drama surrounding the ARM – especially the betrayal by Leftwich and the bombing by John Harris – provoked much anguish, revulsion and reflection among whites, especially among members of the Liberal Party. As the life of the philosopher Rick Turner reveals, the futility of the ARM's activities caused many young white opponents of apartheid to turn their backs on violence and to seek other ways of challenging the apartheid state. But in the main, for the vast majority of South Africans, the ARM was as Wilfrid correctly predicted soon forgotten. In the dominant narrative of the liberation struggle its role has been almost entirely erased in favour of the achievements of Umkhonto we Sizwe, the ANC's armed wing.[14]

In conclusion, it was perhaps of Wilfrid and others like him that John Dugard was reminded when he wrote this passage in his 1978 book on *Human Rights and the South African Legal Order*: 'The South African Bar has a proud record of defending persons charged with political offences. Past leaders of the Bar ensured that however hostile the political mood of the day may have been, the political offender was not without able and dedicated counsel. This laudable tradition has continued since 1948 and distinguished advocates ... ensured that persons of all races charged with treason, terrorism, sabotage and other political crimes have received the best available legal defence ... Although every advocate is obliged to accept a brief for the defence of an alleged political offender, the burden has inevitably fallen upon a small group of skilled trial lawyers whose opposition to government policies is well known.'[15]

NOTES:

[1] The description is from John Kane-Berman, when he was CEO of the South African Institute for Race Relations. He likened the aftermath of the Sharpeville massacre to that which followed the Soweto uprising of 1976; they were both, according to him, 'turning points where South Africa did not turn'.

[2] *Sunday Times*, 1 November 1964

[3] In his book *Inside BOSS: South Africa's Secret Police* (Harmondsworth, Penguin, 1981), Gordon Winter claims that he was told by General HJ van den Bergh of BOSS that the railway police knew about the bomb and had called him and he in turn had called John Vorster on his hotline. Nothing was done to evacuate the area. After the bomb exploded, the government was able to exploit the carnage to the maximum. Harris was tried, found guilty, sentenced to death and executed on 1 April 1965. He was the only white person executed for a political offence in the apartheid era.

[4] It is rumoured that warrant officer Hernus van Wyk earned his nickname from driving a nail, a *spyker* in Afrikaans, through the scrotum of one of his interrogation victims. This appears to be supported by the testimony of Christmas Tinto [TRC Case CT00477] arrested in 1963 and taken to Bellville police station. He testified that Van Wyk took a pair of pliers, squeezed the cover of his penis and pulled out his pubic hairs until he was unconscious.

[5] *TRC Report*, Volume 3, Chapter 5, p. 404

[6] Both Kemp and Brooks later sued the minister of justice, Van Wyk and Zandberg for R4,000 and R2,000 respectively, but received eleventh-hour out-of-court settlements, by which the State avoided having the cases heard in open court.

[7] After the 1964 Rivonia trial, Himie Bernadt looked after the affairs of Nelson Mandela and other members of the ANC on Robben Island. In April 2008 he was posthumously awarded the Order of Luthuli in Silver for 'providing legal defence to anti-apartheid activists and excellent contribution in advancing justice and human rights in the legal field'.

[8] From evidence that came before the Truth and Reconciliation Commission, warrant officer Hernus JP 'Spyker' van Wyk was the individual most consistently associated with torture in the Western Cape over a period of 30 years (*TRC Report*, Volume 3, Chapter 5, p. 402).

[9] *Stephanie on Trial* by Albie Sachs (London, Harvill, 1968)

[10] Wilfrid was correct in his assessment that Leftwich, when faced with the prospect of 20 years in jail, co-operated with the Security Police. In 2002 he would write an eloquent self-confessing essay titled 'I Gave the Names', in which he said: 'In

the gulf that opened up between my reach and my limits, between my knowledge and my self-ignorance, between my fantasies and my capacities, I crashed.' 'The suddenness, speed and near-comprehensiveness of the disintegration of my will and ability to resist interrogation in solitary confinement took me totally by surprise. It took others by surprise, too. I just caved in. It did not happen privately, but publicly and in full view of everyone who knew me.' Stephanie Kemp would meet him in the 1990s and, despite having been betrayed by him, commented about his 'courage in taking on the apartheid state at such a young age and his fortitude in bearing the notoriety of stumbling in the face of enormous state repression' (*The Independent*, 4 April 2015).

[11] Sir Sydney Kentridge is one of South Africa's eminent jurists. Being four years older than Wilfrid, he served in the Second World War and then attended Exeter College, Oxford. He was admitted to the Johannesburg Bar in 1949 and was appointed counsel in 1965. In 1977 he was called to the English Bar and the following year represented the Biko family at the inquest of the death of Steve Biko, where he exposed the lies that the police presented in their attempts to hide their brutal handling of Biko. In 1984 he was appointed Queen's Counsel and he was knighted in 1999. After refusing to act as a judge under apartheid, he took time from his London practice to sit as an acting judge on the Constitutional Court. In 2008 he was awarded the Order of the Baobab in Gold for his exceptional contribution to the fight against unjust apartheid-era laws.

[12] In a court appearance Leftwich told the court, 'I have been stupid; I think we've all been stupid and I think we realise we've been stupid and that we have indirectly and not unintentionally endangered human life.' (Sachs, *Stephanie on Trial*, p. 129).

[13] *Stephanie on Trial* by Sachs (London, Harvill, 1968) p. 130

[14] SADET, *The Road to Democracy in South Africa, Volume 1, 1960–1970* (Pretoria, Unisa Press, 2010), p. 230

[15] John Dugard, *Human Rights and the South African Legal Order* (Princeton, Princeton University Press, 1978), p. 243

CHAPTER 7

'THE TRIAL OF THE CENTURY': THE HEARING INTO THE SANITY OF DEMITRIO TSAFENDAS

Wilfrid's most famous case, the defence of
the assassin of Prime Minister Hendrik Verwoerd

'I have before me, on the evidence, clearly a man with
a diseased mind, subject to delusion, so trammelled, if not
guided, by irrational forces that obviously I cannot begin to
find whether he is guilty or not guilty of a crime at law.'
– JUDGE ANDRIES BEYERS

I n a time of great social and political upheaval around the world, the 1960s was a decade that would come to be marked by a string of high-profile assassinations, from the killing by samurai sword of Inejiro Asanuma, leader of the Japanese Socialist Party, in October 1960 to the shooting of the US presidential candidate Robert F Kennedy in June 1968. As an avid reader, Wilfrid had a particularly strong interest in the most notorious assassination of them all: that of President John F Kennedy in 1963. In the course of his wide reading he came across the book *The Assassins* (1956) by Robert J Donovan in which the author wrote: 'Assassinations and attempted assassinations of American presidents involved neither organised attempts to shift political power from one group to another, nor to perpetuate a particular man or party in office, nor to alter the policy of the government, nor to resolve ideological conflicts … By and large the true story is that the assassins not only were lone operators, but were, most of them, men suffering from mental disease, who pulled the trigger while in the grip of delusion.'

Little did Wilfrid suspect when reading Donovan that just a few years later he would be the lead counsel at an assassination hearing that would have an enormous impact on the politics and history of South Africa, and on his own career. This was the hearing into the sanity of Demitrio Tsafendas, who had dramatically killed Dr Verwoerd in the House of Assembly on 6 September 1966.[1]

On 6 October 1966, after a brief session amid heavy security in a specially constituted court at Caledon Square police station in Cape Town, Demitrio Tsafendas, a messenger of Parliament, was indicted for the murder of the prime minister. The charge sheet read: 'That DEMITRIO TSAFENDAS is guilty of the crime of MURDER IN THAT upon 6th September 1966, and at Cape Town, in the District of the CAPE, he did wrongfully, unlawfully and maliciously kill and murder DR THE HONOURABLE HENDRIK FRENSCH VERWOERD,

Prime Minister of the Republic of South Africa.'

The trial was set down to commence at 10am on Monday, 17 October 1966. As Tsafendas had no legal representation, the Judge President of the Cape Provincial Division, Andries Beyers, called Wilfrid on 26 September and requested him to appear *pro deo* for the accused. In their telephone conversation Judge Beyers commented to Wilfrid that, as Tsafendas had stabbed Verwoerd in front of numerous witnesses, the only defence he thought possible was that he was mad. If not, then 'I will not hesitate to hang him. He will swing.' He then added that he would understand if Wilfrid did not wish to act for Tsafendas. Wilfrid ignored the comment and immediately agreed to being appointed. He requested that the judge appoint Advocate Willie Burger to act as his junior and David Bloomberg of Bloomberg, Baigel & Company as the instructing attorney.

With the trial date only three weeks away, Beyers had made it very clear that it was to be a summary trial with no preparatory examination and that he would not indulge any requests for extensions. After confirming their briefs with Wilfrid and Burger, Bloomberg immediately contacted the police at Caledon Square to arrange to meet their client for the first time that afternoon. Entering the cell, Wilfrid found before him an inert shape sprawled on a dirty blanket on the floor. As it slowly rose, it revealed the swarthy, heavily built, unkempt figure of a middle-aged man who, on the street, might have been taken for a down-and-out hobo. Tsafendas was escorted by a policeman to a secure room set aside for them to consult. There began a process of questioning that lasted many hours and days, to learn his life history and try to understand why he had stabbed Verwoerd. A policeman remained on guard outside throughout the visit.

On being told that Wilfrid had been appointed by Judge Beyers to act for him, Tsafendas answered, in good English, that he did not believe in legal representation as it was contrary to the tenets of his religious beliefs. After Wilfrid emphasised that, given the severity of the charge and the damning evidence against him, it was in his best interests to be represented at his trial, he agreed. Tsafendas then, in an almost reflective manner, muttered that he did not know 'why the Lord should have chosen such a frail person like me'[2] for the deed he had committed. He uttered the words softly and seemed to be in a daze: to Wilfrid, he was a spent force. It was soon apparent that he had limited concentration, would forget the questions asked of him and drift off the subject, giving illogical and absurd replies to such a degree that what he said sometimes sounded amusing to the three lawyers listening to him.

During the first consultation, after admitting to stabbing Dr Verwoerd, he described being overpowered by the members of Parliament who had rushed to the aid of the prime minister. They had, he said, beaten and kicked him before dragging him into the lobby, after which he was taken away in a police van to Caledon Square and then to Groote Schuur hospital to have his wounds seen to. Ironically, this was the same place to which Verwoerd was rushed and where he was pronounced dead. Tsafendas did not complain about the beating. In fact, he was quite philosophical about it and not surprised that he had been handled so roughly. While having no remorse, and as if the killing were part of a dream, he knew he had done something with traumatic consequences to his victim. It was clear to Wilfrid that Tsafendas was grappling within himself to understand why he had committed the murder. Having lived in a race-ridden society, Tsafendas obviously came to the conclusion that his actions had in some way been motivated by the effects of race discrimination.

In later visits Tsafendas appeared a little neater, courteous yet humourless. Wilfrid soon gained the impression that he was an articulate person of above-average intelligence; he spoke good English and had also learnt to speak a number of other languages. He had travelled the world extensively between leaving South Africa in 1942 and his return in 1963.

Slowly the defence team learned of his life. Demitrio Mimikos Tsafendas was born on 14 January 1918 in Lourenço Marques (now Maputo). His father, Michaelis, was from the Greek island of Crete and his mother was a Mozambican woman of colour. She had been his father's servant and there had been a short affair during which she fell pregnant. Shortly after Demitrio's birth, relations between his mother and father ended. Indeed, he never got to know her because at the age of one his father sent him to Egypt where he lived in Alexandria with his paternal grandmother, Katerina, for six years until she was too frail to care for him. She fondly nicknamed him Mimis. He was then sent back to Lourenço Marques, where in the meantime his father had done well for himself. He had married and had two children, with another on the way. Initially, his stepmother, Marika, endeavoured to treat Demitrio much like her own children, but after six months this began to change and he slowly felt he had become an interloper in the family. At nine he was sent to boarding school in Middelburg, Transvaal. Here he would encounter ethnic and racial prejudice for the first time: between English and Afrikaans speakers, between South Africans and Portuguese, and between black and white. It would be here that he was first referred to as 'coloured' by those at his school and was given the nickname 'Blackie'.

At 14 he returned to Lourenço Marques, by which time his father had gone bankrupt. His solitary and odd behaviour eventually led to him being shunned by his family, and at sixteen he moved to South Africa. In 1941 he joined the merchant navy and so started a life of endless travelling around the world – from North America to Europe to the Middle East – in an ongoing saga of poverty, arrest, admission to mental institutions and deportations. He told the defence team that he had not stayed long in any place. They looked at each other in surprise when he casually informed them that his travels were well documented and that the United States government had a thick file on him, which had been handed to the South African government. David Bloomberg arranged a formal appointment with the US ambassador to obtain a copy of the file: it would be used in the defence team's preparation for trial.

When asked how he came to stab Dr Verwoerd, Tsafendas replied that he did not know exactly and then trailed into unrelated rambling: 'quite a few people asked me questions how I got to Cape Town and I gave them…quite a few versions how I got to Cape Town but…my mind…my memory went bad a bit as to how I came to Cape Town as I was working there as a casual interpreter, was the fact that I received a letter through someone in my church, through a person in my church, and his pastor was in Cape Town. Later on, as I was going down the road' – then referring to Durban – 'I passed the racecourse and there must have been the…what do you call? The July Handicap. I have never been to horse racing in all my life because we don't go to racing but I…as I was passing by…I like animals…so I stopped and went to look at the horses running round the course and they were getting round the bend…and two jockeys I remember fell off.' Tsafendas did not appear to be aware that he was not answering the question and was oblivious to the bewilderment of those listening to him.

In the course of the interviews Tsafendas mentioned that he was host to a tapeworm. On being asked when he first became aware of it, he recalled that when he was 15 or 16 in Lourenço Marques he started getting severe pains in his stomach. A pharmacist from whom he sought advice supplied a laxative, which took effect almost immediately and while sitting on the toilet, he looked down into the pan and was horrified to see a monstrous tapeworm in his faeces. He could not, however, see the 'monster's head'. He told his legal team that the tapeworm controlled his life and that he would feel it wriggling inside him. During the course of his travels he had sought treatment to rid himself of the worm at a number of hospitals: on the Isle of Wight, in London, Boston, New York and Hamburg. He believed that without what he called his 'demon', 'dragon' or 'snake', he would have 'gone through life enjoying myself'.

It was clear to Wilfrid and his team that Tsafendas had mental problems, but to confirm their lay observations a trio of local experts was approached to examine him: Dr James MacGregor, a specialist psychiatrist and head of neurology at Groote Schuur hospital; Dr Aubrey Zabow, a specialist psychiatrist; and Dr Harold Cooper (no relation to Wilfrid), who was in private practice and who had a distinguished career working in psychiatric hospitals in Johannesburg and Cape Town. Dr Isaac Sakinofsky, acting head of the department of psychiatry at Groote Schuur, who had examined Tsafendas at 7pm on the day of the assassination, would also testify for the defence as to Tsafendas's mental state. He had come to the conclusion, and noted in his file at the time, that Tsafendas 'was not of sound mind, that his thought processes are grossly impaired and deluded and that he is therefore not in a position to evaluate correctly the consequences of his deed'.

The defence also had to address the physical aspect of the tapeworm and so a specialist physician, Dr Hendrik Muller, was included in the list of expert witnesses. He was chosen not only because he had an impeccable reputation but also because he was known to be the personal doctor of Judge Beyers. It was a strategic selection. Wilfrid recalled from the Rossouw trial that Judge Beyers could vigorously challenge his witnesses, but with the judge knowing Dr Muller he thought this was unlikely to happen in the Tsafendas trial.

Annexed to the charge sheet was a list of State witnesses, which included the names of Tsafendas's friends, co-religionists and other lay persons whom he had known in Cape Town and with whom he had had dealings. In preparation for the trial it was essential for Wilfrid's team to consult with these potential witnesses, but because their names were included in the State's witness list they were precluded from consulting with them without the State's consent. When approached, the prosecutor, the Attorney General Advocate Willem van den Bergh, refused to allow them access.

In view of this refusal, the defence team agreed to approach Judge Beyers to obtain an order permitting the defence to consult the witnesses on the State's list but, given the time limitations, this meant that the meeting would have to take place after hours at the judge's home. Wilfrid later recalled meeting the judge mid-morning on a Saturday in the front garden of his house, which stood on the mountainside above Clifton and looked out over the sparkling Atlantic Ocean. It was a fine spring day. The judge was dressed casually in shorts and *veldskoene*, and he cheerfully wished them a good morning. A charming host, he first took them round his bonsai garden. At the front door, after slipping off his *veldskoene*, he showed them into a drawing room, the floor of which was covered, as Wilfrid recalled, with a cerise Chinese silk carpet from Beijing. The relaxed atmosphere belied the earnest business they had come to discuss.

While still explaining the purpose of their visit, Wilfrid was interrupted by the judge, who said that he did not believe any party had a right to witnesses. But he then proceeded to give them instances when, as counsel, he had consulted with witnesses although their names were on the State's list. After finishing his story, his convivial demeanour ceased. From under his hooded eyes he told them that he did not intend to make an order in this case to allow them to see the State's witnesses but, pausing, added that if they went ahead and consulted with the witnesses and the prosecutor raised the matter with him, they knew what his ruling would be. It was clear that there was nothing further to discuss on the matter and so the team departed, leaving the judge to tend his bonsai garden. The defence consulted with the witnesses without demur from the State.

As the team continued with the preparation for the trial, they learned that Professor AJ van Wyk, the State's psychiatrist, was examining their client without their knowledge or consent. They immediately protested and the professor desisted. Van Wyk had appeared for the State in a number of trials. He was well qualified, being professor of psychiatry at the University of Pretoria, senior psychiatrist at the Pretoria General Hospital and a consulting psychiatrist for the department of prisons. He had examined Tsafendas on three occasions. Later in his report to the attorney general, he clearly stated that during his examinations Tsafendas was attentive and gave a good account of himself. Though he had complained of a tapeworm infestation, behaved peculiarly and had odd ideas, Van Wyk concluded: 'I have found no indications that he is incapable of following the court proceedings or…instructing his legal advisors and assisting them in the conduct of his defence.'[3]

At a pre-trial meeting, the attorney general and his junior, Donald Brunette, gave the defence a copy of Van Wyk's report to underline their contention that Tsafendas was a sane person and could stand trial for murder. Two years earlier, Van Wyk had testified for the State at the politically charged trial of John Harris, member of the African Resistance Movement, who had placed a bomb at the Johannesburg railway station that killed one person and seriously injured 23 others. The attack had aroused the fury of the government. During the trial Harris's defence raised the question of his mental state, claiming he 'was not wholly normal', and called the eminent Professor LA Hurst, professor of psychological medicine at the University of the Witwatersrand, to testify in mitigation that Harris was mentally disordered and not legally responsible for what he had done. Van Wyk in his testimony for the State had rejected this view and his opinion was accepted by the court. Harris was found guilty and condemned to death. Despite an appeal in which the defence established that Harris was unable to distinguish between right and wrong at the time of the bombing, the death sentence was upheld and Harris was executed on 1 April 1965. Would Van Wyk play a similar role in the trial of Demitrio Tsafendas?

The State's position was that while Tsafendas had some peculiar ways, he was neither insane nor mentally impaired and that he was, moreover, an assassin hired by some foreign agency – his purchasing of two knives on the morning of the assassination was, for them, conclusive proof that his actions were premeditated. As the murder of Verwoerd had taken place in full view of numerous members of Parliament, there was little doubt that, if tried as a sane person, he would be found guilty of the murder and Beyers would not hesitate to impose the death penalty.

Bloomberg's team had managed to track down people in Cape Town whom Tsafendas had personally known. These included Mr and Mrs Peter Daniels from Bellville South, who were classified 'coloured' and who were members of a multiracial religious sect, the Followers of Christ, with whom Tsafendas had lived from August to October 1965; Patrick O'Ryan, a coloured man from Lansdowne, and a member of the same sect; and Owen Smorenberg, a white maintenance foreman at the City of Cape Town power station in Dock road, under whom Tsafendas had worked for a short while.

Having just three weeks to prepare, the defence team was under immense pressure to make certain in the last few days before the trial that they had attended to every possible matter. This ranged from taking last-minute statements from witnesses, certifying documents and reports and consulting with overseas doctors to testify if required, to purchasing clothes for Tsafendas so that he was suitably dressed when he stepped into the dock. Preparation for the trial culminated on a Sunday evening, 16 October 1966, when the team met at David Bloomberg's elegant home in Kenilworth. After a final consultation with the expert witnesses and reviewing the evidence to be led the next day, the team members believed that they were ready.

The next morning, Monday, 17 October 1966, it was just getting light when Wilfrid arrived at his chambers in Dorp Street to complete his notes for his opening address to Judge Beyers in Court 1 in a few hours' time. The accuracy and veracity of his address to the court was of great importance and would be pivotal in determining the way the trial proceeded or, given the evidence he was to present, whether there would be a trial at all. Judge Beyers, he knew, had a strong personality but this was combined with a profound knowledge of the law and an inquiring, critical mind. He was a man who did not hesitate to express his views forcefully when he deemed it necessary. He had a powerful intellect and remarkable memory, and did not take notes. His Bench book, it was rumoured, lasted his whole career as a judge and was still in pristine condition when he retired in 1973. If challenged by counsel, he would tear into them and make it quite clear whose court it was. This Wilfrid had experienced five years earlier in his defence of Marthinus Rossouw: he believed that Beyers's comments had influenced the jury and thereby their guilty verdict. Wilfrid knew he had to avoid committing any error in his submissions to the court that would subject him to such exposure from the Bench, as it would affect the fate of his client.

Shortly after eight that Monday morning, Tsafendas was brought under heavy police guard from Caledon Square to the Cape Supreme Court in Keerom Street. Here the security was also tight: sharpshooters were placed on neighbouring rooftops and there was a heavy police presence in and around the court building. Outside the building a crowd of men and women of all ages, races and nationalities had gathered and jostled to catch a glimpse of Tsafendas as he arrived – the first sign of public interest in the trial. When Tsafendas appeared, there were fifty or so people milling around, but an hour later it was estimated this had increased to several hundred and the queue to enter the court stretched down Keerom Street. When again would they see the trial of a man who had assassinated a prime minister?

Around nine o'clock, a full hour before the court was due to sit, one of the four doors of the main entrance was opened and those waiting to file into the public galleries upstairs and downstairs were allowed in until all the seats were filled. Many more were left outside in Keerom Street, disapointed. Inside the court forty reporters, reputedly the most ever to have covered court proceedings in South Africa, were shown to the seats allocated to them. Many were from overseas. Those from South African newspapers had been selected for their expertise in accurate and rapid reporting. The local newspapers, the *Cape Times*, the *Cape Argus* and *Die Burger*, all had their specialist reporters covering the event. Their offices were within a few hundred yards of the court and were ideally situated for the reporters to rush back and present their copy and for the presses to begin rolling with the first reports of the trial.

At ten, Tsafendas came up the steps from the cell below the court and into the dock. He had hardly arrived when he was taken back down by the attending policeman, as the judge and his assessors had not yet taken their seats. Two minutes later, Judge Beyers and his two assessors entered the court. Assessors play an advisory role to the trial judge, and Judge Beyers had appointed a Cape Town advocate, PH Baker SC, and Dr PH Henning, the medical superintendent of the Fort Napier mental hospital in Pietermaritzburg. Advocate Baker had a reputation of being in favour of capital punishment, which was a concern to the defence, though they were heartened by the appointment of Dr Henning, which showed good sense by the judge.

A minute after their arrival, Tsafendas, dressed in a grey double-breasted suit, white shirt and red tie, and flanked by two policemen, was again brought into the dock. Here he stood silently with his hands behind his back, looking at Judge Beyers and waiting for the proceedings to start. Although the court was full to capacity, Tsafendas was quite alone, as he had neither family nor friends present. The local Greek community had closed ranks and distanced themselves from him in the press a few days after his identity and nationality were first made public. Mr A Kallos, the consul for Greece in Cape Town, told the *Sunday Times*[4] that 'Tsafendas was, in fact, a Portuguese citizen, who is reported to have held four Portuguese passports, was born in Lourenço Marques and spent some time in Portugal. He is not of Greek origin at all.' A spokesman for the Greek community in Cape Town went further and said, 'the name is the only indication that he might be of Greek descent, as he is completely unknown to the community and its members'.

Judge Beyers was an awe-inspiring man with a penetrating stare, big broad shoulders and a loud booming voice. He was without doubt a judicial ringmaster and the court was his arena. That this was his court and that this was a trial of importance was immediately brought home to those gathered when, after taking his seat, his first matter of business was to address and caution both the public and the press as to how they were to conduct themselves. In Afrikaans he said:

'You are here in numbers to which we are not accustomed in the courts. You have a right to be here. In this country we believe that justice must be seen to be done in public. It is thus right that the public should be here in a case of this nature. That is how we would like it to be. But there is another side which is important. The courts work in an atmosphere of quiet objectivity as far as this is possible ... Should I find that from the side of the public there is any behaviour which disturbs the calm of this court, I would not hesitate to send you all out of this court and go on with the trial.'[5]

Addressing the press representatives in English, he declared:

'We realise that only a very small part of the public can be in court, and the press represents the many, many others who would have been here had conditions allowed it.' He warned that the case was *sub judice* and added, 'This is not a beer garden. It is a serious business. This man is being tried for his life. There is one thing that will not be allowed – trial by newspaper. I hope it will never be allowed.'

After Beyers's address, Wilfrid rose and announced that before Tsafendas pleaded to the charge he wanted to contend that his client was mentally disordered in terms of the Mental Disorders Act. According to the Act, if it appeared to the judge that the accused was mentally disturbed, he could order that the accused be detained pending a decision by the state president. Wilfrid said further that the defence would lead evidence to show that the accused was mentally disordered and that an inquiry should be held to verify this. When asked by the judge for his opinion, the attorney general referred to the case of David Pratt, who had been tried for the attempted murder of Dr Verwoerd at the Rand Easter Show in April 1960, found to be insane and committed to Bloemfontein mental hospital and said he had no objection to such an inquiry. Beyers frowned and said, 'This is going to take some time. Is there any provision for the accused to be seated?'[6] Tsafendas was then given a chair, as were the two policemen who flanked him, and the court settled down in anticipation of what would be revealed.

Wilfrid then informed the court that the defence would present evidence by specialist psychiatrists that Tsafendas suffered from a psychosis, was a schizophrenic and mentally disordered in terms of the Act and so did not have the capacity, legally, to stand trial for the murder. To prove this, it would be essential to reconstruct his life and history over the past 48 years, but as his travels over the years had covered many countries, it would be impossible to bring witnesses from that part of his life to the court and so the evidence to be presented would concentrate on his immediate past and his life in Cape Town.

As Wilfrid stated succinctly, the defence case was that

Tsafendas's present state was rooted in a deep-seated mental illness of long standing and that he was mentally disordered on the day he attacked and killed Dr Verwoerd. His mental illness, he continued, had spanned many years and was such that he had been a mental patient on numerous occasions in hospitals in America, Portugal, West Germany and Britain. At this point the judge asked Wilfrid if the accused understood the court proceedings, to which he replied that Tsafendas 'understands words'.

The first witness Wilfrid called was Dr Harold Cooper. He informed the court of his qualifications and his experience in diagnosing schizophrenia. He said he had conducted four interviews with Tsafendas, each lasting about an hour-and-a-half. He found Tsafendas to be soft-spoken, polite, cooperative and of normal intelligence. However, the first thing that struck him on seeing Tsafendas was the abnormality of his emotional attitude to his situation and surroundings. He acted incongruously. He was charged with a serious crime, but displayed a singular lack of anxiety. 'One never finds him pacing up and down, he is usually sleeping or he is dozing,' Dr Cooper told the court. Judge Beyers interrupted: 'Have you had other experiences with murderers?' The witness replied that he had, at which the judge commented: 'I have defended many, but I have never found them climbing walls.' This would be the first of many comments to come from the Judge President that morning.

Dr Cooper was not drawn by the judge's comment but elaborated by saying, 'reactions such as frequently asking for sleeping tablets, agitation, asking about his fate and predicament were significantly absent. This kind of action was consistent with schizophrenia.' Tsafendas knew what he had done, that he was going to be tried, but was unable to understand the magnitude of either the situation or its consequences. During his first interview with Tsafendas, while it was evident that he was an intelligent man, Dr Cooper became concerned by his thinking processes. He would vaguely answer the question and then ramble along in a completely disjointed manner and tend to lose his train of thought. Amid laughter Judge Beyers commented, 'I have that difficulty with counsel quite often.'

Dr Cooper retained his composure and continued by saying that when dealing with mental disorder, one was dealing with a question of degree. The degree to which a person rambled was a significant feature of schizophrenia. In the case of Tsafendas it was particularly manifest when he had been talking for some time. Dr Cooper next told the court that the most striking and dramatic feature of Tsafendas's mental state was his fixed belief from an early age that there was a tapeworm inside him, which he could feel crawling around. Tsafendas referred to it as a devil, a dragon, a snake and a demon. It had changed his life and, if it had not been for the tapeworm, he would not have killed Dr Verwoerd.

While there was evidence that Tsafendas was politically resentful and that he disliked Verwoerd as an authority figure, there was no suggestion that Tsafendas had killed Verwoerd for political reasons. 'He was quite open about this but said that his dislike of Dr Verwoerd was not such that he wanted to kill him.' Dr Cooper's final assessment was that Tsafendas was a schizophrenic of such a degree that he was certifiable in terms of the Mental Disorders Act. This opinion provoked Judge Beyers to ask: 'Does he know he's being tried for a crime of murder and does he know that for murder he can swing?' Wilfrid responded, 'M'lord, is it as barbarically simple as that?' The judge did not respond. At the same time he continued to give the word schizophrenia the derisory pronunciation of 'sky-zophrenia' and to interrupt Wilfrid's examination of Dr Cooper with questions of a disbelieving and somewhat hostile nature.

At one o'clock the judge adjourned proceedings and with his two assessors went to the Netherlands Club opposite the Supreme Court for lunch. The judge, the defence team observed, was in a jovial mood as he walked through the crowd and entered the building. They felt this did not augur well for them. As Wilfrid was also a member of the Netherlands Club, the defence team had originally thought of having lunch there too, because of its closeness to the court and chambers so they could have the maximum amount of time to discuss the morning's proceedings. Instead, they now chose to walk to the Café Royal in Church Street. It would afford them the privacy they needed. They knew something had to be done to control the irascible judge, but the question was what. They were still debating this matter when the time arrived for them to return for the afternoon session. On the way it was decided that Wilfrid and Burger should take the unprecedented step of going to see the Judge President in his chambers. Colleagues who learned of this later were dumbfounded that Wilfrid could have thought of confronting the judge in his own chambers. As they walked up the judges' corridor, they saw Judge Beyers ahead, about to enter his room. He heard them, stopped for a moment and waved jovially. Burger said to Wilfrid under his breath, 'Don't smile at the old bastard!'

When they entered his chambers, Judge Beyers was seated behind his desk. Good-humouredly he enquired what he could do for them. Very briefly, Wilfrid said that the defence team felt it was their duty to see him in chambers to tell him of the impression of bias and hostility he was creating, before they raised the matter in open court. Judge Beyers appeared to be momentarily taken aback. He then interrupted Wilfrid, stating that he did not accept that because he was the judge he was not permitted to descend into the arena. When he continued in this vein Wilfrid politely broke in, saying that while they understood his views they adhered to their criticism of his behaviour. The tension rose. At this point Burger audibly whispered, 'Let's fuck off.' The two men then politely excused themselves and left to prepare for court. After donning their robes, they met David

Bloomberg briefly and told him what had happened. Nearby Dr Jim MacGregor and Dr Aubrey Zabow were apprehensively waiting to testify, aware of the hostile reception that Dr Cooper had received that morning. Wilfrid felt that MacGregor and Zabow needed assurance that they would be protected from similar treatment. He now believed, after meeting with Beyers in his chambers, that he could give them that assurance and did so before entering Court 1.

When the trial resumed, Dr Cooper was still in the witness box. Wilfrid made no reference to the complaint made to Judge Beyers at the end of the lunch break and Dr Cooper continued with his evidence. The first change Wilfrid noted was that Beyers no longer pronounced schizophrenia as 'sky-zophrenia', and for the rest of the day there were to be no further acerbic deliverances from the bench. The proceedings were finally adjourned while the attorney general had been painstakingly trying to extract concessions from Dr Cooper that would establish that Tsafendas was fit to stand trial.

Exhilarated by the events of the first day, Wilfrid returned to the Café Royal for a drink at five o'clock. The Café Royal was situated between the offices of the *Cape Times* and the *Cape Argus* and was thus a haunt for many journalists. The building in which it was located was steeped in history, the first dwelling having been built on the site in the early 18th century. Some of the international journalists in town for the trial had also chosen to meet there. Wilfrid was introduced to EJ (Jack) Kahn Jr of the *New Yorker* and Frank Taylor of the *Daily Telegraph*. Both were fascinated by the unconventional Judge Beyers. Taylor had been present at the trial of Jack Ruby in Dallas for the killing of Lee Harvey Oswald, the assassin of President Kennedy, three years before.

Comparing the conduct of Beyers and that of the American judge in the Ruby trial, Joe B Brown Snr, Taylor thought they had much in common. Clearly, Brown was pleased to be in the limelight and the first thing he did was hire a public relations consultant for himself. Despite demands from Ruby's attorney, Melvin Belli, to have the trial moved away from Dallas in the light of overwhelming evidence that he would not receive a fair trial in that city, Brown ruled to the contrary. This virtually guaranteed Ruby a new trial even before the first started. Brown clearly did not want to miss his moment in history.

The following morning when the court reconvened in Keerom Street, the attorney general finished his examination of Dr Cooper. The defence then called the physician Dr Hendrik Muller. With a broad grin Judge Beyers revealed to the court that he had once been a patient of the witness. Dr Muller confirmed that he had examined Tsafendas and could not find a trace of the tapeworm he claimed was inside him. At the same time he stated that the tapeworm remained a reality and that it had dominated Tsafendas's life – he was convinced that the tapeworm influenced Tsafendas but was not prepared to say how.

The next witness was Dr Ralph Kossew, the district surgeon of Cape Town. It was not common practice for a State employee to testify for the defence, but he had been subpoenaed as three months before the assassination he had examined Tsafendas for a disability grant and had noted in his file that he was suffering from a serious form of schizophrenia. He had also examined Tsafendas a few hours after the assassination. Judge Beyers appeared to be impressed by this witness. The attorney general hardly asked him any questions, though he did enquire why he had not certified Tsafendas after his finding in June. Kossew replied that he had not been certifiable and that he appeared to be the type of person who could take care of himself.

Four members of the religious sect the Followers of Jesus Christ were then called as witnesses. Mr and Mrs Peter Daniels and Mr and Mrs Pat O'Ryan, who knew Tsafendas, related their experiences of his abnormal behaviour and his obsession with his tapeworm; that he told them how it it would crawl about in him at night, hungry, and irritate him. O'Ryan, in turn, told him it was a figment of his imagination. The Danielses related that he liked keeping his hat on while having a meal and that he had once sprayed chickens to cool them off. They told of his once gorging himself, using his hands, on three pounds of half-cooked steak. But the Danielses and O'Ryans also testified that, while Tsafendas's behaviour did unnerve them, he was always kind and friendly. They had pity for this homeless wanderer and accepted him as a brother into their faith. O'Ryan even confirmed he took a liking to him and had confidence in him.

Their evidence would also illustrate Tsafendas's ambivalence about his racial identity. On the one hand, he claimed to be a friend of coloured people; at one stage he had wanted to marry a coloured woman and applied to change his official race classification from white to coloured to allow this. Daniels told the court that 'he would like to make himself a coloured man so that he can easily be accepted because he had never really been accepted as a white'. All the same, there was also evidence that at times when with white people he would display hatred and contempt for coloureds. The witness Owen Smorenberg, the power station foreman, testified that he and Tsafendas were working forty feet underground in the water intake for a cooling tower when Smorenberg 'jokingly' said it would be a good place for BJ Vorster, the minister of justice, to keep his political prisoners. Tsafendas replied, 'They should put all the coloureds down here, open the doors and drown the lot.' (Tsafendas evidently believed that Vorster was the right man for minister of justice.)

The next witness Wilfrid called was Dr Isaac Sakinofsky, who had been asked by the police to examine Tsafendas on the evening of the assassination. He had drawn up a detailed report of his examination, which he submitted to the attorney general, but he had not been called as a witness for the State. During his third visit, he told the court, Tsafendas went into grotesque detail about the tapeworm within him, which left him in no doubt he was suffering from a chronic delusional kind of schizophrenia and had been that way for many years. In his final assessment to the court, he said it was quite clear to him that Tsafendas was mentally disordered in terms of the Act and was certifiable. Although the attorney general tried his best to sway Dr Sakinofsky and suggested that he had been confused as a result of concussion from the blow to his head that he received while being subdued in Parliament, Dr Sakinofsky refused to agree and referred to Dr Kossew's report. This found no evidence of Tsafendas being concussed or confused when examined less than an hour after he received the blow.

The defence left court at the end of the second day believing that it had gone well for them. The judge had shown none of the aggression to their witnesses that he had displayed to Dr Cooper on the first day. In fact, his reactions to Dr Kossew and Dr Sakinofsky appeared to have been favourable.

On Wednesday, the defence furnished details of Tsafendas's odyssey, which commenced at Cape Town on 13 June 1942 and ended on his return to the city on 28 August 1965. As Jack Kahn would write in the *New Yorker*, Tsafendas had spent a quarter of a century 'going everywhere and getting nowhere'. The court was given details of his seemingly never-ending trips to various countries and of the mental hospitals at which he had received treatment, including shock treatment at a German institution. They also put before the court as evidence a copy of a letter (referred to for some reason by Judge Beyers as 'the fish and chips letter') that Tsafendas wrote to the British prime minister in September 1959 and signed Staa-Sin-Hah. This, the defence believed, indicated Tsafendas's fragile state of mind already at that time.

The specialists called by the defence on the third day confirmed what had been said by the others on the preceding days. Dr R van Zyl, a clinical psychologist, testified that he had examined

Tsafendas and concluded that Tsafendas was schizophrenic. Dr Aubrey Zabow, a psychiatrist who had much experience in treating and certifying schizophrenic patients, and had examined Tsafendas three times, emphasised in his testimony that Tsafendas was out of touch with reality. 'Although Tsafendas understands words when one speaks to him and, as has been shown in the court, is an intelligent person, his concept of reality is such that basically he is not in the same world as we are,' he said. 'His world is one dominated by a power which at times causes him inconvenience and to act to his detriment.'

When Dr Zabow was asked to comment on the 'fish and chips letter', he described it as the kind of letter that could be used in a psychiatry textbook to illustrate schizophrenic thinking. Dr James MacGregor concurred broadly with Dr Zabow's findings. His observations about Tsafendas's tapeworm were particularly illuminating. 'It did not take long [for me] to realise that this worm was the central theme of his thoughts,' he said. The worm had 'disorganised his real personality and his relationship with the real world'. 'When I asked him what he would want if he could have one wish granted, I expected him to say he wanted to be free. To my surprise, he said it would be to get rid of the worm.'

After Dr MacGregor finished giving evidence, Wilfrid felt they had reached the stage where he had presented sufficient evidence to prove that Tsafendas was not fit to stand trial. But in his own cross-examination of the witnesses, the attorney general did not relent in his questioning to find evidence to refute this. His mind was still clearly set on establishing that Tsafendas was a hired assassin who had committed premeditated murder. There were witnesses that Wilfrid could call who might strengthen the defence's case, but they were overseas and thus unavailable. The defence team debated whether they should apply for leave to take evidence on commission overseas. It was felt, however, that Judge Beyers's attitude appeared to have swung in favour of

Tsafendas, though the judge did have a reputation for sudden changes of mind. In the circumstances they decided to keep their options open and informed the court that the defence was not calling any more witnesses.

The attorney general then applied for a postponement to the next day, which Judge Beyers granted. The defence now expected that the next witness the State would call would be Professor Van Wyk to present the evidence that had been shared with them by the attorney general at the pre-trial meeting – that Tsafendas was fit to stand trial. The fourth day, Thursday, 20 October 1966, was to spring a great surprise.

The session started as usual at ten. Advocate Brunette for the State called AJ Erasmus to testify. Erasmus worked as a clinical psychologist and was employed at Weskoppies hospital in Pretoria. He had interviewed Tsafendas twice at the end of September and subjected him to the same tests as those of Dr R van Zyl, a defence witness from the previous day. From them he concluded that, while an intelligent man with an IQ of 120, Tsafendas believed in his fantasy world and that he displayed thought blocking and a lack of contact with his surroundings. Judge Beyers asked the witness: 'Are these not textbook descriptions of schizophrenia?' Erasmus agreed. In conclusion to Advocate Brunette's questioning, he admitted that he had found signs of schizophrenia in Tsafendas.

With this concession Wilfrid asked Erasmus if he would contest the evidence of doctors Zabow, Cooper and Sakinofsky that Tsafendas was an incurable schizophrenic. No, he would not, he replied, and after a slight hesitation he agreed that Tsafendas was certifiable and should be sent to an asylum.

Then, as the defence had been expecting, the attorney general called Professor Van Wyk to the stand. It should be noted that Van Wyk had been in court when the other psychiatrists had testified. He informed the court that he had observed the accused twice in September and on three occasions in October.

At first he found that Tsafendas was evasive and as a result he was uncertain if the evasiveness was simulation or a symptom of schizophrenia. He then re-tested Tsafendas to see whether he was simulating his behaviour but found he could not have been. When asked why he had travelled around the world, Tsafendas replied: 'In the beginning I thought I went by myself, but then I realised it was the tapeworm.' In another interview Tsafendas told Van Wyk, 'I sometimes say things to people which annoy them, but it is not me but the tapeworm that says that to them.' Then, to the absolute surprise of the defence team, Van Wyk declared that this was a symptom of schizophrenia and that it had become clear to him that 'there was definitely a degree of mental derangement in Tsafendas' and he could not do anything else but certify him. Wilfrid was dumbstruck: the evidence that Van Wyk was now giving was irreconcilable with the attorney general's opening address to the court three days before that he was convinced that Tsafendas was fit to stand trial and that he would call two witnesses to confirm his conviction.

In his cross-examination Wilfrid put it to Van Wyk: 'Do you – on the fourth day – agree with the opinion that Dr Harold Cooper so stoutly defended on the first day of this trial?'

Van Wyk: 'That the man is certifiable in terms of the Act relating to mental disorders?'

Wilfrid: 'Yes, that he suffers from schizophrenia?'

Van Wyk replied: 'Yes, but it is not a conclusion which I only reached today. I came to the conclusion before.'

Wilfrid persisted with his line of questioning and asked if he would now also agree with the evidence of the other psychiatrists who had confirmed Tsafendas's mental state. At this point Judge Beyers interrupted Wilfrid and remarked, 'But this witness has already said what you want. Can you possibly want any more?' and would not allow him to continue. Wilfrid was thus effectively stopped from pursing his questioning of Van Wyk. The matter for Wilfrid was further aggravated when the judge proceeded to compliment Van Wyk for taking his time in coming to his conclusion and said that 'it redounds to your honour that you did not come to a hasty conclusion but that you took your time and gradually reached your conclusion'. It was as if Judge Beyers knew that had he not stepped in and curtailed Wilfrid's questioning,[7] the disingenuousness of Van Wyk's explanation for his volte-face would have been revealed.

Then, to the surprise of all those in Court 1, the attorney general announced that he was closing the case for the State. This brought the inquiry proceedings abruptly to an end. Although the defence team was satisfied that Van Wyk's evidence now supported that of their psychiatric experts, they were left puzzled as to why, if the State had known what their experts were going to say when they took the stand, the attorney general had cross-examined Dr Cooper so aggressively on the first day of the inquiry to try to prove that Tsafendas was able to stand trial. Was the State as surprised as the defence with the testimony of their key witness?

The attorney general then addressed the court: 'The court has taken note of the overwhelming nature of the expert evidence, and even the evidence of the State indicates unequivocally his mental condition is such that he falls within Section 28 of the [Mental Disorders] Act. It is for this court in the light of this evidence to make such findings and make such order as the court deems is justified by the evidence. If the court decides to issue an order in terms of Section 28 (2), I ask that the accused be not detained in an institution but in a jail.'[8]

After a brief discussion with the attorney general, Judge Beyers adjourned the proceedings to decide whether he should deliver his judgment immediately or postpone proceedings to allow for his further deliberations. At 10.45 the court reconvened, and Beyers and his two assessors took their seats. Tsafendas, his head drooping forward and his eyes half-hooded, stood in the dock flanked by two police guards with a third policeman standing close behind him. A court orderly apologised for not having placed a policeman behind Wilfrid: this, he later learned, would have been intended as a precaution against some possible assault from behind.

Word had spread that Judge Beyers was going to deliver one of his impromptu judgments, and many people had come to Court 1 and stood at the door to hear him. The judge started by saying, 'The court is clear in its mind what its order should be and under the circumstances I can see no reason for prolonging the proceedings ... It is incumbent on me to give judgment now.' Having described the nature of the case, he went on to say, 'This court is no less conscious of the momentous background to this case than is anyone else in this country. Once, however, a case is brought in a court of law these considerations of the immensity of the crime and the effect it has upon the people of this country really disappear ... The elements of the crime of murder and the legal processes employed in trying such a crime remain the same and in no wise differ whether it involves the prime minister of the land or the lowest of low. Murder is murder and its elements remain unchanged.'

Referring to the appointment of legal representatives for Tsafendas, Beyers commented: 'My first duty I think is to express to senior counsel and to junior counsel and to their attorneys the deep appreciation of this court for the work they have done. For them it has meant, I think it should be understood, that without any meaningful remuneration they took upon themselves the unenviable and unpopular task of defending this man. Not for one moment did they demur to make the sacrifice of time and the financial sacrifice that goes with it. By their conduct they graced the profession to which they belong and they have acted in accordance with the highest legal traditions of the legal profession of this country.'

After thanking his two assessors, the judge started on a lengthy, somewhat ponderous but detailed explanation as to what had taken place in his court over the past four days. As he delivered his findings, it became clear that he was seeking a path between those who had a desire for revenge and wanted to see the murderer of their beloved prime minister executed and what the law prescribed. And Judge Beyers had a reputation for being a man of the law. He firstly had to make it clear that the inquiry before the court was just that, an inquiry, and not a trial, which rested on 'the simple human civilised principle that a court does not try a madman'.

The judge explained that inquiry into the sanity of an accused person had been established in South African law by way of Section 28 of the Mental Disorders Act of 1916. This Act provided that on the arraignment of any person charged with any criminal offence, if it appeared to the judge presiding that such a person was mentally disturbed, the question of the person's mental condition should be inquired into by the court. Sub-section (2) of the Act provided that if the court found after hearing evidence that the person was mentally disturbed, the presiding judge should record the finding and issue an order committing the person to a jail pending signification of the decision by the state president.

Judge Beyers referred to the history that had been presented that showed that Tsafendas had a long history of mental disorder. He also turned to the matter of how Tsafendas could have been employed at Parliament. He said that thoughts must arise as to how it could have been possible that a man like Tsafendas, with a history of derangement, could find his way into the highest assembly of the land. They were questions, he said, that did not concern the court, but it was 'almost unavoidable that the question arises in one's mind'.

After referring to the host of psychiatrists who had given evidence about Tsafendas's mental state, Beyers said: 'It became clear...that there can be no doubt whatever that the man before me is a schizophrenic; that he is a lunatic –

125

in more direct terms – or, as Roman law would have it, that I have before me a *furiosus*.[9] A *furiosus* is something which I cannot try. I cannot try a man who has not got at least the makings of a rational mind as I could not try a dog or an inert implement...I have before me, on the evidence, clearly a man with a diseased mind, subject to delusion, so trammelled, if not guided, by irrational forces that obviously I cannot begin to find whether he is guilty or not guilty of a crime at law. The process cannot even start. You cannot get to the provisions of the criminal law until you have decided whether he is capable of being tried. So I do not believe it is necessary for me to go into any provisions of the criminal law. I cannot be other than satisfied that on the prehistory of this man and on the evidence of the psychiatrists one after the other who have agreed, that here we have, not a criminal, but a sick man, mentally sick and irresponsible.'

An astute man, Judge Beyers was not unmindful of the sentiment that then prevailed among most of the whites in the country. At this point, switching to Afrikaans, he said: 'Were the court to put a man to death without acting according to the law, it would be murder. We are a law-abiding people. I fully understand that the people of this country have deep feelings about this case. I fully understand when people ask: how can it be that a meaningless creature could have done what he did do. I know, too, that the first reaction of any community through the ages is a feeling of revenge, of retribution. I share that feeling... But one must understand these things a bit more deeply. If this man were to pay for what he has done, that would do nothing for us. It would make no difference to our loss.' Were the court to disregard the law, then Tsafendas would indeed have done greater damage to the life of the country than his act involved.

'To tell the truth people come and go, but if this nation should lose its trust in its legal institutions and the Bench, we would indeed have brought about humiliation and shame which would be an irreparable blot on this country. We must go forward in the deepest knowledge that by giving this man the best legal and medical assistance he could have, and by the order I was forced to make, the honour, prestige and good name of our land remains untarnished and the foundations on which we are building remain unshaken and undamaged. I can expect a certain amount of shock and dissatisfaction among certain people, but I am sure that they will realise that it could not be otherwise and that it is not humane or Christian to condemn mentally ill people…It is my duty to order that this person, Demitrio Tsafendas, be taken from here to jail and be held there at the state president's pleasure.'[10]

During the fifty-five minutes the judge took to deliver his finding, Tsafendas showed no emotion. He sat impassively, as if half asleep, and only towards the end did he nod his head and rock slightly as if he were in a trance. When the court adjourned, he was quickly ushered out to the holding cells below. It was 11:40am on Thursday, 20 October 1966, the fourth day of the trial and 44 days after Dr Verwoerd's assassination.

Shortly after Judge Beyers pronounced his findings, the minister of justice announced that the government accepted them. But at the same time he recommended the appointment of a commission to report on the efficacy of the existing legal rules for the adjudication of criminal cases involving persons suffering from some form of mental derangement. It was apparent that the State had resorted to this face-saving step in the wake of Professor Van Wyk's volte-face.

*

Wilfrid believed that, while Tsafendas did not intend it, nor would he have foreseen it, the assassination of Hendrik Verwoerd was of immense political importance for South Africa. It was equal, he believed, in its consequences to the assassination of John F Kennedy for America. The man who had championed with granite-like conviction and invincible self-righteousness the vision of grand apartheid was dead. With him went the rigid belief that South Africa could be unscrambled into separate ethnic states, and even though his successors tried to hold back the tide of change, in the end they were forced to adapt and then give way. Verwoerd's assassination was a defining event for the generation of which I was part: ever afterwards we could remember where we had been when we heard the news that Verwoerd had been killed. His grandiose funeral drew an estimated quarter of a million people, who lined the streets of Pretoria to view the cortège, an event only surpassed by the funeral of Nelson Mandela in December 2013.

The three weeks leading up to the trial had involved Wilfrid and his team in a monumental amount of work in defending their client. When it ended in their favour, they were elated that despite public pressure justice had been done and their client would not stand trial to face the death penalty.

In the midst of all this, Wilfrid had two further matters to celebrate: the day after Beyers delivered his finding, 21 October, it was his daughter Megan's 10th birthday and on 22 October it was his 17th wedding anniversary. The three events were celebrated simultaneously with great gusto at Riverside. David Bloomberg also celebrated the ruling at his house in Kenilworth where he handed out a tie to all those involved with the defence; the tie was embossed with a small tapeworm emblem.

On the Friday morning Wilfrid was in his chambers, early as usual, and was sorting through the backlog of correspondence on his desk when a messenger arrived with a small parcel with an envelope attached. He opened it and found a short, handwritten letter from David Bloomberg:

Victor and Rose Cooper, Wilfrid's parents.

Wilfrid in his Wynberg Boys' High School uniform, circa 1936.

A sight that remained with Wilfrid all his life: a steam locomotive crossing the bridge at Klawer. *Photograph courtesy of CP Lewis.*

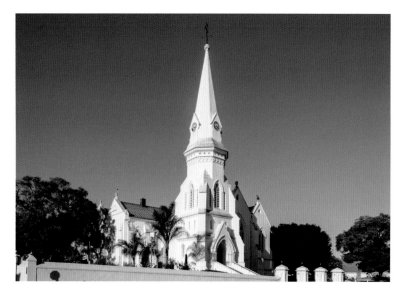

ABOVE The spire of the NG Kerk dominates Malmesbury; it left a lasting impression on both Wilfrid and Stephanie Kemp in their formative years.
BELOW Wynberg Boys' athletics team 1944. Wilfrid, a middle-distance and cross-country runner is in the second row, second from left.

Wilfrid as a first-year student at Stellenbosch University.

ABOVE Wilfrid loved listening to the news on the radio; here with his beloved EL & Co radio, bought for £26.

RIGHT Rambling near Stellenbosch.

View of the Jonkershoek mountains from Wilfrid's room in Stellenbosch.

ABOVE Newlands, with the eastern slopes of Table Mountain and Devil's Peak in the background, circa 1940s.
BELOW Wilfrid and Gertrude on their wedding day, 22 October 1949.

Evidence photograph from Wilfrid's first big case: the murder scene of Jacob 'Kombuis' Hoffman, 31 May 1952.

Baron Dieter von Schauroth and his wife Colleen shortly before his murder in March 1961. The case provoked a media frenzy.

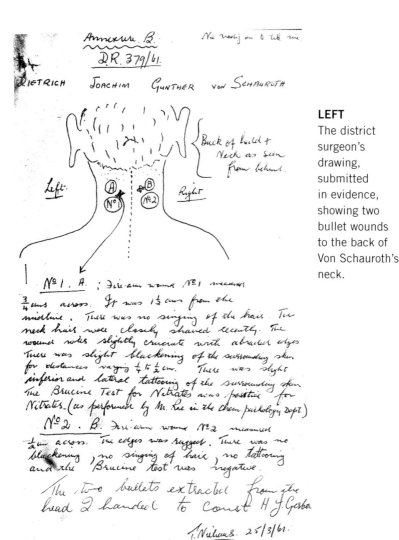

Annexure B.

D.R. 379/61.

DIETRICH   JOACHIM   GUNTHER   VON SCHAUROTH

Back of head + Neck as seen from behind.

Left.   ⒜ No 1   ⒷNo 2   Right

LEFT

The district surgeon's drawing, submitted in evidence, showing two bullet wounds to the back of Von Schauroth's neck.

No 1. A : Entrance wound No 1 measured ¾ cms across. It was 1½ cms from the midline. There was no singing of the hair. The neck hair were closely shaved recently. The wound was slightly cruciate with abraded edges. There was slight blackening of the surrounding skin for distances varying ¼ to ½ cm. There was slight inferior and lateral tattooing of the surrounding skin. The Brucine Test for Nitrates was positive for Nitrates (as performed by Mr Rae in the Chem pathology Dept)

No 2. B. Entrance wound No 2 measured ½ cm across. The edges was rugged. There was no blackening, no singing of hair, no tattooing and the Brucine Test was negative.

The two bullets extracted from the head 2 handed to Const H J Gerba

T. Nilans. 25/3/61.

Marthinus Rossouw, Wilfrid's client, is identified at an identity parade.

Wilfrid on his
appointment to
the Cape Bar,
October 1952.

Parliament Street, the site of Wilfrid's first chambers (on the left).

ABOVE Stephanie Kemp and Albie Sachs. Wilfrid appeared for the former with Sachs as his junior.

RIGHT Robert Kemp (back), who was arrested for protesting against apartheid education, leaving court with attorney Norman Osburn and Wilfrid, 1972.

ABOVE Dr Hendrik Frensch Verwoerd and his assassin Demitrio Tsafendas; Wilfrid appeared for the latter in the most high-profile case of his career. **BELOW** Front page of *The Cape Argus*, 6 September 1966. *Photograph courtesy of Graham Freeling*

ABOVE The queue of people outside the Supreme Court waiting to witness 'the trial of the century'.

RIGHT Tsafendas leaves the Supreme Court in a police van.

ABOVE Attorneys David Bloomberg and Fred Stander with Wilfrid outside the Supreme Court.

LEFT Advocate Willem 'Willie' Burger with Wilfrid before the start of the hearing.

ABOVE Imam Abdullah Haron with his wife Galiema, daughter Shamilah and son Muhammad. *Picture courtesy of Khalid Shamis.*

ABOVE The large crowd on the way to the *janazah* of Imam Haron, 27 September 1969. *Picture courtesy of Khalid Shamis.*

RIGHT Wilfrid in 1965 with his noteworthy publication *Motor Law*.

My Dear Wilfrid,

Although this seems to be the appropriate moment for mutual 'backslapping', believe my sincerity when I say:

I am grateful to you for bringing me into this historic trial (although I originally had misgivings); it has really been a great pleasure working with you.

Your handling of the proceedings was admirable from start to finish. What more can I say? The Judge said it all...!

I hope that the accompanying gift will bring back pleasant memories in future of your great triumph.

In friendship,

Sincerely,

David.

The gift was a handsome Parker gold-plated desk ink pen set, which was inscribed:

To Wilfred [*sic*] from David
'THE TRIAL OF THE CENTURY' OCTOBER 1966

Wilfrid wrote back to David saying that it would always be a precious possession, symbol of the triumph for which they had worked, which they had achieved and which they shared. I know that the gift was important to him, as he used the pens for many years. Later, the set was always on his side table next to the telephone in his chambers and finally in his study at home.[11]

Unfortunately, it appeared that the Cape Bar Council neither took cognisance of his achievements nor shared the sentiments expressed by Judge Beyers that he had acted in accordance with the highest traditions of the legal profession in the country. For on 24 October, the secretary of the Cape Bar Council had a letter delivered admonishing Wilfrid for breaches of Bar protocol with regard to the appearance of several posed photographs of him in local newspapers during the trial, as well as an article about him. The letter came as a complete surprise. On the advice of a colleague, Wilfrid replied, 'It is correct that I posed for the photographs mentioned in your letter. I was not photographed at my request and when I agreed to be photographed I was not aware that this was in any manner contrary to correct Bar practice. Since receiving your letter I have discussed the matter with senior colleagues and I have discovered that press photographs are frowned upon. I now realise that I have breached an unwritten convention and I regret that I have done so.

'As regards the article referred to, the writer thereof did not interview me nor did I furnish her with any information contained therein, and I was unaware of the article before its publication.'

Wilfrid's reply did not satisfy the Bar Council, and there was further correspondence, which led to a meeting in January 1967 between Wilfrid and the chairman, Gerald Gordon, about his alleged touting. The meeting was brief. Wilfrid politely but firmly asked Gordon to inform the Bar Council of his displeasure at the way he had been treated. He never heard from the Council again. The bitterness of the matter was offset when later that month he received a letter from Sydney Kentridge SC, an eminent member of the Johannesburg Bar, congratulating him 'on the extremely impressive way in which you handled the Tsafendas case. It must have been a most difficult case for you. There has been a lot of favourable comment here on the way in which you stood up to the J.P. in the early stages.'

Wilfrid's fee for defending Demitrio Tsafendas was R21 per day or R84 in total for the trial.

In 1996, when interviewed by the *Cape Times* for his 70th birthday, he recalled of Tsafendas that 'He was a messenger in the House of Parliament and was indigent. It was apparent to me he was insane; he was also highly religious, intelligent and articulate. The killing of Verwoerd was a symbolic killing, like St

130

George slaying the dragon. It was not political. Tsafendas was rejected from the word go. During his adolescence he developed a tapeworm and this became his "dragon" – he was ruled by it. I believe he realised that he had travelled everywhere but went nowhere. And there was Verwoerd, the highest in the land, in contrast to his simple position.'

I was too young to remember the details of these times but I was aware that a momentous event had taken place in the history of both the country and my father. I still have his pen set, and look at it from time to time and reflect on his achievement and on the fact that he was only 40 years old at the time of this important event in the history of South Africa.

NOTES:

[1] Other notable assassinations in the 1960s were those of Martin Luther King, Malcolm X and Patrice Lumumba.

[2] Comment by Judge WE Cooper to the Truth and Reconciliation Commission in Durban.

[3] *My Times: The Memoirs of David Bloomberg* by David Bloomberg (Simonstown, Fernwood Press, 2007) p. 81

[4] *Sunday Times*, 11 September 1966

[5] *Cape Argus*, 17 October 1966

[6] *Cape Times*, 17 October 1966

[7] In *The Psychology of Apartheid* (Athens, University of Georgia Press, 1980), p. 239, the psychologist Peter Lambley found 'Several features of the trial puzzling. From the start, all involved appeared to have been given a clear directive that they were to find him insane – this was informally transmitted in Dr Cooper's case as a general consensus of opinion. Secondly, the professionals were discouraged from probing too far into his state of mind or into his activities immediately prior to the assassination – this they were told was a job for the police.'

[8] *Cape Argus*, 20 October 1966

[9] In law a *furiosus* is a madman or lunatic who lacks the legal capacity or will to, for example, enter into a contract.

[10] *Cape Argus*, 20 October 1966

[11] Sadly the apartheid system would be the cause of a schism between Wilfrid and David Bloomberg in the late 1980s when the latter became embroiled in a payment of R2 million he made on behalf of the hotelier Sol Kerzner in what was seen as a bribe paid to the prime minister of the 'independent' Transkei, Chief George Matanzima, for gambling rights. In 1989 Matanzima was sentenced to a nine-year jail sentence for demanding the bribe but would not co-operate in the prosecution sought by Attorney General Christo Nel against Kerzner and Bloomberg. Unfortunately the matter was therefore never resolved between them. Bloomberg wrote of the matter in his biography, and despite Wilfrid having died three years before in 2007, was heavily critical of him for distancing himself from him over the matter. Wilfrid and Gertrude had discussed the matter on many occasions and were, based on what they knew at the time, deeply conflicted as to the way forward. Though the information they had at their disposal was not as clear-cut as Bloomberg made it out to be in his book, perhaps they might have handled it differently; they in no way relished the passing of the friendship they had enjoyed when the Bloombergs lived in Cape Town.

CHAPTER 8

DEATHS IN DETENTION

Notable inquests into the deaths of people in detention, through which Wilfrid sought to expose the lies of the Security Police and the complicity of State doctors

'The magistrates' findings contributed to the creation of a culture of impunity in the South African Police.'
– TRUTH AND RECONCILIATION COMMISSION

After the assassination of Verwoerd, the National Party elected the strong-arm, tough-talking Minister of Justice and Police BJ Vorster as the new prime minister to succeed him. It was Vorster who had been the driving force behind the introduction of detention without trial in South Arica. Under his watch as Minister of Justice, Parliament had passed the 90-day detention law in 1963 and then doubled that in 1965, with the introduction of 180-day detention. Then in 1967 the Terrorism Act empowered the police to prolong detention without trial for an indefinite period, and delivered detainees up to the mercy of the Security Police without any procedural safeguards to protect them against abuse. It was no wonder, then, that many prisoners began to die in detention. From 1963 to 1990, 73 people died while being held under the security laws, the first being Western Cape activist Solwandle Looksmart Ngudle and the last Donald Thabela Madisha. The most prominent death in detention was undoubtedly that of Steve Biko, who died on 16 November 1977.[1] The true callousness of the apartheid government was revealed by the infamous comment at the time of the Minister of Justice, Jimmy Kruger: 'I am not glad and I am not sorry about Mr Biko. It leaves me cold [*Dit laat my koud*].'[2]

In terms of South African law, the death of detainees from unnatural causes required that an inquest be held before a magistrate. But such was their sense of impunity that the Security Police would fabricate stories to explain the sudden deaths of their detainees, in full confidence that the presiding magistrate would accept them. Frequently this was done in collaboration with members of the medical fraternity who, having not rendered the medical attention the detainee required at the time, most likely as per police instructions, would subsequently be less than candid in their court testimony.[3]

Nevertheless, some of the lawyers and advocates appearing for the families of victims had the courage to challenge the lies that the Security Police offered, pick holes in their fanciful stories and provide a convincing explanation of what had happened in the interrogation rooms. Even if, eventually, the magistrates found, as they usually did, that no-one was to blame for the deaths, the efforts of the families' legal representatives pierced the veil of official lies and fabrication and pointed strongly to the culpability and complicity of the Security Police.

The steady stream of deaths in detention in the 1960s peaked in 1969. This was the year in which seven detainees inexplicably died while being held by the police. The most prominent of them was the Imam Abdullah Haron, whose family Wilfrid represented at the inquest hearing.

*

Imam Haron

When I was a boy, Stegman Road in Claremont used to be a through road from Main Road, crossing the railway line at a set of booms and then joining Palmyra Road further down. As a child I would travel regularly along it with my mother in her pale blue Morris Mini-Minor to visit my aunt who lived across the railway line. We would pass the Al-Jamia Mosque where Abdullah Haron, an energetic young Muslim cleric with a sense of compassion for the poor and oppressed, had been appointed Imam in 1956. Haron became known among the wider South African Muslim community for his determined opposition to the threat of closure his mosque faced under the Group Areas Act. But his real political awakening came with Sharpeville. During the state of emergency that followed, Haron was part of a movement of people who smuggled food and other supplies into the military-occupied African townships in Cape Town. In the years that followed, Haron became more outspoken in his support for black South Africans bearing the brunt of apartheid. The Imam's active opposition did not go unnoticed by the

Security Police. On 28 May 1969 he was detained under the dreaded Section 6 of the Terrorism Act and first held at Caledon Square, before being moved to Maitland police station. In all, he would be detained for 123 days without access to his family or the outside world in any way. When his detention was brought to the attention of the United Party MP for Wynberg, Mrs Catherine Taylor, she raised the matter in Parliament with the Minister of Police, Mr SL Muller. On 10 June he blandly confirmed that a 'certain Moslem' was being held, that no charges had been brought and that in terms of the Terrorism Act he was not allowed to see his family or contact his attorney. He also stated that it was not in the public interest to know why he had been detained. A further approach to the minister on 13 June yielded nothing and the Imam continued to languish in detention.

After a silence of four months, the Imam's family was contacted by the police on Saturday, 27 September, to be told that he had died. The police would now go out of their way to 'assist' the family and immediately held a post-mortem, performed by Professor TG Schwär, head of the department of forensic medicine at the Karl Bremer Hospital in Bellville, on Sunday, 28 September. This was most unusual, as in those Calvinistic times work on a Sunday was deeply frowned upon. The authorities went further and even allowed a private pathologist to attend the post-mortem. The Imam was the twelfth detainee to die while in the hands of the Security Police and the bland comments by the minister of police in Parliament in June were now overshadowed by the interest of the press, the outrage of the Muslim community and the dismay and revulsion of many other South Africans. The funeral of the Imam received prominent press coverage: it was attended by about 30,000 people, who came to pay their last respects to the Imam as his body was solemnly carried to its resting place in Mowbray cemetery.

The inquest into the death of the Imam started on Wednesday,

18 February 1970. The family was represented by Wilfrid, assisted by Ben Kies, a well-known left-wing activist, intellectual and friend of Wilfrid's, and instructed by the attorney Himie Bernadt. Mr JW Graan appeared for the State, and the presiding magistrate was Mr JSP Kuhn with Professor LS Smith, the senior State pathologist, as his assessor.

The first person to testify was the officer in charge of the Imam's case, Major Dirk Genis of the Security Police[4]. As the Truth and Reconciliation Commission would later report, Genis was part of a special squad of security policemen who received training in torture techniques in France and Algeria in the early 1960s; subsequently he was associated with a special 'sabotage squad' to deal with 'subversive elements' in the country.

Genis started his testimony by outlining that the Imam had been under investigation for some years and that there had been several reasons for his detention. Based on 'reliable' information, the Security Police believed the Imam was recruiting young Muslim students to be sent to China for training as terrorists; was active in recruiting members for the banned Pan Africanist Congress; had been receiving funds from overseas for unlawful purposes; had contravened foreign exchange control regulations by taking funds out of the country for use by political exiles; had contacted the PAC overseas and visited a terrorist headquarters in Cairo; and was in secret contact with overseas terrorists and had held conferences with them.

In his evidence Genis was almost nonchalant in stating that, while detained, the Imam had been allowed his 'Bible', a prayer rug, an extra blanket and food brought by his wife; that he was not interrogated for more than five or six hours a day; and that he could choose to stand or sit during the sessions. That the Imam had been held incommunicado for a third of a year was lost on Genis. He laboured the point that during his time in detention the Imam had been nervous, emotionally tense and apparently aware that he had been caught out. The Imam, he said, was also worried about his family and feared possible reprisals against them by people who might think he had implicated them while under interrogation. Genis testified that the last time he had questioned the Imam was on the evening of 19 September. When they were finished he, Sergeant 'Spyker' van Wyk and the Imam left his office and went down a dark flight of stairs where the Imam, who was in front of them, slipped and fell. Genis had helped him up and noted that the Imam was only shaken; he neither appeared to have any injuries nor complained of any. He was then taken back to the Maitland police cells.

Genis would see the Imam briefly on the morning of Monday, 22 September and still believed that he looked well. On Wednesday he again visited the Imam, who reported that he had a headache, for which he was given some pills. On Friday, he and Van Wyk saw the Imam for a few minutes: he appeared well and no longer complained of a headache. On the evening of Saturday, 27 September he received a message at home to call the station commander at Maitland and was then told that the Imam had died.

The speciousness of Genis's testimony would not go unchallenged by Wilfrid. In his cross-examination he endeavoured to expose the truth about what had actually happened during the Imam's detention and, more importantly, what had occurred during the last few days of his life while in the care of Genis and Van Wyk. As he knew from his defence of Stephanie Kemp and Alan Brooks, Van Wyk was notorious for using violence to extract confessions from his charges.

Slowly and methodically, Wilfrid drew out the information that the Imam had been interrogated for two to seven hours every day from the end of May to the middle of July. Both Genis and Van Wyk denied that the Imam had been assaulted and, apart from his fall down the stairs, they could offer no explanation about how he had died. When the body of the Imam was examined at the Salt River mortuary it had 26 bruises on various parts, many of them large; a haematoma or swelling caused by trauma near the base of his spine; and a broken rib. In their testimonies both Genis and Van Wyk said they were surprised when told of the Imam's death and puzzled as to how he might have died.

In his testimony the district surgeon for Bellville said that the Imam had been brought to him when he complained of pain in his chest. He examined him, found no injuries and gave him some pain-killing tablets. Cross-examined by Wilfrid, he said he had not asked the Imam what he thought caused the pain because the Imam was a prisoner and did not look as if he was prepared to talk.

Dr DC Gosling, district surgeon for Cape Town, testified that he saw the Imam on 10 July for 10 to 15 minutes and noted tenderness over the ribs. He decided that the pains and malaise that the Imam reported were consistent with an 'influenza-like illness' and gave him the appropriate pills. When questioned by Wilfrid, he admitted that his examination and diagnosis had, remarkably, been undertaken without asking the Imam a single question.

The inquest learned that for three days and two nights, from 17 to 19 September, the Imam had been moved under the supervision of the Security Police from Maitland to another location outside the Peninsula that, in the interests of State security, could not be named. On cross-examining Van Wyk, Wilfrid said, 'I want to put it to you that something strange happened to the deceased during that time and this led to his death, that he did not fall down any stairs and that you know what happened to him.' Van Wyk denied that the Imam had been injured. Wilfrid then reminded him of the broken ankle that Alan Brooks had sustained while in his custody: Van Wyk's explanation at the time had been that Brooks fell down a flight of stairs while trying to escape. Did Van Wyk not find this a strange coincidence? And what of Stephanie Kemp? She had laid a charge of assault against him for which she received an *ex gratia* settlement from the minister of justice. Yes, Van Wyk agreed, there had been allegations, but he had not been charged as a result.

Later in the proceedings, Van Wyk was recalled by the prosecutor in an attempt to give him and his testimony some credibility. Van Wyk then handed in as evidence two letters from detainees, one of whom had turned State's evidence. Both thanked Van Wyk personally for his consideration and kindness while they were detained.

Next to testify was Dr Percy Helman, an eminent surgeon in private practice and a consultant at Groote Schuur hospital, who had studied the report of the autopsy. It appeared to him that a blood clot had formed as a result of the injuries and had entered the artery to the lung. This had led to the death of the Imam. He explained that there was a common danger of blood clotting after surgery or an injury, which usually occurred three to nine days after the event. His experience was that a blood clot would reach the chest about ten days after surgery or an injury – from the report this would have meant between 17 and 19 September. 'I personally think the injuries were partly to blame for the patient's death'. Dr Helman had also been present at the inspection *in loco* of the stairs where the Imam had fallen. He was of the opinion that all the bruises on the Imam's body could not have been caused by the fall. The Imam had bruises all over his body, while a fall would more than likely have resulted in bruises only in one area of his back.

In his examination by the prosecutor, Dr Schwär, the former senior State pathologist in Cape Town, testified that he had conducted a post-mortem on the Imam on 28 September at the police mortuary in Salt River and found various bruises, a haematoma and a fractured seventh right rib. He also found that there were blood clots in the chest wall; the coronary artery had a narrowing; and there were blood clots in the veins of the calves. In his questioning of Schwär, the prosecutor introduced

140

the possibility that the emotional tension that had been reported by the police officers and the Imam's lack of exercise while being detained could also have been responsible for the clots.

It was then Wilfrid's turn to cross-examine the pathologist. In reply, Schwär said it was not possible to determine from the bruises and the haematoma what force had been used to inflict them, but force would have been required. He agreed with Wilfrid that the bruises were not consistent with Van Wyk's testimony that the Imam had fallen on his side and buttocks, but suggested that the other bruising could have been the result of an attempt by the Imam to regain his balance, during which he had turned and fallen against a railing. Wilfrid pointed out that Van Wyk's testimony made no mention of this.

Two constables had independently testified that until about mid-September the Imam had walked around freely, but thereafter they had both observed that this stopped and that from then on he usually stood, sat in the sun or sometimes did not even leave his cell. Wilfrid now asked Dr Schwär if this lack of mobility could have been a cause of his blood clotting. He agreed it was an important factor. With the extensive trauma that the Imam had on his body, would he have been in pain when moving around? Yes, he said. When asked by the assessor, Professor Smith, about two parallel bruises across the Imam's back, the doctor conceded that they were similar to those of a person who had been assaulted with a stick.

In his summation – and quite contrary to what Wilfrid had revealed in his cross-examination – the prosecutor, Mr Van Graan, maintained: 'The general state of health of the deceased was very low and the likelihood that he died of a coronary thrombosis is, in my submission, not improbable. On the other hand, if the injuries Haron sustained did after all contribute to his death and it was accepted that these injuries resulted from his fall down the staircase, nobody could be held responsible.' As to the bruising and injuries which the post-mortem had revealed, 'There is no evidence of assault.'

When Wilfrid's time came to sum up, it was as though he and Van Graan had been examining the evidence of two different inquests. According to Wilfrid, 'the medical evidence, the bruising, the haematoma and the broken rib would have had the following effect upon the deceased: he would have felt considerable pain, movement would have been painful … The medical evidence also infers that the injuries were caused by trauma, i.e. force applied to the person of the deceased.' As to who was responsible for the injuries, Wilfrid finished by saying, 'In so far as the court is concerned, in so far as the identities of the persons who are responsible for this trauma are concerned, it is for the court to decide on the evidence before it whether it can identify these persons. If it cannot identify these persons then it can only say that they were persons whose identity is to the court unknown, they might have been in the employ of the Security Police.'

Finally, on 10 March 1970, the magistrate, Mr Kuhn, announced his findings. Although incredible, they were not unexpected. In his view, the Imam had died from 'a myocardial ischemia, likely contributing cause being a disturbance of the blood clotting mechanism due in part to trauma superimposed on a severe narrowing of the coronary artery. A substantial part of the said trauma was caused by an accidental fall down a flight of stone stairs. On the available evidence I am unable to determine how the balance thereof was caused.'[5]

The Haron family was bitterly disappointed with the finding and the Imam's wife subsequently issued a summons against the ministers of justice and police, claiming R22,125 for her three children 'for loss of support in consequence of the death of the late Imam Haron'. Surprisingly, the minister of police made an *ex gratia* payment in May 1971 of R5,000, which the family accepted. It was scant compensation to the family for their loss, but as further pursuit of the case would take time, money and energy, the family reluctantly decided not to pursue their claim further.

When the settlement became known, Mrs Catherine Taylor raised the matter one last time in Parliament on 9 June 1971. She attacked the government for making an *ex gratia* payment, as in this way they could evade appearing in court to answer claims of death or injury. 'By this means publicity is avoided, the police are not called upon to give evidence and the country is forced into silence and acceptance as a result.'[6]

*

Mapetla Mohapi
The 1970s saw a period of heightened political activity, which would culminate in the Soweto Uprising of 1976. In both that year and the following, 13 detainees died. On five occasions at this time, Wilfrid appeared for the families of the victims, three of which are described here. Each time he tried his utmost to expose the brutality of the Security Police and the complicity of the district surgeons in evading the truth. As Wilfrid later remarked to me, he had known the truth and had fought to the best of his ability for it to be known.

Mapetla Mohapi was a prominent member of the Black Consciousness Movement. After studying at the University of the North, he joined Steve Biko and other leading BC activists in King William's Town. Like his colleagues, he soon attracted the attention of the Security Police. After being detained for 164 days until October 1974 and then released without charge, he was subsequently banned under the Suppression of Communism Act in September 1975 and confined to Zwelitsha Township. Then on 15 July 1976 he was arrested under the Terrorism Act. Not long afterwards, on 5 August, he was found dead in his cell at the Kei Road police station in King William's Town, hanging from his trousers. He was the 24th person to die in detention.

At the inquest, which began in January 1977, Captain A Gerber made a dramatic revelation: he produced a 'suicide note' written on a piece of toilet paper and addressed to Captain Schoeman of the East London Special Branch, which he claimed had been given to him the day after Mohapi's death. It read:

'Death Cell, Kei Road. Mr Schoeman. This is just to say goodbye. You can carry on interrogating my dead body. Perhaps you will get what you want from it. Your friend Mapetla.'

But Wilfrid, who appeared on behalf of the Mohapi family, was entirely sceptical about the document and called a handwriting expert from Durban, Mr HF Allardice, who testified for almost a full day. By the end Allardice had clearly refuted the evidence of the police that the note had been written by Mohapi. 'As a banker I would never have passed the signature on the note as genuine.'

Mohapi's post-mortem had been attended by two Black Consciousness activists, the medical doctors Mamphela Ramphele and Dubs Msauli, both of whom were subsequently detained. They found that Mohapi had died as a result of broad-based force applied to the base of his neck. At the inquest Dr RB Hawking, who had performed the post-mortem, testified that while his findings were consistent with a case of hanging, the pair of jeans that the police said Mohapi had used to hang himself could not have supplied the necessary force. Moreover, if death had been by strangulation from the jeans, there would have been a different pattern of injuries. It was possible, he conceded, that Mohapi died of strangulation before he was hanged from the bars in the cell.

As part of his efforts to reveal the Security Police's methods, Wilfrid made an astute move. He called Thenjiwe Mtintso, then a reporter for the *Daily Dispatch* and a BC activist, to testify about her experience when she was detained in August 1976, a short while after Mohapi's death. She described how she had been repeatedly tortured. A Captain R Hansen made her sit on the floor in front of him. Standing behind her, he wrapped a wet towel over her head and shoulders and then pulled the two ends across her neck, with the result that she felt she could not breathe. While she struggled to free herself, he held her firmly in his thighs. He repeated this on two occasions. Once, when he removed the towel, he said to her, 'Now you see how Mapetla died.' At the inquest she demonstrated this treatment to the court on the family's attorney, Griffiths Mxenge. She also testified that while she was detained Captain Schoeman came into the room where she was being interrogated and said to his colleague, 'If she lies, bring her to me and she will speak the truth, after which she will follow Mohapi.' When asked why she did not report this at the time to the visiting magistrate, she replied that he had been accompanied by a security policeman and she feared further assault if she complained.

In his summation at the inquest, Wilfrid said to a hushed court that there was 'irresistible inference suggesting homicide as the cause of death'. As for the suicide note, he found it extraordinary that the note had been discovered only on the morning after the body was found and said that there were 'grave doubts' as to its authenticity. 'I submit that this is not a genuine note and that with Miss Mtintso's evidence the inference is irresistibly suggesting of homicide.'

But the inquest magistrate, Mr AJ Swart, would not accept this. When he delivered his findings on 18 July 1977, he declared that Mohapi had died of anoxia and suffocation as a result of hanging, which 'was not brought about by any act of commission or omission of any living person'. Once again, to Wilfrid's dismay and anger, no-one was held to blame. As for Mohapi's family, they were not only distraught at hearing the outcome, but their anguish and anger were exacerbated when told that they would be liable for costs of about R250,000 for the inquest hearing.[7]

Twenty years after her husband's death, Mohapi's widow, Nohle Mohapi-Mbetshu, was the first woman to testify at the Truth and Reconciliation Commission hearing in a packed city hall in East London in April 1996. She approached the TRC, she said, in the belief that the commission would shed light on what had happened and she would learn how her husband had died in detention. But no police officer came forward to apply for amnesty for Mohapi's death and to this day no-one has been held responsible for his murder.[8]

*

Hoosen Haffejee

Dr Hoosen Haffejee, a 26-year-old intern at Durban's King George V Hospital, was arrested under the Terrorism Act on 3 August 1977 for being in possession of 'subversive documents'. He was found in his cell less than 24 hours later, hanging from his trousers. Again, the Security Police claimed this was an act of suicide. While the pathologist's report found that his death was consistent with hanging, it also noted that he had some 60 wounds on his body, including his back, knees, arms and head.

The family appointed Dr DH Diggs to examine the body. Diggs told the inquest that he found strong evidence that Haffejee had been tortured. He observed unusual marks on the body and discovered these could be replicated when using an implement, a type of pliers, made to compress lead seals onto string or wire. The assault probably started with a few punches, but as the day progressed it became more violent and Haffejee was hit on his legs, ankles, private parts, buttocks, the back of his body, face, neck, arms and armpits. By that stage he would have been in pain and very bruised. His interrogators would have taken a break from their work and then continued until late into the night, after which Haffejee would have been thrown into a cell.

Haffejee was a slightly built man and weighed 49 kg, but the arresting officers, Lieutenant JB Taylor and Captain PL du Toit, who weighed 82 kg and 104 kg respectively, testified that they had difficulty in arresting him and putting him into their car. The injuries he sustained, they claimed, probably came about from his struggling when being forced into the vehicle. In his cross-examination Wilfrid suggested this was a figment of their imagination: it was highly unlikely that two well-built men like them could not restrain the slight Haffejee. Taylor also denied that Haffejee had been injured while under interrogation. In his closing address to the inquest, Wilfrid emphasised that there was clear evidence that Haffejee's body had substantial bruising and that he had died less than 24 hours after being taken into detention. He asked for a finding that Taylor and Du Toit had used excessive interrogation techniques and deliberately caused Haffejee's injuries.

But once again the conspiracy of silence and perjury by the police succeeded in defeating the ends of justice. The magistrate, Mr TL Blunden, found that Haffejee's injuries were not the result of third-degree interrogation methods and that submissions to the contrary were pure speculation and unsupported by evidence. There is no suggestion that Dr Haffejee's death could be attributed to any homicidal act by any person. No-one seems to have had a motive for killing him.' Haffejee had died by committing suicide and the extensive injuries 'were unconnected and collateral to his death'.

The truth about Dr Haffejee's death would be partly revealed at the Truth and Reconciliation Commission hearings in 1996, when a former Security Branch member, Mohum Gopal, confirmed that he had been present when Haffejee was stripped naked and assaulted by Taylor and Du Toit. He did not believe that Haffejee had committed suicide 'as he was very strong psychologically'. Gopal's statement to the TRC provided further confirmation of the interrogation methods of the Security Police. According to him, if a detainee did not co-operate within the first 48 hours the Security Police would apply for permission to hold him or her for a longer period of time. They would, he told the TRC, routinely use several methods of assault and torture to obtain the information they wanted. These included sleep deprivation and violent forms of assault known as 'panel beating'.

As a result of Gopal's testimony, Taylor was subpoenaed to appear before the TRC, but he denied being involved in the assault of Haffejee, claiming that Haffejee had been in the custody of members of the uniformed police at the time of his death. Once again, truth was evaded and justice was denied. Later, a further injustice was added to his legacy when he was not recorded on the Wall of Names at Freedom Park in the section of those who died in detention, unlike others featured in this chapter. He does, however, have a street in Pietermaritzburg named after him.

*

George Botha

George Botha, a 30-year-old 'coloured' teacher at Paterson High School in Port Elizabeth, was detained on 10 December 1977 under the so-called 90-day detention law. He died five days later at the infamous Sanlam Building, which housed the headquarters of the Security Police in Port Elizabeth.

At the inquest Major Harold Snyman, who had led the interrogation of Steve Biko just before his brutal death, attested that he and Sergeant RF Prinsloo had brought Botha back by car from the Despatch police station, where he was being held, and took the elevator to the sixth floor where the Security Police offices were located. Botha had been cheerful and willing to make a statement. But as Sergeant Prinsloo released his grip on him to unlock the barred gate, Botha suddenly spun around and freed himself from Major Snyman's hold, ran to the stairwell railing and dived head first over it to the foyer below. When Wilfrid asked him in cross-examination why he thought Botha would commit suicide like that, Snyman replied that he was probably scared that the information he had given them during interrogation would be used against him.

The inquest would hear evidence from Dr Gideon Knobel, a senior pathologist, and Dr Benjamin Tucker, district surgeon for Port Elizabeth. They revealed that injuries had been inflicted on Botha two to four hours before his death. However, the magistrate, Mr JA Coetzee, accepted the police version of events without question and declared, with regard to the injuries found on Botha's back, chest, arm and armpit, that 'the court does not know how they were sustained'. Despite Wilfrid's conviction that 'the persons who interrogated him are the ones who can explain how he got the injuries', the inquest magistrate ultimately found that nobody was to blame for Botha's death.

*

The ongoing exposure to the brutality inflicted on detainees by the police and the stress of appearing at their inquests ultimately took a toll on Wilfrid. In mid-1977 he suffered a transient ischaemic attack. Despite being told to take time off to recuperate, he was back in chambers after a week. But stress and high blood pressure would plague him for the rest of his life and probably led to his eventual death.

As any advocate who worked in that time might be expected to, Wilfrid noted the proceedings of the Truth and Reconciliation Commission in the mid-1990s and specifically those related to the cases he acted on. He seemed to me, however, to be always sceptical as to the specific outcomes of the TRC and thus its overall effect; initially, because of his first-hand knowledge of the lengths to which the Security Police would go to protect themselves; and, later, because of the ANC's apparent disinterest in the legacy of the foot soldiers of the struggle. History appears to have borne out his mistrust; in February 2016 the National Prosecuting Authority admitted that there were still 300 pending cases involving slain anti-apartheid victims. In one instance, that of the death in 1983 of Nokuthula Simelane, an MK courier, the NPA only started acting on it once Simelane's family took them to court to force the matter. Were he alive today to comment, Wilfrid would most likely note that had the NPA been less distracted by the affairs of the most senior members of the ANC, it might have been able to administer more justice to the rank and file South Africans who participated – sometimes losing their lives in the process – during the struggle against apartheid.

NOTES:

[1] This paragraph draws on *No One to Blame* by George Bizos (David Philip, 1999)

[2] *Biko* by Donald Woods (Paddington Press, 1978), p. 166

[3] State pathologists, while delivering quite accurate autopsy reports, would often not be candid about their findings at inquests, shoehorning their results into stories concocted by the security policy. Perhaps the most notorious case of medical collaboration involved district surgeons Dr Ivor Lang and Dr Benjamin Tucker, who attended to Steve Biko while he was still alive. Among other things, Biko's medical record and hospital test results indicating evidence of severe brain injury were falsified, preventing him the treatment he needed. The outspoken forensic expert Dr David Klatzow, who assisted Wilfrid in some cases, wrote in his book *Justice Denied*: 'One of the contradictions of those fateful years in South Africa was the fact that, in the heart of the so-called liberal universities of UCT and Wits, there existed forensic departments that seemed to me to be acting outside of the liberal spirit of the institutions in which they were housed. It is inexplicable that, during the worst excesses of the killing squads and the brutality of the SAP towards mainly (but not exclusively) the black citizens of South Africa, not a word was uttered by any of the forensic medicine departments, the sole exception being Wendy Orr. All of this illustrates, in my view, the unhealthy cosiness of the police, the state prosecutors and the forensic pathology services.'

[4] The TRC would reveal aspects of Genis's notorious career. Part of a special squad of security policemen who received training in torture techniques in France and Algeria in the early 1960s, he was later associated with a special 'sabotage squad' to deal 'more effectively with subversive elements in the Republic' (TRC Volume 2, Chapter 3, Subsection 14). In 1972, then commander of the Security Branch in the Orange Free State, he was involved in the abduction of Herbert Mbali, who had sought political asylum in Lesotho and was detained in South Africa. He was handed to Willem Schoon (see chapter 12) who was then a junior major in the Security Branch. After an objection by the Lesotho government, Mbali was returned to Lesotho. Both received amnesty for their deed (TRC AC/2001/236). In May 1985, the TRC records that Genis, now a Major General at SAP HQ in Pretoria, advocated fomenting violence between the UDF and AZAPO in the Eastern Cape. In June 1986 he was sent to Cape Town around the time of attacks by a government-supported counter-revolutionary group, the '*witdoeke*'. (TRC Volume 2, Chapter 3, Subsection 60)

[5] *Cape Times*, 11 March 1970

[6] Lawyers Committee for Civil Rights under Law, *Deaths in Detention in South Africa* (Washington, DC, United Nations Publication 29/77, December 1977).

[7] TRC hearing, East London, 15 April 1996

[8] *City Press*, 16 April 2006

CHAPTER 9

CHAMBERS AND ADVENTURES IN THE CITY

The life of a prominent advocate in Cape Town city chambers

The wide interests of his earlier years – he was now approaching forty – had given way to a passion to be a respected advocate and, one day possibly, a judge.

A fter being appointed to the Cape Bar in October 1952, Wilfrid took rooms in Parliament Chambers and then moved, when space became available, to Temple Chambers at 4 Wale Street. My first recollection of his work environment was of his chambers in Utilitas Building at 1 Dorp Street, where he was on the fifth floor. The Bar had moved there in 1958 from Temple Chambers to accommodate the growing number of advocates. This rather drab building was just around the corner from the entrance to the Supreme Court in Keerom Street, and so was conveniently situated for members of the Bar. From the higher floors there was a glimpse of the Company's Garden and the Houses of Parliament in the distance, but from room 501 the view was of the parking in Dorp Street and the Cape Provincial Administration building on the opposite side.

Every so often on a Saturday the three children would travel into town with Wilfrid for shopping or, in my case, a haircut at Stuttafords department store in Adderley Street. Our first port of call would be his chambers. As you entered his room, the walls from left to right were fronted by bookcases with wooden frames and glass sliding doors, which were packed full of law reports and all manner of legal books. To the right of the door was usually a pile of mostly unopened *Government Gazettes* and newspapers, mainly copies of *Die Burger*, which Wilfrid bought every morning and read without fail. Next to that was a round table with six chairs for consultations and trial preparations with attorneys. His desk, which faced the door as you walked in, was not particularly big so the overflow of papers, especially when he was writing a book, spilled onto the table or stood in piles spread out on the floor. Under the windows on the far right were more bookshelves and, close by, a large easy chair where he used to read and take a nap at lunch time.

All the furniture was of dark wood, the carpet was dark blue, and the covering fabrics on the furniture and the curtains were an elegant, legal-looking purple with a green stripe, which gave a lovely sense of cool in summer. But the overall impression was of stern professionalism befitting the chambers of a senior criminal advocate.

The office had a low-armed swivel-and-tilt chair behind the desk, to the left of which was a side table with two black Bakelite phones, one his private line and the other an elongated contraption with a crank handle and a number of buttons that connected him to his colleagues on the floor and to Mr Jubelin, the floor clerk. To me Mr Jubelin seemed an old man, possibly a war veteran. He had a small office midway down the passage onto which it opened with a counter where he would receive visitors, post and briefs delivered by attorneys. At the back was a kitchenette, with a magnificent view of Table Mountain, where he would prepare tea for the advocates and their visitors. Two of Wilfrid's colleagues, Ben Kies and Gerald Friedman, whom we knew, had offices on the eighth floor. We were allowed to venture up the stairs or in the lift to visit them and enjoy the better views of the city.

Alongside the telephone there was usually a Hermes typewriter on which Wilfrid, an accomplished typist, used to type the drafts of most of his books, as well as heads of argument and general notes as his handwriting was legible only to him. Another of his 'tools' was a long, brass letter opener that lay in front of him and that he used to tap or play with when thinking. After the Tsafendas trial, the Parker fountain pen set given to him by the attorney David Bloomberg for his defence of the assassin would occupy a prominent position and was used for making notes and signing documents.

On the wall there were various paintings. One of them made a profound impression on me from an early stage. It was a painting of the Pont Neuf, one of the oldest bridges over the River Seine, close to the Palace of Justice. This now hangs in my office as a reminder of those wonderful chambers.

There was always a ritual to be followed when we visited. We would first be sent down the passage to Mr Jubelin and spend some time with him while Wilfrid was busy with his papers. Mr Jubelin would make Wilfrid a cup of tea and take it to him, and discuss the matters of the day. Then we would leave on our errands in the city. In those days Wilfrid was a brisk walker and my sisters and I had to scamper to keep up with him. Only when we came to the Argus Building in St George's Street would he slow down to allow us a moment to look at the newspaper photographs that used to be displayed on pinboards behind glass. Diagonally opposite was Marks Coffee House, where we would occasionally stop for tea on the return journey. At other times he would take us to the Company's Garden to feed the squirrels and see the goldfish in the ponds near the museum. It was all quite an adventure for a young boy.

Utilitas Building was next to Cranford's book shop, which at one time was reputed to be the largest second-hand book shop in the southern hemisphere. Sometimes Susan, an avid reader, would be left there to explore its shelves and enclaves, while Megan and I, the younger siblings, went with Wilfrid into town. There is no doubt that Wilfrid's chambers and Cranford's book shop in particular fostered our love of books. There was a wonderful smell that permeated Cranford's and visiting the shop was an intoxicating experience. Despite its being a warren of rooms on two or three floors with dozens of shelves, the staff could always direct you with great accuracy to the shelf that held the book you were looking for. On one of our forays into the shop in 1966, just before the Tsafendas hearing, I bought a copy of the *Stories of Robin Hood & His Merry Outlaws* by J Walker McSpadden. It was elegantly bound in tan leather, with gold embossing on the spine – quite a find for a seven-year-old. Sadly, the shop is no more, but I still have the *Stories of Robin Hood & His Merry Outlaws* on my book shelf. When I want to remember Cranford's and the Saturday mornings we spent there, I open it and smell the slightly blemished pages.

In early 1974 the Bar moved to Huguenot Chambers in Queen Victoria Street. Given his seniority, Wilfrid had first choice of chambers. He chose no. 1301, which took up a whole corner of the thirteenth floor with magnificent views of Table Mountain and the Company's Garden on one side and Signal Hill and the Bo-Kaap on the other. The office was lovely and airy and provided a splendid new home for Wilfrid's furniture, bookcases and extensive library. When the *Cape Times* digitised its operations and converted to an open-plan layout, Gertrude bought her large, antique partners' desk for a few rands and moved it to no. 1301. Wilfrid's old desk continued to do service in his study at home. While more modern and with plenty of natural light that flowed in from the large windows, no. 1301 still maintained the ambience befitting Wilfrid's position at the Bar.

In the late 1980s, when he was permanently appointed to the Bench, it was a sad task to dispose of the unneeded books and furniture. Some went home, but I immediately took over the partners' desk. It has been my place to work at for most of my business career and has continued to serve me well even though it is at least a century old.

CHAPTER 10

THE MARLENE LEHNBERG APPEAL

Wilfrid's involvement in the cause célèbre of the 1970s, the sensational 'Scissors Murder', in which he saved a young woman from the gallows

'He obtained a powerful hold over her when she was no more than 16 and he used her to gratify and satisfy his sexual desires. This gave rise to an unholy love which in time led to murder.'

– CHIEF JUSTICE FLH RUMPFF

I n 2014 two murder trials captured the attention of the public and held it obsessively for their duration. The first was that of Oscar Pistorius, the world-famous Paralympic athlete, who was accused of shooting his girlfriend Reeva Steenkamp on Valentine's Day in 2013. The other was of the British businessman Shrien Dewani, who it was alleged had arranged for the murder of his new wife, Anni, while on honeymoon in Cape Town in November 2010. These trials completely absorbed the public's interest, and the trial proceedings were followed avidly and covered in detail by the media. Much the same kind of attention was drawn in 1975 to the sensational trial of Marlene Lehnberg, an attractive young woman who had an affair with a man old enough to be her father and had then cajoled the poor, disabled Marthinus Choegoe to brutally murder her lover's wife. This case soon became known as the 'Scissors Murder'.

Marlene Lehnberg was born in Cape Town on 13 October 1955, the second of five children. Her parents had married in 1952 when her father was 22 and her mother 19. For the first years of their marriage they lived with his parents as he was unemployed at the time. But her mother did not get on with her parents-in-law so they moved out after a while. When Marlene was born, her parents were living in straitened circumstances in a single room in Maitland and, as a result of her birth, had to move back to her father's family home. It is highly likely that her birth was unplanned and that she was unwelcome and unwanted by her parents.

Marlene was brought up in a strict and conservative home. Her father was a puritanical man who hardly communicated with her and showed none of the usual fatherly affection. He did not allow her to socialise like other girls of her age; by the time she reached high school she had not been to a cinema. She was naive and innocent; but she was also very intelligent and came first in her class. Her teachers thought her a well-behaved and hard-working pupil, quiet and passive – she was described as 'blotting paper', absorbing everything but never giving of herself. She would come home from school, go to her room, do her school work and keep to herself.

Despite her good performance at school – indeed, her headmaster thought she was university material – she decided to leave at the end of Standard 8 and did so without consulting her parents. At the same time, her leaving school did not meet with any protest from them and she took up employment with an insurance company in January 1972. In February she began working as a receptionist and telephonist in the orthopaedic workshop at the Red Cross Children's hospital in Rondebosch. At this time she was 16 years of age; a bright, attractive, intelligent young woman. With her new-found freedom she underwent a great transformation, especially given her background. She started to use make-up, dyed her hair, wore tops with lower necklines and shorter skirts, and smoked. She now socialised regularly, dating two young men with whom she had sexual relations, and soon was no longer attending church.

Also working in the orthopaedic workshop was Christiaan van der Linde, a tall, self-assured man of 47, who was a senior technician and Marlene's superior. A short while after meeting, they started seeing each other socially. She was drawn to Van der Linde and he responded to her. It appears she saw him as a father figure, the older man who had been largely lacking in her own family life while she was growing up. They would meet after hours in the workshop and soon a physical relationship developed. In all probability Van der Linde seduced her and groomed her to be his sexual partner. Even while she was still living at home with her parents, the relationship had essentially developed into a full-blown affair. To those who knew her, it was clear that she was in love with Van der Linde and wanted to marry him.

In October 1973, at the age of 18, she made the decision to leave home and hired a room in a boarding house in Observatory.

Again, there was no opposition from her parents; they did not even know where she was living after she moved out. From then on, from Monday to Friday, Van der Linde would take her home after work. They would drink in a local hotel or in her room and then have sex.

As the relationship proceeded, Lehnberg fell intensely in love with Van der Linde. He became a pivotal part of her life and she took no interest in other men. But Van der Linde was a family man who had been married for just over 25 years, had three children and lived in a comfortable house in Boston Estate. He spent the weekends with his family and went to church on Sundays, leaving Marlene alone in her boarding-house room. During this time the two discussed the possibility of his divorcing his wife, but he was not prepared to do this. All the same, he led her to understand that should he survive his wife, he would then accept her. The inference was quite clear to Marlene: if his wife should die, he would be hers. It is certain that the idea of murdering Van der Linde's wife, Susana, developed from this.

In early 1974 Van der Linde became suspicious that the two were being watched and he terminated their intimate meetings after work. There is no doubt that this sudden cessation of relations had a marked effect on Marlene; by July 1974 she began to consider leaving Cape Town. Van der Linde persuaded her not to, even though he still made it clear that he would not leave his wife and family. In September Marlene, exasperated with the situation, decided to meet Susana van der Linde and talk with her. Marlene initially tried to speak to her on the phone but Susana wouldn't hear her out and put the phone down on her. Then, in October, Susana agreed to meet her in Bellville. But the meeting did not go as Marlene had wanted. Her expectation was that she and Susana would work out some arrangement, but it soon became clear that Susana would do anything to keep her husband. She told Marlene that she would never divorce him, but conceded that if Christiaan was amenable they could establish some compromise. It appears that she was even prepared to share her husband with Marlene, but would not give him up.

Around this time Marlene Lehnberg's accomplice in the eventual murder became known to her. Marthinus Choegoe was a disabled coloured man who had lost his left leg above the knee in a car accident. He was ill-educated, extremely poor and unemployed and had low self-esteem, his injuries having affected his mobility and dexterity. As his prosthetic leg was uncomfortable, he came to the orthopaedic workshop at the Red Cross hospital to have it attended to. Here he met Marlene.

As Marlene's plan to murder Susana developed in her mind, she approached Choegoe by way of a letter in which she suggested that he could earn money if he were good with his hands, implying some kind of legitimate work. They then met one evening at Rondebosch station and, after some conversation and an inducement of gin, she came out with it and asked him to kill a woman, adding that he would not be suspected as he was a cripple. In order to get away from her, according to his subsequent testimony in court, he agreed to this and Marlene gave him Susana van der Linde's address. Some days later Choegoe went to Boston Estate to warn Susana of the threat to her life, he would later claim, though he did not carry out his intention.

Marlene persisted with her requests and made him a variety of promises: money, a car, a house, even to have sex with him. There is no doubt that Choegoe must have found the attentions of an attractive young woman, and the material promises she made, difficult to resist. Marlene did not give up in her efforts. She went as far as picking him up in Bellville and dropping him off near the Van der Linde house with a hammer with which to hit Susana. Choegoe rang the doorbell but there was no reply, and so he left. But he was noticed by a neighbour and was picked up by the police, but then released.

In view of Choegoe's lack of success, Marlene tried another tack and approached an engineering student, Rob Newman, asking him if she could borrow a pistol he owned. He refused. In the end she stole the weapon, which was later used to strike Susana.

By this time Marlene wanted to end the relationship with Van der Linde and leave Cape Town to start a new life, but he persuaded her to stay. At the end of September 1974 she resigned from the orthopaedic centre and told Van der Linde that she was going to work for a certain Vigus. By then Van der Linde had informed his wife about the affair and broken off the relationship after Marlene let him know that she was pregnant. (It seems she was not.) Yet, when she started to work for Vigus, Van der Linde continued to take her out at lunch time in his car.

Finally, Marlene decided to move to Johannesburg. She packed her things and, as far as her family knew, she was to leave by car at midnight on 3/4 November. However, early on the morning of 4 November she went unannounced to fetch Choegoe at his home in Retreat and took him to the Van der Linde house in Boston Estate, where they arrived just after 7.30am She said she wanted to have him as her witness when she told Susana that she was leaving for Johannesburg.

What happened when they came to the house was later the subject of dispute between Marlene and Choegoe in court. She claimed that she dropped him at the house and waited in the car, while he testified that they entered the house together. According to a witness who walked past the house at the time of the murder, there was no-one inside Marlene's white Ford Anglia, which was parked outside the house. Choegoe testified that when they entered the house Susana took fright and tried to get away, but Marlene tripped her and she fell, hitting her head. Marlene then struck her with the stolen pistol on the jaw, breaking it in two places. Choegoe further noted that on Marlene's instructions he started throttling Susana. Marlene then handed him a pair of scissors that were on the sideboard and he proceeded to stab Susana seven times in the chest, four of them to the heart. After the murder Marlene took Choegoe back to his house and she immediately left for Johannesburg.

During the day of 4 November, Van der Linde tried to contact his wife a few times and finally sent his daughter, Zelda, who worked close by, to try the house during her lunch hour. Around one o'clock she found her mother dead on the living-room floor and called the police. Van der Linde was notified. When he arrived at the house the police were surprised by his casual disregard for his dead wife. He apparently turned her body over with his foot in an attempt to identify her.

Initially, Van der Linde was suspected of the murder, but he had a solid alibi. Marlene was not immediately under suspicion as she was out of town; but when a piece of evidence came to the attention of the police she was questioned in Johannesburg by the Brixton Murder and Robbery Squad. She appeared nervous and finally, when asked if she knew 'Marthinus', she blurted out that she had taken him to the house, waited outside and then afterwards brought him back home. She was then arrested and gave a full statement before being flown back to Cape Town. In the light of her statement, Choegoe was arrested later that day.

On Tuesday, 4 March 1975, the sensational trial of Lehnberg and Choegoe started before Judge Diemont with two assessors, Mr AJ van Niekerk, a retired senior magistrate, and Mr F van Zyl Smit, a legal adviser from the department of justice. The State was represented by Attorney General Ted Harwood KC and Advocate Nic Treurnicht. The accused were represented *pro deo* by counsel: Advocate Dennis Delahunt appeared for Marlene Lehnberg and Advocate Roelf van Riet for Marthinus Choegoe; they acted without the support of attorneys.

The trial drew hundreds of Capetonians to the Supreme Court in Keerom Street. They packed the court every day in their eagerness to see the two accused. On the second day of the trial the *Cape Times* reported: 'In scenes reminiscent of pop-star arrivals, smartly dressed women, middle-aged and older, secretaries and typists, housewives, mothers and daughters, queued, quarrelled, punched, or tried to bribe their way into the courtroom.' There were reports that people even climbed onto nearby roofs to take photographs. Marlene Lehnberg's parents' home in Plumstead was almost in a state of siege, and the police had to shield them from photographers and a stream of curious onlookers. It was an event made for the newspapers and the trial became front-page news for its duration.

Over seven days the State called 33 witnesses. Neither Lehnberg nor Choegoe took the stand to give testimony and, importantly, no psychiatric medical evidence was led by the defence counsel for the accused. With all the damning evidence presented by the prosecution Judge Diemont, after due deliberation with his two assessors, found them both guilty. In his summing up, the judge said of Marlene Lehnberg: 'I accept that this young woman became infatuated with a middle-aged man. I accept that he must have had some influence over her and that he may even have encouraged her to hope that they might at some time get married. And I accept that this infatuation was what led to what counsel described as a crime of passion ... In this particular case it was, as the Attorney General said, not committed in hot blood on the spur of the moment, but it was planned over a matter of months and it must be remembered that the accused was not the innocent party in this triangle. She knew that Van der Linde was married; she knew he had a wife and two sons and a daughter. She was the one who took the initiative and tried to persuade Mrs Van der Linde to give up her husband after they had been married for many years, and when she failed to persuade her on the telephone she went to see her and tried to persuade her to grant a divorce, and again she failed. When this was refused, she decided to satisfy her passion by killing the woman who stood in her way. Stated in those blunt terms, one may well ask how her conduct may be described as being in any way extenuating.'

On 14 March 1975 the court found there to be no mitigating circumstances and they were both sentenced to death. After the conviction only Choegoe entered a plea in mitigation of sentence; but, again, nothing was heard from Marlene Lehnberg.

Almost immediately after the trial ended, a number of people stepped forward, wanting to give their expert assistance for the accused. Both Lehnberg and Choegoe then lodged appeals against their sentences to lead further evidence. Since their counsel, Advocates Delahunt and Van Riet, would be tendering affidavits to the court, and might even have to appear as witnesses to support the appeal, they could not appear for the accused. The evidence was therefore led by Advocate Gerald Friedman SC for Lehnberg, with Advocate Ismail Mahomed SC acting for Choegoe. Both Friedman and Mahomed presented various affidavits to the court from a number of experts that introduced psychiatric evidence not heard in the original trial. In his ruling Judge Diemont first noted with some irritation: 'It is a strange fact that expert witnesses who may be qualified to assist the Court will follow the conduct of a murder trial closely in the press and then after sentence come forward with belated offers of assistance.' All the same, he granted the application for leave to appeal.

As Friedman was not available, Wilfrid was briefed to take the matter, on a *pro deo* basis, to the Appellate Division in Bloemfontein and introduce the new evidence in mitigation. He was assisted by Advocates Delahunt and Michael Odes. Advocate Mahomed continued to act for Choegoe. The appeal, which attracted almost as much press coverage as the trial itself, was heard on 23 July 1975 by Chief Justice FLH Rumpff, assisted by Acting Judges R Muller and B Galgut. Judge Rumpff made it clear that the appeal would have to be heard in one day, as he had to hear another case the following day.

Although the trial judge, Judge Diemont, had given Lehnberg and Choegoe leave to appeal in Bloemfontein, Wilfrid first had to present argument that the evidence adduced after their trial should now be considered by the Appeal Court in mitigation of the death sentence handed down. This he successfully did. Wilfrid could then proceed to present the evidence. He started by giving the court the salient details of Lehnberg's life and of the relationship that developed with Van der Linde, who became the central driving force in her life. Around the time of the murder, her judgement was clearly disturbed, as evidenced by a letter she wrote to Van der Linde on 23 October 1974: 'My darling, what have you done to me? You've ruined me forever. The man I loved so much, whom I could talk to, who meant the world to me, who comforted me, has just discarded me. I am probably going to have a nervous breakdown any moment. I just can't face it. I wish I could die. I will never forgive you for what you've done to me. I was so sure that you loved me. You proved it so many times. How you can just say, thank you, I can't get over it. This past six months has been hell for me. I gave up everything I had for you.'

Wilfrid then introduced the evidence as to her psychopathy. Dr Pascoe, for the State and also a specialist psychiatrist, was of the opinion that although she was not a psychopath she had the characteristics of psychopathy, which included being cold and callous, showing a lack of remorse and guilt, an indifference to her predicament and untruthfulness. Pascoe felt that she had a 'psychopathic disorder'. However, after some discussion with Judges Rumpff and Galgut, Wilfrid had to concede that on the evidence before the court it could only be argued that Lehnberg was not a psychopath but that she showed psychopathic tendencies. The expert evidence did show, however, that on the balance of probabilities she was emotionally immature.

In closing his argument, Wilfrid said that the court should see that the cumulative effect of the mitigating factors made

Lehnberg's actions less morally reprehensible. 'It is submitted that the mitigating factors outlined above – signifying her youth, her emotional immaturity, her psychopathic personality and the resultant deep emotional involvement with Van der Linde which gravely impaired her judgement – made her conduct morally less reprehensible. The fact that the Appellant acted with callous disregard of the feelings of the deceased, and shows no remorse, does not, it is submitted, negate the existence of extenuating circumstances, since these are the very features of a psychopathic personality.

'In the final analysis, this Honourable Court is dealing with a vulnerable young girl, who, because of circumstances not of her making, found herself in a deep emotional involvement which disturbed her judgement. If she had not had the misfortune to meet Van der Linde, but instead had met a young man who was warm and compassionate, who took her to his home and introduced her to warm and caring parents, Marlene Lehnberg may well have identified with that kind of environment, and would probably never have committed a crime of this nature. Marlene Lehnberg is not a menace to society. There is good reason to believe that she will respond to treatment and undergo a process of maturation, and in time she will be restored to society as a useful and socially acceptable person.'

The ruling of the appeal judges was a landmark decision in respect of the pivotal role of expert evidence when the defence of psychopathy is raised. It further established that, depending on the circumstances of the case, psychopathy could be admitted as a mitigating factor, albeit in conjunction with youthfulness. In his findings Chief Justice Rumpff stated that, although Lehnberg was cold-blooded, callous and cruel and her actions were premeditated, the evidence showed she had committed the murder not out of inherent evil but because her personality was undermined at a very impressionable stage of the relationship with Van der Linde. About the latter, the judge was scathing;

'The true source of the evil was her lover Van der Linde. He obtained a powerful hold over her when she was no more than 16 and he used her to gratify and satisfy his sexual desires. This gave rise to an unholy love which in time led to murder.' Coupled with the effect that Van der Linde had on her, her youthfulness served as a mitigating circumstance, and the judge altered her sentence to twenty years' imprisonment.

With regard to Choegoe, Judge Rumpff said that when consideration was given to all the mitigating factors it could fairly be said that he was in a very vulnerable position and his willingness to become involved in the crime became understandable, if not excusable. He changed his sentence to fifteen years' imprisonment.

*

Wilfrid had appeared for Marlene Lehnberg on a *pro deo* basis as he was not only against the death sentence but he regarded the original sentence imposed on her as unjust. When we talked about the trial at the time, he told me that she had lost her childhood because of the puritanical behaviour of her loveless parents. Van der Linde had then come into her life and exploited her innocence to satisfy his physical needs. Wilfrid could not abide seeing this emotionally misdirected young woman lose her life on the gallows as a result.

After the appeal, he received a letter from a woman from Paardeberg Prison. It is not clear from the letter whether she worked there or was an inmate. She wrote, 'That I only want to thank you for all that you did for your fellow human being, Marlene Lehnberg. You have said you never knew her or her family but I also did not know her or her family and never met them. But day and night I prayed for her. In my simple handwriting I also pleaded to the Chief Justice of Bloemfontein and even pleaded for mercy for her from the

President. Anyway many, many thanks from an unknown grandmother, Cecilia Vercniel.'

Though unrepentant, Van der Linde would not be unscathed in the matter: he lost his job and moved away from Cape Town to his wife's smallholding in the Magaliesberg, where she had been born and where she wanted to be buried. By all accounts he lived a hermit's life on the property and died a lonely man in 1983. Marthinus Choegoe was released on 13 July 1985 and Marlene Lehnberg on 17 December 1986, after serving eleven years and nine months of her sentence. According to newspaper reports, she had 'become a Christian and wanted to start a new life'. Later, having suffered from osteoporosis for a number of years, she was diagnosed with breast cancer. The pain became intolerable and she evidently committed suicide at her home in October 2015 just days before her 60th birthday.

CHAPTER 11

A WOMAN, WINE AND CULINARY DELIGHTS

Wilfrid, the conversationalist,
breaking the bounds of formality and snobbery,
of language barriers and distance

'One Grahamstown Bar dinner was enlivened by the presence
of the rumbustious Cooper, in town on a case.'
– FROM BAR, BENCH AND BULLSHIFTERS

Through Gertrude's career at the *Cape Times*, she and Wilfrid had developed a keen interest in food and wine. They regularly dined out or visited various wine estates in the Western Cape and so came to know many of the restaurateurs and winemakers in and around Cape Town. Food and wine were important to Wilfrid and Gertrude, but what it was really all about was the pleasure and enjoyment of being with their friends, of engaging in conversation and discussion, and of conviviality.

In their courting days the Café Royal in Church Street, just around the corner from the newspaper, was one of their regular haunts. It was here that Wilfrid proposed to Gertrude. Another restaurant that I associate with Wilfrid was the Harlequin in Parow. Owned by Angelo Inzadi, it was situated opposite the Magistrate's Court on Voortrekker Road. When Wilfrid appeared there, he would make a point of crossing the road and having lunch at the restaurant. This could sometimes end quite late, especially if he was with his friend, the attorney Hasie Haasbroek. The Harlequin was also the venue for occasions in the evenings for family, friends and overseas visitors. The Italian delights that poured out of the kitchen still enliven my memory.

Given the nature of both Wilfrid's and Gertrude's occupations, they often socialised with all sorts of people: celebrities, politicians, diplomats, wine farmers, hoteliers, lawyers and businessmen, who in turn frequently became personal friends – and so the number of social events they attended multiplied accordingly. When it started to become a challenge to see everyone as often as they wanted, they decided to hold champagne brunches in the garden at Riverside. The first of these took place on a still summer Sunday morning in about 1970. Caterers, barmen and waiters were arranged to attend to the hundred or so invitees who gathered round tables and under umbrellas placed around the garden, which Gertrude had slaved over for many weekends to ensure it was in peak condition. After much champagne,

Black Velvet, food and an impromptu cricket match on the lawn, the last guests finally left at midnight. It was undoubtedly a success and more would be held at irregular intervals in the years to come.

Wilfrid loved a party, with the chance it offered to enjoy conversation and wine. One of the more memorable occasions I recall was my thirtieth birthday, which was held at Riverside. The evening was flowing well when I noticed that Wilfrid was missing, along with three of his friends: Felix Ernst, the managing director of the company I then worked for, Gernot Boker and Basie Maarten. Gertrude then told me they were 'held up' in the TV room. On approaching the door, I heard Wilfrid's voice followed by raucous laughter from within. I entered the room and came upon the four, like naughty school boys bunking class. The centre table was full of plates and wine bottles in various stages of demise; the conversation was flowing like a torrent and Wilfrid was holding forth. Later I observed Wilfrid scuttling down to the garage and covertly returning with another bottle of wine for the quartet. When the party ended, the four emerged looking decidedly worse for wear.

The annual Bar dinners were also occasions for festivity. The following anecdote from the compilation *Bar, Bench and Bullshifters* can stand for many: 'One Grahamstown Bar dinner was enlivened by the presence of the rumbustious Cooper, in town on a case. At the end of the dinner some juniors found him insensible under a table. They assiduously carried him out and helped him to his hostelry. In the morning the Settlers' Inn received a call. The indistinct enquiry was whether perhaps a full set of dentures had been found under the table. The Tiger was toothless.'[1]

In 1987 the Tastevin restaurant at the Cape Sun Hotel hosted a series of 'Men of Distinction' dinners at which an illustrious group of Cape Town men – such as the artist Vladimir Tretchikoff and the winemaker Günter Brözl – were asked to prepare the meals. Our family was highly amused when Wilfrid was invited to contribute to the series, as we knew his culinary skills did not stretch much beyond making instant coffee, badly, and burning toast. We guessed that the invitation had been extended not because of his culinary skills but rather because he was a well-known criminal lawyer and a good after-dinner speaker. He ended the series of dinners with an interesting menu titled 'An Infamous Last Meal', which included chicken cream soup 'Sing Sing', Breakwater Lobster Salad and Venison San Quentin. This was followed by 'George Appel' and Coffee in Mitigation. The meal was excellently prepared by the renowned Swiss chef Markus Iten, leaving Wilfrid free to do what best befitted his gregarious personality after a good meal and with a captive audience.

While Wilfrid loved to socialise, he equally loved to intellectualise. In 1955 he joined the Owl Club, which describes itself as 'remarkable remnant of the Victorian period of Cape Town, South Africa, being a gentleman's dining club formed in 1894 to provide a social meeting-place for those with an interest in the liberal arts and science. The members are entertained and informed by a strong tradition of excellent speakers and a high standard of music. The Owl Club maintains a tradition of monthly dinners for Members and their male guests; "black tie" is the customary plumage.' I have vivid memories of Wilfrid donning his 'black tie' to head off to Kelvin Grove, where the dinners were then generally held, and his arriving back home in the early hours. An Owls evening was sometimes followed by one of his characteristic excursions into the swimming pool the next morning, where he would submerge himself with much splashing and blowing – always surefire evidence of a good time the night before.

In his youth Wilfrid had played cricket for the University of Stellenbosch. Once he was settled in his career, he joined the Western Province Cricket Club in 1958. When I was very young, he still played a game or two. He would come home at lunch time to dress in his now not-so-white whites and go down the road with his somewhat elderly cricket bag to play. The reports on the matches to the family afterwards were vague, but despite there being no floodlights for night cricket in those days, it was usually well after dark when he arrived back home. All this came to an end when he came home one evening and dejectedly reported that he had been bowled first ball – a golden duck.

One event he always tried to attend was the New Year's cricket match at Newlands cricket ground, where he would sit in the members' stand and meet his friends. His friend Mickey Giles related to me how, at the lunch break, he would dine with his companions and, of course, take a glass or two of wine. The following session would inevitably pass rather quietly as those present, now facing the hot afternoon sun, would gather their strength by dozing in their seats until tea-time. After the second day, Wilfrid's face, not used to such exposure to the sun, would be lobster pink.

Once his interest in playing cricket ended, Wilfrid turned to golf as his sporting activity. His home course was Rondebosch. On a Saturday – in those days a men-only day – he would play regularly at various courses around the Peninsula; or on a Sunday, after family lunch, he and Gertrude would play a round with friends. I would sometimes walk with them. It was clear to me that my father would not be leaving his career in law to become a golfer: the caddies and I would be sent regularly into the rough to look for his ball.

Abandoning golf in later life, Wilfrid's exercise regime returned to what he had enjoyed in his youth and he would roam the paths and tracks of Table Mountain. He usually walked on a Sunday morning. His standard dress was either shorts, if it was hot, or a navy-blue tracksuit, which would be worn for many years until it became so ragged that Gertrude would be forced to confiscate it and buy a new one. He also wore a floppy canvas hat, usually blue, which would also see lengthy service before being retired. One of his quirks on his walks was to pick up litter and discard it in the nearest refuse bin. But on the many occasions when no bin could be found, he would return home attired in his worn tracksuit and laden with a bounty of packets, papers and plastic bottles that had been picked up en route. This would draw strange looks from people he knew or, when he lived in Constantia, arouse the great mirth of the local farm labourers.

Wilfrid had a rigorous work routine. He would rise at 5 or 5.30am and have a light breakfast. Both Wilfrid and Gertrude were frugal people so, to save the cost of having two cars in town, he would catch one of the first trains from Newlands station into the city to be in chambers by seven. Walking up from the station he got to know many of the coloured workers and newspaper sellers who were also around at that hour, always buying *Die Burger* en route. He loved this regular walk, as the city would be almost empty and it gave him time to think before the rigours of the day ahead.

Gertrude would then drop us three children off at school and then proceed to town. At the end of the day she and Wilfrid would drive home together and have supper with us. Such was Gertrude's busy schedule that there were times when they would have to go directly to a function after work and we children would have a nanny to look after us. As we got older we came to look after ourselves.

Wilfrid rarely took holidays or was away from chambers for any length of time. While many of our friends had regular family holidays, we only ever had two. The first was to East London on my fifth birthday. The second, in June 1976, was a driving tour around South Africa in preparation for my sister Susan's Rotary student exchange to New York State the following year; my parents wanted her to be informed about the country so she would make a good ambassador for the family – and even then, Wilfrid left us halfway in Durban to attend a trial.

NOTE:

[1] *Bar, Bench and Bullshifters, Cape Tales 1950–1990* Gerald Friedman and Jeremy Gauntlett (comp.) (Cape Town, Syberink, 2013)

CHAPTER 12

THE SWAKOPMUND SWAPO TRIAL

A forgotten but critical trial of the 1970s
in which the prosecution of six accused of
murdering a homeland chief in
South West Africa served as the apartheid state's
proxy trial of SWAPO

'However strongly the court may disapprove
of their conduct, nevertheless the court is aware that history is a
long wheel that turns, and the criminals of today are frequently the
patriots of tomorrow. We have seen this
in our country since 1945.'

– WILFRID COOPER

One Sunday morning in early December 1975, the phone rang at home. Gertrude was working in the garden and Wilfrid was at his chambers. When I answered, the man on the other side introduced himself as Colin du Preez from the firm Lorentz & Bone in Windhoek, South West Africa.[1] He told me he needed Advocate Cooper to act for six members of SWAPO who were accused of assassinating a tribal chief in Ovamboland, one Filemon Shuumbwa Elifas. All faced the death penalty under the Terrorism Act.

Not long afterwards Wilfrid arrived home; on receiving the message he immediately phoned Du Preez. There followed a lengthy conversation, after which we sat down for lunch. Wilfrid was quiet and reflective and briefly shared with us what he had been told, commenting that this was going to be a lengthy and difficult trial. Little did he know that it would span fifteen months and have a profound effect on the history of Namibia. It would also expose the lengths to which the South African government was prepared to go in trying to subvert the struggle for independence in South West Africa. It was a trial that would have been common in Moscow in the late 1930s or in Eastern Bloc countries in the 1950s: a political trial staged to discredit a regime's opponents rather than determine the guilt or innocence of the accused.

The opponent in question was the South West Africa People's Organisation, better known as SWAPO. Formed in 1960 in Windhoek, its primary support base was in fact in Ovamboland in the extreme north of the country. In time SWAPO would become recognised by the United Nations as the sole liberation organisation for the independence of Namibia from South Africa, which had governed the territory as a mandate from the League of Nations since the 1920s. Initially, SWAPO limited itself to peaceful methods of working for change but in August 1966, in view of South Africa's refusal to relinquish its occupation of the country and indeed its determination to extend grand apartheid there, SWAPO turned from being solely an 'internal' political organisation to launch an armed struggle by establishing an 'external' military wing, the People's Liberation Army of Namibia (PLAN). PLAN was a guerrilla army that operated initially from bases in Zambia and later in central southern Angola. After PLAN's first major contact with the South African Police and Defence Force troops in August 1966, the conflict escalated over the next 22 years into a major local war that drew South Africa militarily into Angola. It came to be known as the South African Border War or, more commonly, the Angolan Bush War. Armed incursions by SWAPO took place along the entire northern border of South West Africa but particularly in the populous area of Ovamboland, where most of the country's population resides and where the need on both sides of the conflict to establish support and credibility was greatest.

I myself came to know this area as a conscript in 1979 when I was sent as a photojournalist for the official Defence Force magazine, *Paratus*, to cover events in Ovamboland. My task, over the course of some months, was to photograph and write about incidents, landmine explosions and 'contacts' by South African troops with SWAPO insurgents, or other matters of interest, for publication. As a photographer weighed down with camera equipment, I carried only a 9mm Star pistol and I travelled unescorted in the area in a soft-skinned Land Cruiser. After seeing first-hand what a Russian landmine could do to such a vehicle, I would leave the relative safety of the tarred main roads and travel to assignments down gravel side roads with extreme trepidation. One gruesome scene I photographed involved a Ford bakkie: the vehicle, along with its occupants – a father, mother and young child – had been blown to pieces. Images like that are never forgotten and such devastation brought home to me the indiscriminate nature of the Border War on the local population going about their daily business. The truth of the political situation was perhaps harder for a young conscript, a small cog in the political mechanics of the time, to discern: that Ovamboland in particular, and South West Africa in general, was a frontline in the apartheid state's battle against its 'terrorist' enemies.

About 200 metres from the army camp where I was stationed lay the base of Koevoet, the recently established, secretive police unit. Years later the truth of this unit's activities would emerge in terrible detail: it was the platform for Eugene de Kock to cut his counter-terrorism teeth, developing the skills he would later use with such horrific effect at Vlakplaas. When I was first signed into camp and shown around, I was warned that the Koevoet area was strictly out of bounds because the men stationed there were *'befok'*. This was Ovamboland of the 1970s.

*

One consequence of the struggle for Namibian independence was the extension to the country of the Terrorism Act of 1967.[2] This gave the police far-reaching powers to detain anyone they believed to be a terrorist, have information about a terrorist or was believed to be withholding information relating to terrorists. It also allowed that 'no court of law shall pronounce upon the validity of any action taken under this section, or order the release of any detainee'. The Act also presumed that those accused of committing an offence had to prove beyond a reasonable doubt that they had not committed it – unlike the common presumption of innocence until proven guilty. The use of the Act by South Africa in what was deemed to be an international territory was deplored by both the United Nations General Assembly and the Security Council, which saw it as a denigration of the rule of law.

Filemon Elifas was the hereditary chief of the Ondonga tribe in Ovamboland. In August 1973, as part of the apartheid government's drive to grant 'self-government' to separate ethnic 'homelands' in South West Africa, Elifas was elected Chief Minister of Ovamboland. In the elections he secured the support of fewer than three per cent of eligible voters – an indication of his unpopularity among the Ovambo people, who largely saw him as a stooge of the government. In order to retain power and maintain order, he fell back on harsh emergency powers, and after the elections detained many people, specifically members of SWAPO. Several were held for months without charge before being brought before a tribal court. If found to be members of SWAPO, they were sentenced to flogging despite protests from the Lutheran and Anglican churches and court actions inspired by SWAPO. In June 1974 Judge J Strydom, who two years later would preside over the Swakopmund trial, refused to impose a temporary interdict on the floggings before the outcome of an application to the appeal court. It was only in February 1975 that Chief Justice Rumpff interdicted the Ovamboland Tribal Authority from arresting, detaining or inflicting punishment on any person who might be a member of SWAPO.

Clearly there were many in Ovamboland, as well as in the rest of South West Africa for that matter, who did not support Elifas. There were more than likely some who had sufficient reason to see him dead. But immediately after his assassination on the night of Saturday, 16 August 1975, at a liquor store at a place called Onamagongwa, a few kilometres south of Ondangwa, it became clear that SWAPO would be held responsible for the deed. Speaking two weeks after Elifas's killing and just before the first meeting of the Turnhalle Conference, a controversial initiative by the South African government to reach an internal political settlement for South West Africa that excluded SWAPO and international bodies like the United Nations, Prime Minister BJ Vorster opined that 'the assassination is the work of an undermining organisation, and that its aim was to wreck the forthcoming constitutional talks.[3] Action will be taken against them, whoever they are and regardless of the consequences.'[4]

In the weeks after the assassination, the police proceeded to detain more than 200 men and women, mainly members of SWAPO but also members of the Evangelical Lutheran Church. The inclusion of Lutheran pastors and lay members in the dragnet only showed that the police were not particularly interested in the actual perpetrators of the murder but rather in the broader spectrum of those who were opposed to the South African government. Finally, six people were charged under the Terrorism Act with 'intent to endanger the maintenance of law and order' by engaging in terrorism or for harbouring, concealing or rendering assistance to terrorists.

Advocates Hans Berker and Colin du Preez were engaged for the accused while the State was represented by a young, ambitious prosecutor from Grahamstown, Advocate Chris Jansen. Acceding to a surprise request from Jansen to hold the trial in Swakopmund, the Judge President set the proceedings to commence on 16 February 1976. He gave no reason for agreeing to move the trial from the Supreme Court in Windhoek to the small, cramped Magistrate's Court at the seaside resort. Though it was a picturesque and popular holiday destination, Swakopmund was far away from the capital, almost five hours' drive from South West Africa's principal airport, and even further from Ovamboland. Perhaps the judge was merely being considerate to those involved by ordering the holding of the trial in the cooler climate of the coast, which would be more agreeable for an event of this duration and sensitive nature. A more probable motivation, however, was the desire to hold a politically sensitive trial in an isolated town that could be more easily policed, thus preventing the likelihood of protest and unwanted media attention. As with the obscure towns of Delmas and Bethal that would see two prominent political trials of the 1980s, Swakopmund had only one main, tarred road. The trial of the SWAPO six was, in many ways, a forerunner of things to come.

The six whom the police delivered to the court in Swakopmund were the following:

Aaron Mushimba, 29, a travelling salesman from Windhoek who was charged with having purchased a Land Rover, which he subsequently handed over to the SWAPO member Victor Nkandi.[5] (Nkandi was later forced to become a State witness in the trial.) Eventually, the Land Rover came into the hands of alleged terrorists and was involved in a skirmish with the South African Defence Force (SADF) some distance from Ondangwa. Mushimba was the brother-in-law of Sam Nujoma and the SWAPO national organising secretary in Windhoek.

Andreas Nangolo, 53, a shopkeeper from Windhoek, who was also charged with having purchased a Land Rover, which was handed over to one Usko Nambinga for delivery 'to a person or persons whose purpose it was to overthrow the South West African administration by force'.

Hendrik Shikongo, 28, a clerk at a general dealer's shop at Ondandjo, who was the only accused whose alleged crimes were directly related to the murder of Chief Elifas. He was charged with providing transport to three men, Nicodemus Mauhi and two unnamed others, who were known to him, aware that they wanted to abduct or kill Chief Elifas. During the trial the prosecution would also claim that far from being an ordinary member of SWAPO, Shikongo had a much greater involvement in the organisation's local planning and strategies; that, in fact, he was part of a conspiracy to kidnap ethnic homeland leaders such as Elifas and take them across the border to Zambia, where they would be forced to make subversive propaganda broadcasts over Radio Zambia. This plot went awry, however, and Elifas was not as initially intended abducted on Friday, 15 August 1975, but was murdered instead on the Saturday night. Shikongo steadfastly denied his involvement in such a conspiracy and maintained that while he might be a member of SWAPO, he knew very little about its plans and strategies – he was certainly not involved in the conspiracy that the prosecution believed to have existed.

The other accused were three nurses, Rauna Nambinga, Naimi Nombowa and Anna Nghihondjwa, who worked at the Engela Hospital, 60 kilometres from Ondangwa and eight kilometres from the Angolan border. They were charged with having given money to Usko Nambinga (who had also received the Land Rover from the second accused, Nangolo) for delivery to conspirators who wanted to overthrow the South West African administration. In addition, Rauna Nambinga was charged with crossing the border into Angola to meet with people with a similar subversive intention. Both Rauna Nambinga and Anna Nghihondjwa were sisters of Usko Nambinga.

All six accused were members of SWAPO and all, apart from Shikongo, were members of the Evangelical Lutheran church.

*

Swakopmund in the 1970s was a quaint seaside town with a strong German colonial influence where not much ruffled the calm and quiet way of life. But on the Sunday before the trial, the tension in the town was palpable. There were police roadblocks on the main road from Windhoek and black travellers were pulled over and searched. The Namibian National Convention held a meeting in the town to show solidarity with the six accused. On the Monday morning there was a crowd of about 200 demonstrators outside the court with placards, chanting slogans and singing the SWAPO anthem of independent Namibia. Although at the end of the first day as the trial judge was about to leave the building the demonstrators were charged by policemen with dogs, they would remain a regular presence throughout the trial, which lasted four months, with thirty-five days in court. There would also be a contingent of journalists and foreign observers whose numbers ebbed and flowed during the course of the hearing.

The State would call thirty-three witnesses in all, seven of whom had been held in detention since Elifas's death. It soon became apparent that some of the witnesses had been tortured by the police in order to extract information and make statements under duress, and then forced to testify for the State against fellow members of SWAPO. All the same, not all of the witnesses detained by the police had given statements or were prepared to give testimony for the prosecution. Upon entering the witness stand Victor Nkandi, a SWAPO member who had been arrested in the police sweep after Elifas's murder, said to the judge, 'Before I am sworn in, I stand in this case, if today I am not an accused then I am not a witness.' The judge was nonplussed. 'I am not a witness,' Nkandi stated emphatically. After some further discussion the judge made it clear that he had been brought to the trial to testify as a witness for the State and he was expected to do this and tell the truth. To which Nkandi replied, 'As far as I am concerned I do not know what the truth is and what truth I have to speak I do not know.' He also told the court about the abuse he had suffered after being detained in September the previous year. After relentless beatings and sleep deprivation he had finally given the police a statement. But, he told the court, this statement was not true as 'I gave them the statement because I was afraid, as I was told that they would hang me up if I didn't speak'. After Nkandi again refused to testify and remained silent, the judge, ignoring his claims of abuse at the hands of the police, sentenced him to twelve months in jail for contempt of court.

The prosecution also called Axel Johannes, secretary-general of SWAPO, as a State witness, but upon taking the witness stand and being asked to take the oath, he said to the court, 'How can I swear while I have not heard why I am here and being tried?'

After a lengthy statement about the despicable treatment meted out to the witnesses, the judge responded that the law required he should answer all questions put to him. Defiantly, he replied, 'I will tell the court that I have been held for 200 days because I have broken the laws of South West Africa. I was not arrested to give evidence … If I was not guilty then I would not have been held for 200 days. Therefore I feel that I am guilty, therefore I was arrested.' He too was sentenced to twelve months in jail for contempt of court.

During her testimony, accused no. 4, Rauna Nambinga, told the court of her torture at the hands of the Security Police to compel her to make statements. She had eventually done so merely to put an end to her ill-treatment though this, it was later revealed, did not prevent her from miscarrying her unborn child. The inhumanity of the police did not stop there, as the body of her dead child was then thrown into a cesspool and left to putrefy in the hot sun. Once again the judge would show himself indifferent to her plight.

The initial string of witnesses called by the State testified to the purchase of the blue Land Rover by Aaron Mushimba and its involvement in an exchange of fire with a South African Army patrol, under Major JP Human, ten days after the murder of Elifas. Under cross-examination Wilfrid tried to extract specific information from the Major as to where exactly the contact with the 'terrorists' had taken place. But apart from stating that it had been in the operational area in Ovamboland, the Major insisted that he was not authorised to reveal the details of the incident in terms of the Official Secrets Act. The court therefore had to be satisfied with his word that the contact had in fact been inside Ovamboland.

Having presented evidence to link Mushimba to the purchase of the Land Rover and its later use 'in the operational area', the prosecutor then turned his attention to the third accused, Hendrik Shikongo. Not only did he seek to establish that

Shikongo had transported the three conspirators to the liquor store where Chief Elifas was shot, but also that he had entered the store and acted as a scout to ascertain Elifas's whereabouts and movements for the sake of the killers waiting outside.

Crucial for the State was the evidence-in-chief of Elizabeth 'Queen' Namunjembo, a 38-year-old unmarried mother of four, a witness whom Wilfrid described as 'a figure who would have not been out of place in the French Revolution'. She had been a member of SWAPO for a number of years and had been held in detention since shortly after the murder of Elifas. On taking the stand and commencing with her testimony, she spoke very softly, almost as though she did not want the world to hear what she had to say. In her testimony Namunjembo denied that she had heard at any time of a plot to abduct or harm Elifas and said that the killers, Nicodemus Mauhi and the two strangers, desired only to 'speak to' the Chief. Yet in the face of this alleged ignorance, Wilfrid revealed a number of inconsistencies in his cross-examination of her. Firstly, contrary to her evidence that Nicodemus had arrived at her house on the morning of the murder, saying he wanted to speak to Shikongo, it turned out that he had visited her twice on the day before; the first occasion in the morning, when she had been instrumental in putting him in touch with Shikongo, and the second that night, when he came and asked her for accommodation for his two visitors. This revelation seemed, to the defence at least, to create the grave suspicion that Namunjembo was more implicated in the conspiracy to murder Elifas than Shikongo was.

Namunjembo went on to testify that Shikongo came to her place on the Saturday evening when the murder occurred. Nicodemus and the two strangers had then climbed into Shikongo's vehicle and were driven to the liquor store. According to Shikongo's own testimony, however, she had been the one to ask him to take the three men to the liquor store, as they wanted to speak to Elifas. This was corroborated by a defence witness, Dr Ihuhua, who told the court that Namunjembo had asked him on the Saturday morning if he could take two of her friends to the liquor store that evening. As it happened he could not assist her, but three or four days later Namunjembo had contacted him and asked that he forget about this conversation. At this point, the prosecutor was swift to debunk his evidence and challenged the reliability of Dr Ihuhua as a witness, asking the court to ignore his testimony.

Despite being uncorroborated, one of the most harmful parts of Namunjembo's evidence-in-chief was that Shikongo had returned to her house late on the night of the murder, looking for Nicodemus and the two strangers. He then told her they had murdered the Chief, saying, 'The Chief is finished, we killed him.' On cross-examination by Wilfrid, she professed to have been shocked initially by what Shikongo said but then soon afterwards thought it was a lie. When asked by Wilfrid why Shikongo would tell her this and why, if she thought it was false, she had been frightened by a story she believed to be untrue, her response was: 'I did not think of anything and I can't answer the question.' In addition to her damning evidence about Shikongo, she also gave testimony that implicated Aaron Mushimba.

The case against the other accused, the three nurses from Engela Hospital, was equally flawed and unlikely. When Wilfrid called them to the witness stand, they spoke of meeting Usko Nambinga during their breaks outside or in the eating hall at the Engela Hospital. He told them of the people, their 'brothers and sisters', who had fled Ovamboland across the border into Angola to avoid the arrests and beatings that had been taking place under Elifas's rule. Having abandoned most of the things they owned, they were now suffering hardship across the border, without food, clothing and other basic necessities of life. He had appealed to the nurses to give money, food, clothing or anything they could spare to assist the refugees and alleviate their misery. The three nurses all told the court of walking across the border, which was close to the hospital, and meeting up with people there, people in need of aid and not soldiers, as the prosecution witnesses had consistently alleged. They were emphatic that the only soldiers they had seen were members of the Angolan rebel group UNITA at the border crossing.

This simple story came under rigorous cross-examination by the prosecutor, who contended that the nurses had not met refugees across the border but 'terrorists' and SWAPO soldiers. Furthermore, the R10 they admitted giving, together with donations from other nurses, they knew would be used by people who wanted to overthrow the South West African administration. Indeed, the prosecutor dogmatically insisted that Usko Nambinga had convened the meetings with the nurses at Engela Hospital under the banner of SWAPO. But Rauna Nambinga, like her fellow nurses, never wavered in her replies. She was emphatic that the 'meetings' with Usko had merely coincided with the times when the nurses were already gathered for a break or for lunch – they had not been specially organised by her brother. Despite Wilfrid's objection that there was no evidence on record from any State witness that Usko had organised meetings among the nurses on SWAPO business, the judge merely replied that the prosecutor was entitled to 'put anything on the basis of conjecture to the witness' and overruled Wilfrid's objection. All the same, as Wilfrid later contended, the State failed to prove the essential element of the main charge as it was required to do under the Terrorism Act, that when handing over money to Nambinga the accused had intended it should be used to endanger the maintenance of law and order in South West Africa. All that had been testified to by both the defendants and the State's witnesses was that their offering had been given out of compassion to help people in need.

The trial was long and complex, and it required herculean labours on the part of the defence to surmount all the difficulties thrown in their path. One such was the basic meaning of the testimony, which was largely given by witnesses in Oshivambo, and then translated by an interpreter into Afrikaans for the benefit of the court. The way key terms were translated could very easily prejudice the defence's case. Thus, while arresting Elizabeth 'Queen' Namunjembo, the police seized three cassette tapes with items recorded on them that the State alleged were SWAPO songs. On being questioned, she said they were hymns and some were about SWAPO, but she had not listened to them very often. These tapes and the interpretation of the songs were later the subject of extensive discussion in court as the prosecution looked for the most sinister meanings in the words. The interpretation of the tapes proved laborious, as it was necessary to establish the literal, colloquial and contextual meanings of the original Oshivambo words with the help of the court interpreter. In one instance Wilfrid engaged in a lengthy debate as to the use of the Afrikaans word for 'soldiers' (*soldate*) in a context where the word could also have meant just 'men' (*manne*): the interpreter conceded that he used 'soldiers' only because it fitted the context of the piece he was interpreting. Two other disputed words were 'landmines' and 'terrorists', where the latter could also have meant simply 'people'.

Another disadvantage that the defence team faced was the plainly biased nature of the presiding judge in favouring the prosecution. He was unmoved by the stories by witnesses of their torture by the Security Police. He ignored the testimony not only that witnesses were made to give false statements to the police, but even that the investigating officer, Lt Gert Dippenaar, had coached a witness just before she entered court. The judge's partiality was particularly apparent when he allowed extensive evidence to be presented by State witnesses that was hostile to SWAPO and its policies and had no relevance to the specific charges faced by the accused. Another instance of his partiality was his handling of the defence's application for an inspection *in loco*.

To Wilfrid and the defence team it soon became clear that

to mount a more informed defence for their clients they had to see for themselves the various places in and around Ondangwa to which the State witnesses had so extensively referred in their testimony. Such a visit would enable them to place this testimony in context and enable them to better challenge it when they presented their defence. So, after consulting with the prosecutor, Wilfrid requested the court be adjourned in order to allow the defence team time to conduct its inspection. The judge agreed and the defence team left the following day for Ovamboland.

The trip was not made easy for the team by the police. During their journey, they were shadowed by members of the Security Police and this made interviewing prospective witnesses more difficult. Most of the local people had no wish to be seen with them or co-operate with them in case they were accused of assisting 'terrorists'. The team was also forbidden to stay at a guesthouse in this militarised area and so had to fly to Tsumeb, 250 kilometres to the south, to find lodgings, which added further time and expense to the trip.

When the court reconvened, Wilfrid approached the judge on the matter of the court conducting an inspection *in loco*. The judge, he said, would be able to see for himself the places involved in the case and how the testimony of two of the State's key witnesses that Shikongo had acted as a spy for the murderers of Elifas was plainly ridiculous. Their testimony that from the liquor store they had seen Shikongo's parked vehicle some distance away on the night of the murder was simply not possible, as an inspection *in loco* would reveal. But the judge denied the request out of hand.

Later in the trial, after calling his last witness, Wilfrid once again raised the matter of the court conducting an inspection. There was now, he said, 'positive evidence' from the defence witnesses and from the testimony of Shikongo that was clearly in conflict with the evidence led by certain of the State's witnesses. Wilfrid concluded: 'I submit that your Lordship cannot remove from your Lordship's mind at this point of time that you might be doing the accused an injustice if you did not hold an inspection *in loco.*' But after a brief adjournment the judge ruled on Wilfrid's application and again summarily dismissed it.

It had by now become abundantly clear to Wilfrid that the trial was not about determining the guilt or innocence of the six on trial for murdering Elifas, but about SWAPO, an as yet unbanned political organisation. A large part of the prosecution's case was intended to put SWAPO on trial by collapsing the activities of SWAPO 'internal' into those of SWAPO 'external' and its military wing, PLAN, with its commitment to armed struggle against the South West African administration. The first witness to introduce evidence of this nature was Colonel Willem Schoon, who was later promoted to become commander of Vlakplaas and then head of the Security Police's covert Section C, which was responsible for numerous human rights violations, including the abduction and murder of ANC and PAC operatives. Schoon's entire evidence to the court would involve reading out the December 1975 issue of the SWAPO magazine *Kalahari Pilot,* which was published in London. The magazine covered a variety of topics and included articles about SWAPO engagements with the South African Army and pictures of weapons claimed to have been captured from South African forces. Interestingly, in a timetable of operations for 1975 there was no mention of the Elifas assassination, though there was a lengthy article on the 200 arrests made by the police afterwards and a call for solidarity for the six accused who were being held for trial. Wilfrid reserved the defence's right to study the document in detail to try to establish what there was in it which specifically linked it to their clients. But the absurdity of Schoon's evidence was such that Wilfrid eventually chose not to cross-examine him.

The investigating officer, Lt Gert Dippenaar, likewise set out to highlight the role of SWAPO when he was called to testify about the arrest of Shikongo and the nurses. When the blue Land Rover, originally purchased by the accused Aaron Mushimba, was searched after its involvement in a skirmish with a South African Army patrol, a cardboard box of documents had allegedly been discovered inside it, together with two Russian-made submachine guns. Dippenaar proceeded to read from some of the documents that had been found in the box. A draft copy of the SWAPO constitution included the statement that the taking up of arms was 'the only effective means to liberate Namibia'. A memorandum dated 16 August 1975 recorded that 'Today is a great day to remember for all the people of Namibia as we see the death of Chief Elifas at 8.30pm by SWAPO soldiers. Four brothers are fulfilling this task.' A pocketbook contained an entry celebrating the death of Elifas. A press release, dated 2 February 1973 and issued in Lusaka, described SWAPO operations, including details of damage and casualties inflicted on the SADF and a map plotting the position of South African forces in Ovamboland. Wilfrid cross-examined Lt Dippenaar for two days on every aspect of his evidence-in-chief, in particular the various documents that had been found in the box from the blue Land Rover, and tried to establish their authenticity and relevance to the murder of Elifas.[6]

The third witness to put SWAPO on trial was Petrus Ferreira, who had been a captain in the Security Police and had had dealings with SWAPO from 1966 until his retirement in October 1970. He presented himself to the court as an expert on SWAPO, and for ninety minutes proceeded to enlighten those present on the history and evils of SWAPO external – where its support came from, where the training of recruits took place, how they were armed and a summary of their attacks on targets within South West Africa.

Once the prosecutor had finished his examination of Ferreira, Wilfrid immediately informed the court that he would 'have to receive very full instructions from our clients and consider the position that we are faced with now because in fact what the State has done is to put SWAPO into the dock as an accused'. He requested an adjournment in order for them to prepare. There was some discussion within the defence team as to whether they should even cross-examine Ferreira, for his testimony essentially had no relevance to the charges facing the six accused. Colin du Preez felt that Wilfrid should object to his testimony, as the information he had presented was based on SWAPO publications and from 'interviews' with SWAPO guerrillas and indigenous locals, almost certainly under duress or torture. Wilfrid disagreed, however, and after two weeks of preparation the defence was ready to cross-examine Ferreira.

Wilfrid slowly had him concede that little of his information was first-hand. While Ferreira might have acquired some knowledge of SWAPO's political activities while stationed in Ovamboland and from his reading of its literature, he had no deep knowledge of the workings of the organisation. He did not even have a fundamental understanding of SWAPO's constitution, which contained its aims and objectives. As to his claim that the internal and external wings of SWAPO were one and the same organisation under Sam Nujoma, Wilfrid referred to a SWAPO congress held in 1974–5 in Walvis Bay, where an executive had been elected for both wings. It therefore could not be suggested that the external wing was directing the internal wing, and it had been clear from the evidence that the internal wing was against the use of violence – they were organisations with similar objectives but their means differed. While the accused were members of SWAPO, this should not allow the court to draw the inference that they were intent on violently overthrowing or subverting the South West African administration.

Unrepentant, Ferreira responded by trying to read to the court from a document, a photocopy of an original that had been published in London in *The Namibia News*[7] in early 1974, entitled 'Central Organ for the SWAPO Youth League of Namibia'. As with other documents, this had not been made available to the defence and so had not been entered into the evidence. The copy then given to Wilfrid and the court was illegible. Ignoring the authenticity and relevance of the document, the judge allowed Ferreira to read excerpts from it.

In his testimony, Ferreira clearly and unequivocally laid the blame for the flight of local people across the border into Angola at the feet of SWAPO. Wilfrid then asked Ferreira to read from a memorandum compiled by the Anglican and Catholic churches in Ovamboland in 1974 that reported their findings as to why people were leaving the area and fleeing to Angola. It outlined the enforced carrying of identity cards bearing their fingerprints, which made people feel like criminals, and referred to laws and proclamations under which people could be flogged and tortured. After Ferreira finished reading the churches' report, Wilfrid commented: 'According to this memorandum there seems to be a great deal of dissatisfaction among the Ovamboland people. Attributing all the problems in Ovamboland to SWAPO is therefore grossly oversimplifying matters.'

After a meeting with the judge in his chambers, the court was adjourned until 26 April to allow the prosecutor and defence to prepare their final arguments.

The prosecutor commenced his closing argument by outlining the evidence that the State witnesses had presented to the court over the preceeding months, which he said proved the guilt of the accused. In conclusion, he argued that in the event that the court did not accept the main charge against the accused (that they had engaged in terrorist activities), then there was sufficient evidence to support the alternative charge that they had rendered aid to people whose intention it was to overthrow by violence the lawful administration of South West Africa.

During the course of the prosecutor's argument, Wilfrid, for the second time, requested that the court dismiss the charge against Andreas Nangolo, the second accused, as the State had not proved its case against him. The defence was now to have its first major success of the trial, as the judge, despite having turned down a similar application three weeks before, almost immediately agreed and pronounced that the State had not proved its case beyond a reasonable doubt. After months of work the defence was pleased that at least one of their clients was now free. After the prosecutor had finished, Wilfrid then addressed the court. As usual, he was thorough and meticulous in his argument. It was, he told the court, only during the prosecutor's cross-examination of Shikongo that the allegations were made of a political conspiracy in which SWAPO was involved. No details, he said, were put to the accused as to where and when the alleged master plan had been hatched and if in fact there had even been such a political conspiracy. If there had been, then it was strange that the State's indictment against the accused did not refer to it. There was in reality not a shred of evidence to support the allegations of a conspiracy nor any visible evidence that SWAPO had been involved in it. As Wilfrid argued, there was a great deal of suspicion in the case, but that suspicion was not proof and there was not enough proof to convict the remaining accused.

Wilfrid maintained that the identity of the person or persons responsible for the assassination of Chief Elifas was, almost a year later, still unknown. In the current politically charged atmosphere of the country, the alleged role of SWAPO was an emotive factor that the court should not allow to cloud the facts that had been presented over the past months. The State, Wilfrid observed, was more interested in trying and convicting SWAPO than establishing who murdered Elifas. In his view, the court had to decide exactly what the State had actually proved against the accused.

In analysing the State's case, Wilfrid argued that it had chosen not to call certain witnesses who had been present on the night of the shooting. Written statements had not been taken by the police from a number of the witnesses the defence had called and a blood sample had not been taken from the Chief and sent for analysis. In the light of this and especially after the defence team's inspection in Ovamboland, there was a far more complex picture about the shooting than the State had presented to the court.

After 33 days in court, the State and the defence closed their cases and the court was adjourned until 11 May. Wilfrid's notes for 11 May 1976 start simply '9.03 Court assembles' and from then until 3pm, with a twenty-minute morning tea break and an hour for lunch, Judge Strydom delivered his 94-page judgment. Despite the courtroom being packed and overflowing with spectators, both black and white, and with many from overseas, he delivered his judgment in Afrikaans.

It became clear from early on that the fears of the defence that the judge had an obvious deference to the State's case were well founded. He started by summarising the evidence presented about SWAPO, both oral and documentary, noting that the accused were members of the organisation, which, while not banned, was abhorrent to him: 'Despite SWAPO, according to their exhibits, claiming or proclaiming that it is an organisation which enjoys worldwide recognition, I do not find here any profession of God, who through his omnipotence and guidance controls the destiny of things and people.' He proceeded to accept the evidence of the State's expert witness, Petrus Ferreira, and argued that the defence had not furnished any evidence to refute it and that leaders of SWAPO internal had not been called to testify that they were against violence. He accepted the documents found in the Land Rover as evidence, confirming that SWAPO was a militant organisation and wanted to overthrow the legitimate government of SWA.

He also accepted the testimony of the State's witnesses in general – there was no impression that he thought they had told a fabricated story. However, he was contemptuous and dismissive of the defence witnesses and regarded the evidence of Hendrik Shikongo, whom he described as an arrogant and presumptuous young man, as 'simply laughable'. He was equally contemptuous of the defence presented by the three nurses and damned Aaron Mushimba for not testifying in his own defence: his failure to do so implied his guilt.[8]

Wilfrid noted at three o'clock the judge's findings:

Accd No. 1   Guilty Main Count
Accd No. 3   Guilty Main Count
Accd No. 4   Guilty Main Count
Accd No. 5   Not Guilty
Accd No. 6   Guilty Main Count

At three minutes past three the court adjourned.

The defence team and their clients had prepared themselves for this outcome, but all the same it was a devastating blow and there was little consolation to be found in the blatant bias of the judge.

Shortly afterwards the court reconvened to hear two witnesses whom the prosecutor called in aggravation of sentence. The first was Colonel Carel Coetzee, a 'master' detective from the Brixton Murder and Robbery Squad, who was investigating seven cases in northern South West Africa that he ascribed to terrorist activity. He was on the stand for seven minutes. The second witness was Colonel Schoon. As with his first testimony, he merely proceeded to read out to the court for twenty minutes a list of fifty-seven recent criminal acts in Ovamboland. Starting with the murder of Elifas, which he described as an act of terrorism, they also involved landmine explosions and an attack on national servicemen, as well as several cases of theft. Schoon was emphatic the police had evidence that proved that SWAPO was guilty of all these deeds. It was clear that the prosecution wanted the (unproven) acts of SWAPO to affect not only public sentiment, but that of the court. There was little that Wilfrid could do to change this. Indeed, the newspapers lapped up the disclosures, and headlines such as 'The full picture of terror in SWA' (*Cape Argus*) and '59 Ovambo terror raids' (*Windhoek Advertiser*) appeared on the streets the following day.

When the prosecutor finally rested the State's case, it was not lost on Wilfrid that Jansen had not fulfilled his promise, undertaken at a pre-trial meeting, not to seek the death penalty for the remaining accused.

Wilfrid then announced that he would not be calling any witnesses in mitigation of sentence. He commenced his closing argument by saying that the court should consider history: 'however strongly the court may disapprove of their conduct, nevertheless the court is aware that history is a long wheel that turns, and the criminals of today are frequently the patriots of tomorrow. We have seen this in our country since 1945.'[9] He appealed to the court that it should show mercy to the accused and should be dispassionate with its sentencing: all were young, first-time offenders and some had families. He pointed out that neither Mushimba nor Shikongo had been found to be directly involved with the acts of terrorism or the death of Elifas, to which they were supposedly linked. He reiterated how much of the evidence presented did not show that they even knew they were part of the conspiracy to murder Elifas. As for the nurses, 'they are trained to serve society in a more honourable way than many of us' and each one was of good character and had sympathy for those who had left Ovamboland. Referring to the testimony of the previous day, he said, 'the very act of calling the two witnesses yesterday afternoon creates the impression that the State is calling for vengeance' and admonished the judge to heed the Bible, which stated, 'Vengeance is mine, said the Lord.' In closing, he again referred to the history of the country: it had been 'splattered' with *'kragdadigheid'* [force] since the turn of the century and in most instances such action had been counterproductive. And referring to case law, he said the courts had always held that 'punishment should fit the criminal, as well as the crime, be fair to the State and to the accused and be blended with mercy'.

The court adjourned for the judge to deliberate.

After ninety minutes, with police lining the walls of the court and the accused standing, Judge Strydom returned. He took his seat and started to read from his four-page judgment. He gave an overview of the 'terroristic' activities the State's two witnesses in aggravation had introduced into evidence the day before. This had affected him deeply, he said, and the court had no mercy on people associated with the assassination of a chief minister or an attack on a Defence Force patrol. The evil of terrorism must be torn out by the roots; law and order must be maintained.

The fact that Mushimba and Shikongo had neither elected to give evidence in mitigation nor shown a glimmer of remorse nor dissociated themselves from the crime was all evidence of an evil disposition. The two men were guilty of extremely serious acts and he found nothing in mitigation. The interests of the community had to be protected and the court had no option other than to impose the 'supreme penalty' for high treason. With regard to the two nurses, their conduct was aggravated by the size of their donations, being a fifth of their salaries, and by the fact that they had given the money voluntarily. In mitigation, he said they were young and had been influenced by Usko Nambinga. He sentenced them to seven and five years' imprisonment respectively.

There was stunned silence in the court after the judge's barrage. A few cries could be heard, and Wilfrid and his team stared glumly ahead of them to avoid looking at the judge. Their clients were ashen. The clerk of the court then stood and asked if Mushimba and Shikongo had anything to say as to why the death sentence should not be pronounced. They were simple men and therefore had no experience and no words to enable them to counter the savage pronouncement the judge had just made. After all that had been said, all the evidence that had been led and all the efforts of their defence over the past four months, how would their few words offer them any salvation?

Rising on weak legs but with a brave voice, Mushimba told the court that he had bought the Land Rover for a friend, and had no idea what he would do with it. He did not want to violate any law, was not a violent man and did not want to kill or harm anyone. He had a family and he pleaded for the mercy of the court. Shikongo acknowledged that he had given a lift to Nicodemus and the two other men, but he had had no idea of their intentions on the night Elifas was murdered. He did not feel guilty as he had no wish to murder anyone or endanger the maintenance of law and order. He asked for mercy and that the court sentence him to a term in prison.

In reply, the judge did not mince his words: the court had no authority to give mercy. As though at last his moment of triumph had arrived, Strydom drew himself up and pronounced that the sentence of the court was that Mushimba and Shikongo be taken to a place of custody where they would be hanged by the neck until dead.

Wilfrid lodged an application to appeal against the finding and the sentences of the accused. But Judge Strydom saw no reason that after three months in court there was any merit for an appeal and dismissed the application.

Newspaper headlines the following day read 'First SWA political leaders to hang' and '2 SWAPO men sentenced to death' and were followed by 'UN anger over death sentences'. The churches in the country were also vocal and asked how the sentences could contribute to Prime Minister Vorster's current policy of détente in southern Africa. 'We can only see a hardening of fronts.'

*

The defence team had been working on their appeal even before the trial ended, but as Judge Strydom had not given leave to appeal, there would now have to be a petition to the Appeal Court in Bloemfontein. However, just over two weeks after the sentencing, on 28 May 1976, the *Windhoek Advertiser* carried the astonishing front-page headline 'Leak to police – Attorney fired'. Below it ran the story that one of the partners of Lorentz & Bone, Anthony Smit, had dissolved his partnership in the firm following allegations that he had been giving highly confidential information to the Security Police. The journalist who wrote the piece ended his article by saying: 'Smiling members of the secret service told me last week that they now knew everything that they wanted to know about SWAPO. They refused to tell me who their sources were.'[10]

Wilfrid had been forewarned about what was brewing. With the eminent advocate Issy Maisels, he had flown to Windhoek earlier in the week to file a motion for a special entry to be made on the record of the trial about 'irregular and illegal departures from the rules' required for a fair trial; these had resulted in a failure of justice. Judge Strydom should have heard the application, but as he had just left for Pretoria the matter – to the relief of the defence team – would be heard by another judge. The entry of an irregularity could only bode well for their application to the Appellate Division, as this would circumvent Judge Strydom's refusal to grant leave to appeal. On 2 June the affidavits of Wilfrid and of Catharina de Beer, Colin du Preez's secretary, who did all the typing for the defence team, were presented to Judge MJ Hart, on the same day that their petition to the Chief Justice in Bloemfontein for leave to appeal was lodged.

In her affidavit De Beer stated that she had been telephoned in December 1975 by an anonymous male caller who, after asking if she was working on the 'terrorist case', wanted to know if she would provide him with information. She refused. A week later the switchboard and telex operator, Elsie Ellis, admitted to her that she had been approached in January 1975 by Captain Nel of the Security Police to give information. She then started to pass on documents to Nel at lunch-time meetings at the Windhoek Public Library, including statements of witnesses and the accused from the Swakopmund trial. This had continued right through the trial; even the defence team's heads of argument at the end of the trial were handed over. De Beer said that she, as well as everybody else in the office, was scared of Ellis and that she had recently received threats from her. She was so scared that she had collapsed and had to be treated in hospital for a threatened miscarriage.

Colin du Preez's statement outlined how in early February, either before or after the Swakopmund trial started, he had gone to a police holiday house in Swakopmund where the prosecutor, Advocate Jansen, was staying to obtain some information for the trial from him. Lt Dippenaar was also present. After completing their business they went for a drink, which turned into a social occasion. While they were having drinks, Du Preez said to Dippenaar that he had heard alarming reports about the methods the police used to obtain information from witnesses. In the ensuing conversation the braggard Dippenaar divulged that the police believed the accused had not been truthful because, as he explained, they knew everything that Lorentz & Bone had on their files, even who was paying their fees for the trial. Du Preez had reported the matter to Wilfrid, but it was decided that the conversation had taken place 'off the record' and, as there was no corroboration or proof, there seemed no point in taking the matter further. On his return to Windhoek after the trial, Du Preez had told his staff of his concerns about leakages of information from their offices. De Beer then came to him and related her story.

In his affidavit Bernd Mautschke, an articled clerk with Lorentz & Bone, said he had been asked by the partner Anthony Smit if he would assist the Security Police with information. Smit told him that he had a friend in the Security Police, Captain Nel, who later visited Mautschke and sought his assistance, but Mautschke had declined, saying it would 'violate my code of ethics'. In December 1975 Smit had been told that the firm was going to be involved in the defence of the six SWAPO members accused of murdering Chief Elifas. Smit was opposed to this and had, in Mautschke's presence, made a number of calls to Nel, telling him, for example, the details of defence counsel's trip to London to meet senior members of SWAPO.

Early on in the court proceedings before Judge Hart, the Attorney General lodged an application that the matter be heard by the original trial judge. When Judge Hart dismissed the application, Maisels, for Wilfrid's defence team, began questioning the various police witnesses. First was Major Koos Myburgh, divisional head of the Security Police, who denied any knowledge of the information contained in the papers before the court. It was only after a visit by a senior partner of Lorentz & Bone, complaining that the Security Police had tried to obtain information from members of staff, that he had called in Captain Nel, who then admitted that he had approached Ellis and Anthony Smit.

The central figure in the whole matter, Captain Nel, also submitted a sworn affidavit, in which he declared that one of his responsibilities was to observe the activities of SWAPO, its supporters and anyone associated with it. He had known Smit and Ellis for a number of years, the purpose of his liaisons with the two being to obtain information on SWAPO. Smit and Ellis had not known of each other's involvement with the Security Police. But he had not given instructions to them to pass on documents or information from the defence in the Swakopmund Trial.

In his testimony to the court the prosecutor Advocate Jansen, under cross-examination, insisted that his case had not been based on documents or information from the defence attorneys.

While he agreed that he was a close friend of Myburgh, Nel and Dippenaar and that he had obtained information from them, he could not say where they had obtained it, but he was sure that none had been from the office of Lorentz & Bone.

After all the damning testimony about Ellis, there was much anticipation as to what she would say when she took the stand. Maisels, who dubbed her a modern-day Mata Hari – the press called her the Kaiser Street Mata Hari – questioned her relentlessly for two days. While admitting to having been a police informant since 1972, she said she only worked for BOSS, the Bureau of State Security, when instructed to do so. When she approached De Beer to give information to the Security Police she had, she told the court, been acting on her own initiative. She agreed with Maisels that the request she made to De Beer was something that a loyal employee ought not to do. When asked by Maisels how she could say that she had not solicited or passed on information about what was the most important SWAPO case to come before the courts, she could give no explanation and merely claimed that she was confused.

On the fifth day of the hearing Anthony Smit took the stand. He said that while he was not proud of lying to his partners about his activities for the Special Branch, he was proud of what he had done for the national interest. He revealed he had first become a police informer seven years before, when employed in the office of the State Attorney, but he claimed that while he was at Lorentz & Bone he had not given the Security Police information that would prejudice the firm's clients. He had only given them details of the movements of SWAPO members and people they were associated with. This he regarded as his duty as a good citizen. Maisels commented: 'I am reminded of certain legal practitioners in another country in the time of a dictator, that dictator is now happily deceased.'

In his closing argument, Wilfrid declared that the Security Police had their own standard of morality and that the evidence given by this select brotherhood was exceedingly dangerous. It would be asking too much to believe that if the Security Police had two informers within Lorentz & Bone, they would not avail themselves of the opportunity to secure information from them. 'Our complaint strikes at the very root of an individual's right to be able to communicate in confidence with his legal adviser, and it is fundamental to a fair trial. It strikes at the very core of the administration of justice.' He said it was quite clear that information was first passed to Nel and then on to Dippenaar. 'It would have required qualities of sainthood to admit this happened, and neither officer appears to have displayed these qualities.'

After months of not seeing justice being done, 25 June was a euphoric day when Judge Hart made his finding on the defence team's application. Commenting that the matter had the characteristic intrigue of a James Bond novel, he granted the defence's application that a special entry be made on the court record of the Swakopmund trial. He was satisfied that Elsie Ellis, who he believed had left the witness box completely discredited, made copies of documents from the defence files and conveyed them to Captain Nel. These had then somehow come into the possession of the investigating officer, Lt Dippenaar. He found Nel to be an evasive and unimpressive witness and rejected his denial that any leaking of documents had taken place. 'From this it follows that the privilege between client and attorney was seriously breached and a special entry must be made.'

In August the defence's application for leave to appeal was granted by the Appellate Division in Bloemfontein and argument was heard in February 1977. On 17 March Chief Justice Rumpff in his 33-page judgment found that the leaking of documents had been not only an irregularity but a gross irregularity as far as privilege was concerned. The breach of privilege affected the proceedings of the trial and justice had therefore not been done. The sentences of Mushimba, Shikongo, Nambinga and

Nghihondjwa were set aside. They were released from prison in Pretoria and returned to South West Africa, where they were greeted by jubilant crowds in Windhoek.

Because of the finding of irregularity, the Appeal Court judges did not deal with any other aspect of the trial as contained in the application. This deprived the world of having an independent review of what had taken place in the courtroom of Judge Strydom. From the trial record and Wilfrid's application, it is quite clear that the judge was neither impartial nor objective in his handling of the trial. In 1989, after a rare public rebuke by the Johannesburg Bar Council, he would achieve the distinction of being the only judge to be impugned in Parliament – by the stalwart opposition member, Helen Suzman – for handing down an excessively lenient sentence on a white farmer who had tortured and killed one of his labourers for running over the farmer's dog with a tractor.

*

The Swakopmund trial of the six accused and the assassination of Chief Elifas remain two unrelated events. The defendants were certainly not charged in terms of criminal statute for the murder of Elifas but rather as members of SWAPO, under the Terrorism Act, for intending to endanger the maintenance of law and order. Despite the lengths to which the government went to achieve its political objectives through a judicial trial, it failed spectacularly on all fronts: no-one was found guilty of the murder of Elifas; and the ultimate acquittal of all the accused meant that the government lost any grounds on which to proceed with the 'legitimate' banning of SWAPO, which would have removed the organisation from the internal political settlement it was then trying to orchestrate with the Turnhalle Conference.

The question still remains, who murdered Elifas? Since its accession to power in Namibia, SWAPO has never publicly acknowledged its involvement or that of its members in the shooting of Elifas that August night at the Onamagongwa liquor store. It is not apparent that the murder of Elifas would have advanced the SWAPO cause at the time; in fact, quite the contrary.

This then raises the question whether the murder of Elifas was engineered by the South African government. It certainly did create the immediate excuse for the police to detain large numbers of SWAPO members, while many not detained fled the country. The consequent disruption to the 'internal' SWAPO was considerable at an important time. The murder of Elifas also assisted the government in two other ways. First, it created the opportunity for a trial which, if successful, would ensure that its major political opponent was removed from the political scene, probably by banning, as had happened to the ANC in 1960. Second, it also appears that Elifas, while demanding more powers from the government, was not really delivering much in the way of increased popular support, public legitimacy or effective control in Ovamboland. In fact, his brutal reign over the Ovambo people probably hardened their resolve for independence and gave weight to the UN's continued recognition of SWAPO as the legitimate organisation representing the people of South West Africa. The fact that, after the release of the six accused, the police neither arrested nor brought charges against anyone else in connection with the death of Chief Elifas speaks volumes about their desire to find the actual killers.

NOTES:

[1] Lorentz & Bone was the oldest law first in South West Africa, having been founded in November 1919 by Dr Theodor Lorentz, who was of Dutch origin, and Edgar Bone, of Welsh origin. They both served as magistrates after South Africa took over control of the German colony in July 1915. In the 1970s and 1980s, with the struggle for Namibian independence escalating, they were one of the few firms to take on politically related work. The firm finally closed in 2006.

[2] The lawyer Joel Carlson believed that the Act was drafted and passed specifically to bring members of SWAPO to trial. The Act was passed with retrospective effect to 27 June 1962, which is when SWAPO formed PLAN and started training for armed struggle.

[3] The Turnhalle Conference, named after the historic Turnhalle building in Windhoek, was held between 1975 and 1977, with the first meeting of 134 members of 11 ethnic groups of South West Africa being held on 1 September 1975. In October 1977, after four plenary sessions and a number of committee meetings, the conference was dissolved. On 5 November 1977 the Democratic Turnhalle Alliance (DTA) was formed by a number of the smaller ethnically defined parties and proceeded to win 41 of the 50 seats in the 1978 legislative elections. SWAPO, SWAPO-D and the National Namibian Front boycotted the elections.

[4] www.wikileaks.org/plusd/cables/1975PRETORIA03093

[5] Nkandi had an unfortunate history. He was sentenced to flogging in 1973 in terms of the proclamations that gave extreme powers to traditional leaders to detain people. Then he was detained in August 1976 in connection with the Elifas murder. Released on 28 February 1977, he was immediately redetained at the Security Police's main interrogation centre at Oshakati, where he was tortured by the police to obtain a confession. Defended by Advocate David Soggot, he was charged with terrorist activities and with transporting people between Angola and Ovamboland with the knowledge that they were planning to murder Elifas. He was released when the trial collapsed, with the judge blaming unreliable witnesses. He went into exile and rose through the ranks of SWAPO. But during a 'spy crisis', he was detained by SWAPO at one of their camps in Lubango, Angola, and possibly tortured. He became one of 708 SWAPO people whose deaths have not been accounted for. SWAPO has steadfastly maintained a 'barrier of silence' as to what happened to these members.

[6] Colin du Preez was involved in an unrelated trial in which Dippenaar gave evidence of a document seized in a raid on SWAPO premises. The document set out in great detail SWAPO's objectives and the methods it would use to destabilise the country. Du Preez had, however, recently read a newspaper report detailing that the same document Dippenaar had just submitted as evidence had been found in the Natal

Supreme Court to be a forgery. Dippenaar immediately retracted his evidence.

[7] A publication of the marginal South West Africa National United Front (SWANUF), an organisation that sought to merge SWANU (South West Africa National Union) and SWAPO but, having no support in Namibia, ceased to exist in the 1970s.

[8] The reason why Mushimba was not called to testify was that in taking statements from him the defence team found his versions of events varied quite considerably. They felt that to call him could have unexpected, disastrous consequences.

[9] Wilfrid's words were prophetic, as after going into exile in the 1980s Aaron Mushimba represented SWAPO in various countries, advocating Namibia's independence from South Africa. After independence Mushimba played a crucial role in promoting trade and commerce, managed several businesses and helped to address the social and economic challenges of the new nation. He died in Cape Town on 31 August 2014.

[10] *Windhoek Advertiser*, 28 May 1976

CHAPTER 13

POLITICAL TRIALS OF THE 1970s

A series of political trials in the 1970s, defending Steve Biko, Jeremy Cronin and others, which reaffirmed Wilfrid's belief in the importance of protest as integral to a democratic society

'It is a principle of Western democracy that people should be able to air their views in private and in public. Protest is an integral part of efficient government and democracy such that a certain amount of public inconvenience is not reason to stop such protest.'

– WILFRID COOPER

After the dramatic events of the early 1960s – starting with the Sharpeville massacre and ending with the Rivonia trial, at which the leaders of the ANC were sentenced to life imprisonment on Robben Island, South Africa entered a period of political quiescence and economic prosperity. It was apartheid's Indian summer. But beneath the placid surface, new forces of protest and opposition were incubating that would erupt in the 1970s to challenge the apartheid government. Wilfrid's firm convictions about the value and necessity of public protest – as the epigraph to this chapter reveals – would ensure his involvement in a number of prominent political trials that took place in the 1970s.

By far the greatest political figure to emerge in the period between Mandela's imprisonment in 1964 and his return in 1990 was Steve Biko. A charismatic, engaging, articulate and fearless young man, he first came to public notice as a student leader while studying medicine at the University of Natal. With a group of talented colleagues, Biko developed ideas of black consciousness – with an emphasis on promoting black initiative and a sense of black pride and identity – that would prove inspirational to a whole new generation of young people. He soon attracted followers and visitors of all kinds, including journalists and diplomats, who came to hear his views and draw strength and encouragement from them. He also drew the attention of the Security Police and the apartheid government, which banned him in 1973 and restricted him to his home town of King William's Town. In 1976 he was detained for 101 days and then, on 21 March 1977, he was arrested again and charged with defeating the ends of justice.

According to the State, Biko had persuaded five students 'to perjure themselves by contradicting their free and voluntary confessions to police officers'. These five had appeared as State witnesses the previous year in a trial relating to the burning of Forbes Grant Secondary School in Ginsberg township outside

King William's Town, which Biko had himself attended for a while. When Biko appeared in the King William's Town regional court the day after his detention, he was refused bail and remanded in custody at Fort Glamorgan in East London until the 30th. On the 28th, however, he again appeared in the King William's Town regional court on charges that he had contravened a restriction order by leaving the area and attending a gathering without permission of a magistrate. On the 29th, Wilfrid's great friend and colleague John Whitehead, then living in Grahamstown, appeared for Biko and successfully applied for a postponement of the matter.

In the meantime Wilfrid had been briefed on the charge of defeating the ends of justice and rushed to East London to appear in court. His junior was Advocate Denis Kuny. At Biko's first appearance on the morning of the 30th, the prosecutor, Mr JG Muller, told the court that the original charge was to be withdrawn and a new charge sheet was to be introduced containing more particulars of what Biko was alleged to have done. This charge sheet was only made available that afternoon, which gave Wilfrid little time to study it, but the defence had already asked the State for more details. Wilfrid then applied for a postponement to the following day. He did manage, however – contrary to the contentions of the prosecutor that Biko would abscond and interfere with witnesses – to persuade the magistrate that Biko be granted bail of R5,000 and released. There was another peculiarity, as Wilfrid pointed out to the court, in that Biko's movements were restricted to the magisterial district of King William's Town, though this trial would be held in East London. Consequently, Biko had to seek the permission of the magistrate in King William's Town to attend the court in East London.

The new charge sheet against Biko had as its main charge that he had personally, or through three others, persuaded five students, then appearing as State witnesses, to change their evidence and say that they knew nothing of a meeting at Forbes Grant where it was agreed to set fire to the school, nor of the intention to burn or damage the school, nor anything about the accused in the case. As a result of their false evidence six people had been found not guilty and acquitted. As an alternative, Biko was charged with suborning the witnesses to commit perjury by persuading them to change their evidence at the trial. In terms of possible sentence, these were by far the most serious charges Biko had yet faced but there were also other penalties involved in terms of the significant time that would have to be spent in court and the expense of legal fees incurred. The police were no doubt aware of these costs to Biko and his movement and saw the trial as a ploy to drain the reserves of the movement with continual court appearances and attendant legal costs.

The matter of Biko's banning order was a serious impediment to the trial. Hoping for some reasonableness from the State, Wilfrid went to discuss the matter with the magistrate in King William's Town with a view to persuading him to relax the onerous conditions. This was not to be. The magistrate merely said that his hands were tied: Biko could not leave his home before 7am each day of the trial and had to return home immediately after the trial by the shortest possible route. Before he left he had to report to the King William's Town police station and again when he returned; and the same procedure had to be followed when arriving in or leaving East London. The prosecutor in East London was equally inflexible in insisting that the trial had to be held there, as that was where the witnesses were being detained. Wilfrid then appealed to the sensibilities of the presiding magistrate, but his response was equally unaccommodating: if the defence encountered difficulties with the arrangements, he said, then, and only then, might he consider moving the trial to King William's Town.

When the trial started, the first witness was Warrant Officer GA Hattingh of the Security Police, who had investigated the fire at Forbes Grant Secondary School the previous year. He told the court that originally there had been twelve people, mostly juveniles except for two who were in their twenties, accused of burning the school. He had supervised the interrogation of the witnesses, which took place from 11.30pm on 28 September until 4am the next day. While some of them had been smacked, he denied that they had been assaulted, as most had proved co-operative. Any allegations of assault were groundless. When Wilfrid told him that a summons had been issued against him, the minister of police and six others for wrongful assault, he said he was unaware of this.

Over the next few days the State trotted out a procession of youths as witnesses, who would testify in their evidence-in-chief that they had been detained by the police and made statements in connection with the Forbes Grant fire. They later met with Steve Biko, who, they said, had encouraged them to change their statements in order to assist those who had been charged.

Under cross-examination by Wilfrid and Denis Kuny, their stories changed. They told how they had been taken from their homes late at night, beaten with a baton the police called 'Black Power' and then made to sign statements, whose contents they never saw. One 14-year-old told the court that he had been detained for almost a month before the present hearing, with no access to his parents, and had only had contact with prison warders and a magistrate. Although he had been detained on 7 March, his statement, which was presented to the court, was dated 18 March and he could give no coherent explanation as to why it had taken so long before he made it. He could only say that when you are confined in a prison, you are lonely, you constantly think about people outside and you do not know what day it is.

Another witness told how he was the first student to be assaulted by the police, but in an effort to downplay his experience, he said that he had not felt fear. Under cross-examination, he conceded to Wilfrid that he had felt pains on his body. When pushed by Wilfrid – 'You claim that you volunteered to make a statement to the police after being beaten and hearing screams. Was it not that you dared not refuse to make a statement?' – the boy replied that he had intended to make a statement, but after further questioning from Wilfrid he conceded that the statement he had made to the police had not been read out to him at the time. He therefore had no idea what his statement was about.

One young witness was still in detention, having been held since 10 March. He faced the ordeal of testifying in court with the policeman who had interrogated him, Warrant Officer Hattingh, sitting in the same courtroom, staring at him, and having no idea when he would be released. He told the court how he was arrested at 4.30am and taken to the King William's Town police station. He had been made to sit and wait for three hours while others arrested at the time were taken into the Security Police offices to make statements. He had heard shouting and screaming from behind the doors and noted one youth coming out with a swollen forehead. Under cross-examination by Kuny, when asked if the statement he made on 12 March was true, he reluctantly told the court that it had not been made under oath as Hattingh had not asked him to swear.

The trial was postponed until 11 July. Before the court rose, it was pointed out to Biko that the proceedings would continue at the new East London Magistrate's Court, at which Wilfrid quipped that Hattingh should assist Biko in showing him the way to ensure he did not get lost. The police appeared not to have a sense of humour or else were miffed that the case was not going their way for in the early hours of 5 July Biko, as well as his close associates in the Black Consciousness movement, Mamphela Ramphele and Thenjiwe Mtintso, who had been staying with him, were detained by eight security policemen. They were taken to the infamous Kei Road police station in King

William's Town. Wilfrid and the attorney Griffiths Mxenge had just arrived in King William's Town for the inquest of another leading Black Consciousness figure, Mapetla Mohapi, who had died in the Kei Road cells in August the previous year. Ramphele and Mtintso were due to give evidence at Mohapi's inquest so Mxenge immediately contacted the police and, after lengthy discussions, secured their release by the end of the day on R200 bail. Their release was subject to the conditions that they could not be in the same house together, they could not communicate with each other and they had to be fingerprinted by the police. They also had to appear later before the chief magistrate for a formal remand while the charges were being drawn up by the police.

When the trial resumed, Biko would have his voice heard – for the only time – in a court of law as to what had happened after the burning of Forbes Grant Secondary School. He said he had been contacted by the parents of two of the youths who had been detained and who faced charges of arson. Biko learned that the detained youths were under constant pressure and intimidation by the Security Police and they had eventually signed statements. One had been told that if he did not sign, he would be kept in solitary confinement. When another of the youths finally came home, he informed Biko that after being assaulted by the police he had signed a statement that he had neither seen nor was allowed to read. Biko denied in court that he had asked the youths to make false statements or change their statements. He had, however, told them to make statements to give to the attorney whom he had arranged to represent them. When cross-examined by the prosecutor, Biko said that when he learned that the youths were being intimidated and assaulted while in detention, he had acted out of a real concern for their wellbeing. As the court knew he had also been detained and could understand what they were going through.

Wilfrid's closing argument took the best part of a day. Clearly, he told the court, there were factors that were unique to the trial inasmuch as the witnesses that the State had called were all accomplices. They had all been detained for a long period until called to testify. The testimony the court had heard revealed the unlawful conduct of the police in making the youths sign statements they had never seen and, by doing this, binding them to the statements from which they were then not free to depart. The youths were also in an invidious position in that their release, or prospect of release, from detention was dependent on how closely they adhered to the statements they had made to the police. Biko, he said, had given evidence under oath in an exemplary manner and it was significant that none of the witnesses in their testimony had referred to Biko, yet 'the type of statements they made were with intent to implicate the accused and for them not to be convicted'. In closing, he said it was clear that the State had wanted a united front, co-operation and solidarity from its witnesses. 'One thing is clear from this case, the man the State wanted to nail was the accused. Each witness is trying to ingratiate himself with the authorities, but each was trying to extricate himself from the predicament he found himself in.'

While in his judgment Magistrate Van Zyl found Biko's evidence under oath more satisfactory than that of the State's witnesses, he was unsure of Biko's culpability; but under the circumstances he gave him the benefit of the doubt and found him not guilty. He also found that there was collaboration between the witnesses, but even though there was evidence of considerable interference by the Security Police with the witnesses in making their statements, the magistrate rejected the claim that the police had been involved in fabricating the evidence.

As Biko's biographer, the newspaper editor Donald Woods, wrote, 'Wilfrid Cooper probed the Security Police explanation and alibis and their version sounded highly unconvincing, yet the magistrate ruled that no clear evidence existed to indicate blame on any person. Steve had expected this finding but said it didn't matter, that the important thing was to publish the evidence as we were doing, so that people could know what was going on in political prisons.'[1]

In conclusion, one can speculate that in failing to secure Biko's conviction in this trial and so being able to send him to jail, the Security Police became more determined than ever that at the next opportunity they would 'get' him. Indeed, he was detained just over a month later on 18 August in a roadblock near Grahamstown and, less than a month after that, he died on 12 September after being barbarically assaulted by the Security Police while in detention. His death would have an enormous impact, not only in South Africa, but throughout the world. As Biko had himself prophetically said: 'You are either alive and proud or you are dead, and your method of death can itself be politicising. So if you can overcome the fear of death, which is irrational, you're on your way.'

*

One of the legal instruments to which the State increasingly resorted in the 1970s to deal with its political opponents was the ferocious Terrorism Act of 1967, which allowed for detention without trial for an indefinite period on the suspicion of 'terrorism'. The Act withheld the basic rights of those detained: the right to be told what the charges were, the right to see a lawyer, the right to bail and the right to appear in court within a reasonable time. The Criminal Procedure Act of 1977 tipped the scales even further against those arrested by giving judges the power to hear evidence in camera. It was Wilfrid's principled aversion to the assault on the rule of law, embodied in these Acts, that drew him into some significant political trials during the 1970s.

On 22 September 1976, the trial commenced in the Cape Supreme Court of three young activists: Dr David Rabkin, a *Cape Argus* journalist who had been born in South Africa but had left for England with his parents because of their opposition to apartheid; his pregnant wife, Susan, who was British-born; and Jeremy Cronin, a political science lecturer at the University of Cape Town. Proceedings the day before had had to be postponed as the judge set to hear the trial, Jack Watermeyer, inadvertently saw documents that he should not have had sight of before the trial. While the defence had no objection to Watermeyer's action, the Judge President, JW (Helm) van Zijl, reconstituted the court under Judge Marius Diemont, who sat with two assessors.

The three, who had been arrested at the end of July, were charged under the Terrorism Act and the Internal Security Act for endangering the maintenance of law and order, and for having conspired with members of the Communist Party, the African National Congress and its military wing, Umkhonto we Sizwe, to print and distribute subversive literature from January 1973 to July 1976. As the three had pleaded guilty, Wilfrid and the defence team made certain admissions to the Attorney General, Advocate Ted Harwood, to limit the evidence to be presented to the court.

In the well of the courtroom there was a pile of pamphlets, blank paper, stationery, Roneo ink, stencils, duplicating machines, typewriters and materials to make bucket bombs for scattering the pamphlets in public places. These had been found in a rented garage in Green Point, as well as in flats in Wynberg and Clifton where Rabkin and Cronin resided. The pamphlets had headings like 'Inkululeko – Freedom', 'The Communist', 'Vukani – Awake' and 'A Message to the Workers' from the South African Communist Party. The Attorney General told the court that this extensive evidence and the admissions from the three on trial would 'indicate that the accused not only conspired with others to produce the Communist Party and ANC propaganda contained in the various documents, but, in addition, did in fact combine to produce these documents and distribute them'.

The Attorney General called a number of policemen who testified as to where and what they had found. On the second day he introduced a mystery witness, a black detective constable, called Mr X to protect his identity. The press had a field day with his testimony. As with the State witnesses in the Swakopmund SWAPO trial, the evidence that Mr X gave to the court had little direct relevance to the actual charges against the accused. Instead, he told how he had been recruited by the ANC in 1959 and detailed his subsequent experiences with the organisation overseas. After it was banned in 1960, he fled across the border to Botswana and in July 1964 went to Dar es Salaam for preliminary training. During the course of the morning Mr X told the court how he and more than 70 other comrades were flown to Odessa on the Black Sea in the Soviet Union where they were trained in combat tactics, topography, artillery control, the use of small arms, such as the AK47, and motor mechanics. They also received instruction in Marxism and Leninism and the history of the Communist Party in the Soviet Union and elsewhere. The group then moved east to the city of Baku for further training. Over the next eight years he was deployed to various ANC camps in Angola and Tanzania, until finally he was sent back into South Africa in 1972. He was arrested within a month of arriving in the country and after capture and interrogation,was 'turned' and joined the Security Police as an askari in February 1974. He also told the court that he had left South Africa without knowing the aims and objectives of the ANC but with the desire to overthrow the apartheid government. However, he discovered that what had been offered to him by the ANC was not what he had been seeking.

Given the damning evidence against the accused and their guilty pleas, Wilfrid and his team closed their case without leading any evidence in defence, leaving the Attorney General to make his closing argument. He mainly reviewed the various documents and pamphlets that had been found in the Green Point garage, stating to the court that it was this type of inflammatory propaganda that had contributed to the recent Soweto uprising. Wilfrid asked that the court take no notice of this *ex parte* statement, as there was no evidence of this contention and none of the people who had received the pamphlets had been called by the State to testify to this effect. The State, he said, could not assume how people had reacted when they received and read the material. The judge advised that 'judicial notice' would be taken of the fact that there had been recent rioting in the country.

In addition, the judge would not merely take judicial notice of the countrywide unrest but, later in his judgment, would quote from a number of the pamphlets, which, he said, made unpleasant reading in that they advocated violence and insurrection again and again. The final pamphlet he read from was 'crude' in its insistence on violence, he declared: the first sentence read 'Death to the murderous oppressors' and the last 'Free Mandela, hang Vorster'. Staring intently at the three accused, he said: 'This is strong meat. It is stuff which could have far-reaching consequences. It amounts to terrorism which could endanger the law and order in South Africa.' Rabkin and Cronin were both found guilty in terms of the charges under the Terrorism Act and the Internal Security Act.

To limit what the State alleged against Mrs Rabkin, Wilfrid objected to an assumption by the Attorney General that she had known what was happening in the Green Point garage. While the State had evidence to link Rabkin and Cronin, there was, he pointed out, no evidence that Mrs Rabkin had even visited the garage and so there was little probability that she knew what was transpiring. The judge must have listened, as he acquitted her on the main charge under the Terrorism Act.

All the same, it was clear that the charges against the three were not to be underestimated, for they carried the death penalty or at least a lengthy prison sentence. The strain on the accused and their families was no doubt immense. Rabkin's mother, Joan, who lived in London, wrote to Wilfrid after the trial to say: 'I left Cape Town two days before the end of the trial because I knew it could be easier for both Gerald [her husband] and David if I wasn't there crying like a drain all through the evidence. And better for Jobie [her grandson] to say goodbye to me while his mother was still there.'

When finding the three guilty, Judge Diemont, rather than merely making reference to the 'terroristic activities' with which they had been charged, read the full list of charges to the court, the trial having been a summary one. As the Terrorism Act carried the death penalty, it was essential for evidence in mitigation of sentence to be presented. Wilfrid called a number of witnesses to offer such evidence. This included, and was agreed to by the Attorney General, affidavits from three people in England brought by Mr Arthur Ravenscroft, a senior lecturer at Leeds University, where Rabkin had gained his doctorate in English literature in 1972.

Both Rabkin and Cronin gave unsworn statements to the court. Rabkin told of his ideals and said he had great regrets in involving his family in his activities. He pleaded to the court to show leniency to his wife and unborn child. He was, however, unrepentant in his view that the ANC, and all those affiliated to it, provided the only hope for all the people of South Africa and he expressed no remorse for his political actions. Cronin also regretted that, while his wife and mother did not share his views, they had suffered considerably from his actions. He was steadfast, too, in holding that what he had done had not been anti-South Africa but for the advancement of a South Africa free of racial division and exploitation.

Arguing in aggravation of sentence, the Attorney General was quick to respond. Rabkin and Cronin were two married men with family responsibilities, and statements the defence had submitted to the court emphasised the compassion they had shown in their youth and their brilliant academic careers ahead of them. But the picture painted of them was at loggerheads with their promotion of violent activities in the inflammatory articles they wrote and the pamphlets they distributed. As for Mrs Rabkin, he drew the attention of the court to the fact that her diary had the word 'garage' written in it on several occasions, which must have had some significance. In closing, he told the court that people who disseminated 'poisonous literature' that could incite others to riot must, if apprehended, expect to receive severe sentences, even the death penalty. The law, he said, had teeth and these teeth must be shown.

Wilfrid focused his address on Mrs Rabkin and the power the court had to suspend part of her minimum one-year sentence laid down by the Act. Citing several cases, he argued that the court should suspend the whole sentence as she had played a very minor role in the matter, and it was her loyalty and love for her husband that had led to her involvement. He also put it that society does not require that a pregnant woman be imprisoned and said he had been instructed to give the court an undertaking that she would, as a British citizen, leave South Africa if she were not imprisoned. That her husband was going to be sentenced to a long period in prison was punishment itself. With regards to Rabkin and Cronin, he urged the court not to see them as monsters and said that they were not professional terrorists or saboteurs. He urged the court to consider that the minimum prescribed sentence of the Act, of five years, was severe enough.

Early in his sentencing address, Judge Diemont remarked: 'Counsel for the defence took it upon himself to admonish me not to sentence in anger and not to sentence in haste. I do not know why he presumed to read me this homily; I have been sentencing in this court for many years and I am only too aware of the problems which beset a sentencing judge. But since he has raised the matter, let me assure the accused that I have given deep and anxious thought to the matter of the sentences which I am going to impose.' He was moved by the compassion of Rabkin's father's plea to the court, as well as that of Cronin's mother, a widow. He was not, however, impressed with the strong principles of the two accused to promote armed struggle against the government: 'Inciting people to violence and bloodshed, acting with intent to endanger law and order – and that is what they pleaded guilty to – will not solve the problems of the underprivileged.' This, he declared, was a crime in South Africa and in Western countries and 'such conduct would receive scant sympathy in a communist regime'.

While he did not believe Mrs Rabkin to be as innocent as she made out, he sentenced her to twelve months' imprisonment, with eleven months being suspended on condition that she leave South Africa. 'You are an unwelcome visitor in this country,' he told her. As for her husband, he could find no reason to deal with him leniently, as his actions were aggravated by the fact that he had conducted his 'subversive activities' for a period of three years. He was sentenced to ten years. As Cronin was involved for less time, he was sentenced to seven years.

In her letter to Wilfrid, Joan Rabkin finished by saying: 'I have been told that you had the courage of a lion in our service and I will forever be grateful to you. I was told before I met you that you were courageous but some people found you abrasive! I only found you kind and understanding.'

David Rabkin served seven years of his sentence and was released in 1983. He was killed in an accident in November 1985 in Angola while training with Umkhonto we Sizwe. In an obituary, Joe Slovo, general secretary of the Communist Party and an MK commander, praised his achievements for the struggle against apartheid: 'If we are where we are today, it is because of the likes of Dave.' Jeremy Cronin served his full sentence and upon release he joined the United Democratic Front. Since 1994 he has been Deputy Minister of Transport and of Public Works, a member of the ANC National Executive Committee, deputy general secretary of the South African Communist Party and a member of Parliament.

*

As the argument of the attorney general during the trial of the Rabkins and Cronin made clear, events off stage had a marked impact on the conduct and tenor of the case. These events were sparked by the Soweto uprising of June 1976, when students at secondary schools in the Johannesburg township took to the streets to protest against the introduction of Afrikaans as a language of instruction and were met with a violent police response. The demonstration soon turned into a revolt and spread to other towns and cities throughout the country. What was noticeable about the protest was its generational aspect: this was a rebellion of the young and Wilfrid acted in a number of court cases in the 1970s on their behalf.

Perhaps the first of its kind arose from a demonstration of white students from the University of Cape Town in 1972. In June of that year a group of a few hundred students held a protest against apartheid education on the steps of St George's Cathedral in the city centre, believing that this being a church and private property, the police would refrain from attacking them. This was not to be and they were baton-charged and tear-gassed and fifty-one were detained for breach of municipal by-laws. The police had even followed some fleeing students into the cathedral and dragged them outside. One of the students arrested was 20-year-old Robert Kemp. While not a leader of the demonstration, he had briefly addressed the crowd through a loud-hailer and was then arrested and charged with inciting or encouraging a public meeting without permission from the city council. Wilfrid appeared for him.

The prosecution's chief witness was the police District Commandant of Cape Town, Colonel PA Crous, who had been on the scene of the protest and who had arrested Kemp. He agreed that the students were amiable and in good humour and that he had had no objection to the meeting though he had insisted on their keeping off the pavement. There were fifty policemen present, all carrying batons: according to Crous, it was a policeman's duty always to be prepared. Unusually, Brigadier MC Lamprecht, head of criminal investigation, was also on the scene. When Wilfrid questioned Crous as to why it should have been that two senior officers were present at a small demonstration, he replied that he could not comment on the activities of his superior officers. As the court proceedings would reveal, the baton charge by the police was probably the result of miscommunication between these two senior officers. Kemp was initially fined R50 (or forty days), which on appeal was reduced by Judge Jack Watermeyer to R20 (or fourteen days). The judge found that it was clear from remarks during his sentencing that the presiding magistrate disapproved of the purpose of the demonstration. This was a political consideration that should not have been taken into account. As Wilfrid had said in his closing argument during the trial, 'It is a principle of Western democracy that people should be able to air their views in private and in public. Protest is an integral part of efficient government and democracy such that a certain amount of public inconvenience is not reason to stop such protest.'

During the aftermath of the Soweto uprising, Wilfrid was again drawn into the defence of young people caught up in the nationwide unrest. In August 1976 there was a student boycott at the University of the Western Cape in Bellville. In the early hours of 30 August, a room in the women's residence at the university was set alight and damaged. Four female students were charged with sabotage or, alternatively, with arson and malicious damage to property. Wilfrid was briefed by Dullah Omar's firm of attorneys, with Ben Kies acting as his junior, and the case commenced on 1 December in the Supreme Court before Judge Diemont. Cross-examination by Wilfrid revealed discrepancies in the testimony of the State witnesses and on the fifth day Judge Diemont ruled that the State had failed to prove its case.

The unrest continued into September 1976 on the Cape Flats and also drew in three brothers, Hassan, Abdul and Abdurahman Allie, who lived with their parents in Ravensmead, close to Modderdam Road, where popular protests were taking place. Abdurahman was mortally wounded when he stepped outside the family home. A neighbour would later tell the family that she had seen four policemen hiding behind a wall outside their house.

The family's nightmare was just beginning for as Abdul and Hassan tried to pick up the body of their bleeding brother to take him inside, the four policemen rushed down the driveway and clubbed Abdul to the ground. The brothers stopped them and called an ambulance, which took Abdurahman to Tygerberg Hospital, where he was pronounced dead. Being of the Muslim faith, Abdurahman needed to be buried the following day but the body was taken away to the State mortuary and an autopsy conducted without the family's permission. When the family was finally allowed to bury Abdurahman the police were present and fired into the gathered mourners.

A few days later the police arrived at the Allie home, surrounded it and proceeded to search it from top to bottom, looking, they said, for explosives. They found nothing. Two weeks after that the police came to Abdul's place of work and told him that he and his brother were being arrested and charged with public violence. They were taken to Ravensmead police station and detained for the night without food, even though it was Ramadan. Fortunately, family members could raise the bail money required and through donations, including R2,000 from the World Council of Churches, they were able to put together the funds needed to mount a defence. It was Wilfrid whom they asked to represent them.

The hearing of the case against Abdul and Hassan commenced in the Bellville regional court on 10 November. The prosecution alleged that they had acted in concert with their dead brother and had joined a gathering with the intention of disturbing the peace. The State further alleged that members of the gathering threw stones and petrol bombs at vehicles and blocked roads with burning tyres. The brothers pleaded not guilty to the charges.

In the early stages of the hearing Wilfrid submitted to the magistrate, Mr MMC Symington, that the charges against Abdul and Hassan should be dropped as the State had no evidence to show that the brothers took part in the alleged riot. The application was turned down and the brothers' ordeal continued. They would have to see evidentiary photographs of their dead brother riddled with 21 shotgun wounds to his left arm and chest. Unfortunately, the case was then postponed and Wilfrid had to withdraw because of other obligations. But the foundations of the defence had been set in place and eventually the brothers were acquitted due to lack of evidence.

*

There were numerous other trials in this period in which Wilfrid appeared for the defence. In each case it was his incisive cross-examination of witnesses, guided by his belief that the accused were entitled to a fair trial, that secured favourable outcomes. In March 1977 he appeared in Grahamstown for a trial under the Terrorism Act of two youths, as well as the person who had allegedly recruited them for the Pan Africanist Congress to undergo military training outside the country. After hearing the evidence of three witnesses for the State, Wilfrid applied for the accused to be discharged. One witness, suspected of being a police trap, had been thoroughly discredited on cross-examination by Wilfrid. The presiding judge agreed with

Wilfrid's application and ruled that the State had not shown that the men were members of the unlawful PAC.

In another trial held in the Grahamstown Supreme Court in 1977, Wilfrid defended Lawrence Mene on charges that he was a member of the banned PAC, which had held PAC meetings at his house and incited people to undergo military training. Mene had been detained for almost a year under the Terrorism Act. Even before the State led its evidence, Wilfrid challenged the indictment as prejudicial and vague: it did not state who had attended the meetings, when the meetings were held or how many meetings had taken place. He commenced by asking that the State furnish more information to enable him to prepare a defence for his client. The prosecutor was not pleased with this challenge, but after robust argument from Wilfrid the judge upheld his application. When the prosecutor then failed to produce the evidence, the charges against Wilfrid's client were quashed. Mene, the judge said, was entitled to a fair trial and he was not satisfied that justice would be done on the vaguely particularised charges of the indictment. Mene was then released.

In the same year Wilfrid was also successful in defending Abdul Sayed, publisher of the *Muslim News*, on charges under the Terrorism Act. Again he was briefed by Dullah Omar. The trip to Bloemfontein would be a short one as the two key witnesses who had been subpoenaed refused to testify and the prosecutor was forced to drop the case. A week later Wilfrid was in Port Elizabeth at a special court hearing for the trial of three New Brighton men charged with incitement to commit public violence. One of the accused was Thozamile Botha, a teacher and later founder of PEBCO, one of the first township 'civic organisations', which would become the backbone of the United Democratic Front when it was established in 1983.

Under cross-examination by Wilfrid, one witness told the court how the police had arrived at his house at three in the morning, dragged him by the scruff of his neck and thrown him into the back of a police van. He had then been taken to a gymnasium attached to the Algoa police station where he was questioned at length by Gideon Nieuwoudt, one of the feared security policemen who had been involved in the murder of Steve Biko. Nieuwoudt threatened him and hit him across his back with a sjambok on numerous occasions. After being detained for ten days, he was told that he had a 'last chance' to make a statement: by this he understood that if he did not do so the police would charge him under the Terrorism Act.

Another witness, still clearly nervous and biting his nails in the witness box, told of being taken from his home at one in the morning to the notorious Sanlam Building where, it was common knowledge, the teacher George Botha had died and where Steve Biko had been held that September before his death. He was threatened by the police that if he did not tell 'the truth', he would be detained for six months or longer.

The magistrate, Mr JB Robinson, dismissed the charges against the accused and said that he had strong suspicions that the witnesses had been pressured by the police. Six witnesses were arrested after the trial and charged with perjury.

*

In early 1978 the anti-apartheid activist and attorney Griffiths Mxenge again briefed Wilfrid, this time as senior counsel to lead the defence team in the Bethal treason trial of Zephaniah Mothopeng and 17 other members of the PAC. This highly politicised trial had already commenced some time before so relationships between the accused and the existing defence team had been established. Whenever he accepted a brief, the representation of the accused in court was always a matter of importance to Wilfrid. In this case it was settled in consultation with Mxenge that as leader of the defence Wilfrid would represent, with two juniors, accused numbers 1, 2 and 13 to

18. The representation was arranged in this manner to enable Wilfrid to have the right to cross-examine any State witness.

Notwithstanding the brief in terms of which he had been engaged, Wilfrid was taken aback to be contacted by Mxenge at the end of March and told that accused numbers 13 to 18 wanted to revert to the positon where the two junior counsel also had the right to cross-examination. This, Wilfrid was told, was because the accused believed he had not been effective in his cross-examination of a certain State witness; had the two junior counsel cross-examined the witness the outcome might have been different in their view. Wilfrid pointed out to Mxenge that any change in representation should be settled between Mxenge and the accused and was at pains to remind him that his duty as an attorney was to his clients' best interests and not to identify with their wishes. Accused number 1 then spoke to Mxenge and said he had not been consulted about the change of representation and wanted the original senior counsel, Advocate Andrew Wilson, to represent him as before and to become a joint defence leader.

The request of the accused was unexpected and came as a shock to Wilfrid: none had raised any objections to the rearrangement of representation when he had taken over as lead counsel. He was to be further surprised when the accused insisted that cross-examination of witnesses should henceforth be decided by the team as a whole and by a majority vote. This was for Wilfrid a clear intrusion into what was properly the province of counsel. Despite expressing their confidence in Wilfrid and wanting him to remain, the accused had effectively terminated his brief. After a number of discussions with Mxenge to resolve matters with the accused, it appeared he could not do so and Wilfrid therefore had no alternative but to formally withdraw from the defence.

The Bethal trial would drag on behind closed doors for another 18 months and accumulate a court record of 7,000 pages. Behind the scenes a team of Security Police torture specialists, which included the notorious 'Spyker' van Wyk, conducted a reign of

Wilfrid, in PhD doctoral gown,
with his son, the author, 1972.

A model-shoot photograph of Marlene Lehnberg taken before the scandalous murder of Susana van der Linde in 1974.

BELOW Advocates Denis Delahunt and Michael Odes with Wilfrid at DF Malan Airport in July 1975. They were returning from Bloemfontein, where they had successfully appealed against Lehnberg's death sentence.

Lehnberg, once notorious as the 'Scissors Murderer', after her release from prison in 1999.

A Ford bakkie after an encounter with a SWAPO landmine in Ovamboland, one of the apartheid state's fronts in its battle against 'terrorism', 1979.

Exhibit D4, the liquor store at Onamagongwa where Chief Filemon Elifas was murdered. Elifas's vehicle was parked at D and Hendrik Shikongo's at A; the arrows depict how he reversed away from the building.

Wilfrid and Advocate Issy Maisels leave the Windhoek Supreme Court.

Police dogs are set on demonstrators near the Swakopmund Magistrate's Court, where the trial of the SWAPO Six was heard.

ABOVE Attorney Eliot Osrin, Susan Rabkin, Wilfrid and Advocate Edwin 'Sharky' King make their way to the Supreme Court for the trial of David and Susan Rabkin and Jeremy Cronin.

ABOVE Poster marking the death in detention of activist Mapetla Mohapi in 1976.

LEFT Steve Biko and Mamphela Ramphele outside court.

ABOVE Wilfrid, wearing his trademark hat, at the inspection in loco of the railway line near Malmesbury, August 1973.

BELOW In judge's robes in his chambers at the Supreme Court.

Champagne brunch at Riverside, 1976: Wilfrid is far left; son-in-law Mike Gent at rear with Ben Kies to the right; author second from right.

Wilfrid and friends on a hunt in the Kalahari in the early 1970s. Long-time friend Izak Strauss is in the middle.

Hunting group, late 1991: Jimmy, James and Michael Reid, Douglas Legg, Wilfrid and author.

ABOVE Wilfrid and Gertrude celebrate her birthday at the Winchester Mansions.

RIGHT Angelo Inzadi, owner of Harlequin restaurant in Parow, serenades Wilfrid on his birthday, circa 1980s.

Wilfrid and Gertrude visiting son-in-law Mike Gent and daughter Megan in the UK.

The author, Wilfrid and Gertrude celebrating the launch of *Motor Law Volume II*, in 1987.

Enjoying lunch at La Colombe on the Constantia Uitsig farm: Gertrude, daughter Susan-Ann, the author and Wilfrid.

Gertrude and Wilfrid at the Fish River Canyon lookout point, July 1997.

Gertrude and Wilfrid
outside Jameson Hall
after he received
his LLD from UCT,
December 1987.

POLITICAL TRIALS OF THE 1970s

brutality. Accused number 14, Johnson Nyathi, was thrown from a fourth-floor window, but miraculously survived and attended the trial with both legs in plaster and on crutches. Four PAC members linked to the trial were also murdered.

As he had been briefed by Griffiths on a number of occasions it was a great disappointment to Wilfrid that, after the Bethal trial, this came to an end. Then one morning in November 1981 Wilfrid came to my room, stood for a moment at the door looking stunned and said very quietly, 'They got Griffiths', before he walked out. 'They' clearly referred to the Security Police. Mxenge had on several occasions shared with Wilfrid his concerns at the attention he was getting from the police. While he had not seen eye to eye with Mxenge on the way he handled the Bethal accused, Wilfrid respected him as a colleague of the law who also pursued his convictions of finding justice within the legal system and mourned that he had been so brutally murdered.[2]

Mxenge's death struck a chord with Wilfrid. During Wilfrid's trials and inquest hearings in the 1970s the family always suspected that the telephone at home was tapped and strange things happened from time to time at Wilfrid's chambers. During the Swakopmund SWAPO trial we knew that the house had been entered on at least one occasion: one evening when we came home there was a window open in my bedroom that should have been closed and papers had been moved in various parts of the house. That Wilfrid was white mattered little; four months after Biko's death the academic and anti-apartheid activist Richard Turner had been shot at his house in Durban in front of his daughter; and later, in September 1989, Anton Lubowski, an advocate and member of SWAPO, was gunned down outside his Windhoek home. Wilfrid and Gertrude were always cautious about voicing their thoughts about such matters in front of us children. We did not fully appreciate at the time that the trials Wilfrid was involved in were very much matters of life and death for all concerned.

NOTES:

[1] *Asking for Trouble: Autobiography of a Banned Journalist* by Donald Woods (London, Gollancz, 1980) p. 289

[2] Wilfrid was of course right. In 1996 at the TRC the truth of the brutal murder was confirmed: Mxenge was stabbed 45 times, with three okapi knives and a hunting knife, bludgeoned with a car's wheel spanner, disembowelled, his throat slit and his ears cut off. His execution had been undertaken by Vlakplaas death squad operatives Dirk Coetzee, Brian Ngqulunga, Joe Mamasela, David Tshikalanga and Almond Nofomela.

CHAPTER 14

A TUNA, A TOLLIE AND A BEY-EM-VEY

Wilfrid at ease and at play in the world

'That ebullient barrister from the Cape, Dr Wilfrid Cooper,
was walking around this week with the same expression you
see on Florrie's face when Andy Capp has just inflicted
one of his chauvinistic injustices upon her.'

– DONALD WOODS

My interest in fishing started when I was very young. It had not come from Wilfrid, as his limited experience had been confined to the Olifants River at Klawer and, by all accounts, he was not very successful. At the age of four, equipped with a stick, a piece of line, a home-made hook and periwinkle as bait, I managed to catch a large *klipvis* in one of the rock pools at Surfers' Corner during a family excursion to Muizenberg beach. Despite the protests of my sisters, the catch was triumphantly taken home. This set my mind to bigger things.

Wilfrid then bought me my first proper rod and reel and would take me down to Kalk Bay harbour on a Saturday afternoon to fish from the breakwater. The era of making big catches from the breakwater had passed, but that was no deterrent to a determined young angler who still believed that there was, or had to be, something out there. After unpacking the fishing gear, Wilfrid would amble off down the harbour wall, ostensibly to see if the fish were biting elsewhere, though I am sure it was more to relieve the boredom of watching me throwing away hooks and sinkers. In his meandering he would engage in conversation, comfortably in Afrikaans, with any local coloured fishermen he encountered. There was also the hidden agenda of scrounging some fresh bait, as we usually arrived at Kalk Bay with old frozen stuff from a previous visit. He always managed to obtain something fresher for the afternoon's fishing, not that there was much biting and even less so was there anything to catch.

Wilfrid had a great friend, the attorney Vic Cohen, who was one of those responsible for the establishment of the sport of game fishing from boats in the Cape. When I was young, he converted an old navy launch, *La Morva*, on which we went out into False Bay a few times to catch bottom fish off the Glencairn quarry or the Bullnose just outside the Simonstown naval base. For a six-year-old it was an immensely exciting experience to

236

be out on the water and actually catching fish of some size. On one trip to Smitswinkel Bay, nothing happened until the late afternoon when Cape salmon and mackerel came on the bite, and so we stayed on, catching well into the night. As *La Morva* was not a fast boat, we had to chug back to Kalk Bay and finally arrived home only in the early hours of the morning, tired, smelling of fish and bait, but with a large Cape salmon in the Volvo boot. Gertrude was waiting up, worried sick about where we had been, and tore a strip off Wilfrid for having been out so long. We still went to bed smiling and had fried and pickled fish for a week thereafter.

Vic then built a new, dedicated sport fishing boat, *King Fisher*, which was a more serious affair. I was too young to go deep-sea fishing, but Wilfrid went out from time to time. After one trip he returned home and proudly opened the Volvo's boot to reveal a yellowfin tuna that filled the entire space. My mother was furious – this time, by the thought of what to do with the huge fish. She was a wonderful cook, loved fish but hated waste, and clearly saw that the tuna was far in excess of what the family would be able to consume – it could clearly feed a small army. So after a few calls Wilfrid was back in the car, heading off to a friend, the owner of the International Hotel in Gardens, who butchered the fish and took a great deal of the beautiful flesh in exchange. We still ate tuna for many weeks thereafter. Something similar occurred a few years later upon Wilfrid's return from Upington, where a grateful client had given him a '*tollie*' (a young ox), which again filled the boot of the Volvo. This time the chest freezer that Gertrude had bought in the interim was filled with meat and we ate beef in many and various forms for months afterwards.

One September in the 1970s, together with my school friend Sandy Calder, we camped on the banks of the Titus River in the Ceres Valley, where we planned to fish the morning rise. There was a labourer from a nearby cottage who assisted us in setting up the tent, getting firewood and even serving us tea early in the morning before we went to fish. Wilfrid always entered into a warm conversation with him and, while it was never about matters of great importance, I was struck by the way in which he spoke to the man as an equal. The animated conversations covered a whole range of topics from which both derived great pleasure.

Throughout his life Wilfrid continued to engage with people from humble backgrounds and helped a number of them where he could. He once represented in court a railway engine driver, Frederik van Niekerk, who had been involved in the derailment of a passenger train at an S-bend between Malmesbury and Moorreesburg on 29 September 1972, in which fifty people were killed and many injured. Van Niekerk, who looked a little like my grandfather, faced charges of culpable homicide for allegedly driving the train while under the influence of alcohol. The trial was held in August 1973. It was a drawn-out affair with the experts called by the State and the defence failing to agree on what might have happened. While the evidence of Van Niekerk's stoker, Mr ML Kotze, was damaging, Acting Judge President van Winsen found it to be uncorroborated and so, to Van Niekerk's great relief, he was acquitted. He was so thankful that he embraced and shook the hands of his family, his friends and the defence team in court. Outside he pulled Wilfrid aside and asked if Wilfrid would give him his hat as a souvenir – this was something of a trademark for Wilfrid in the 1960s and 1970s – but Wilfrid declined to part with it. I have no doubt that the fact that both Wilfrid's father and grandfather had been engine drivers could account for the vigor with which he acted for Van Niekerk – and at a reduced fee.

Wilfrid had the ability to talk to anybody and everybody. He was also something of a peacock and, when occasion arose, he would be more than happy to regale those present with stories of his experiences. This was noted by the journalist Donald Woods in an article entitled 'Many misfortunes'. It appeared in the

Cape Times in July 1977, shortly after Wilfrid had acquired a brand-new metallic-silver BMW 528i, which he had to drive from the dealer in Port Elizabeth to Cape Town. The frugal Gertrude was opposed to the purchase of such a vehicle, as she believed it to be an extravagance; Wilfrid, however, saw it to be a fine automobile befitting an eminent advocate and so relished the chance to get behind the wheel for the first time.

That ebullient barrister from the Cape, Dr Wilfrid Cooper, was walking around this week with the same expression you see on Florrie's face when Andy Capp has just inflicted one of his chauvinistic injustices upon her.

Reason for Wilfrid's chagrin (yes Wilfrid, not Wilfred) was that a journey he recently undertook produced some unexpected side-effects.

Having bought an exciting new car (of a type known in Bavarian phonetics as a "Bey-em-vey") he set out to drive from Port Elizabeth to Cape Town and was well-disposed to give a lift to any hitchhiker likely to ask a barrage of pleasing questions about the treasured vehicle.

Nearing the Karoo he espied the sort of hitchhiker he was looking for. The fellow who had the appearance of a man would appreciate a ride in an above-average car; a man who could reasonably be expected to want to know about horsepower, gadgetry, performance and so forth – Wilfrid had all the details ready. In fact they were almost bursting out of him.

But the chap simply climbed into the car, sat down, and stared glumly ahead of him. He might as well have been riding in a *tjorrie* for all the notice he took of Wilfrid's automotive pride and joy.

After a few kilometres of mounting frustration, Wilfrid thought he would steer the conversation in the right direction and asked if the fellow had a car of his own.

Well, he had had one, the chap said, but it was *'stukkend'* [broken]. It was *stukkend* because he had been involved in a collision with a car driven by *''n Kaffer'*. The fellow went into detail about the damage to the car, which was in fact a complete write-off.

Had the accident been the fault of the, er, other motorist? Wilfrid asked. Well, no, not according to the Supreme Court, allowed the hitchhiker, who disclosed that Mr Justice Jennett had sentenced him to six years' imprisonment, three suspended, for his culpability.

Good heavens, said Wilfrid, that was a heavy sentence. Well, the chap explained, his wife and child had been killed in the crash. They had been to a dance, and his wife had danced with another man, and he had had a lot to drink because he wasn't a sissy, and he had been very cross with her and had driven off very fast with her and the child, and that's how it all happened.

The hitchhiker then disclosed that he was now returning from a visit to his brother, who had sustained irreparable brain damage in an incident on the border.

Wilfrid's condolences took the line that the man's parents must be shattered at all this grief, whereupon the man said that his father was dead and his mother in jail.

In jail?

Yes. She was serving 15 years in Kroonstad for killing a Mr Nel by pouring petrol on him and setting him alight.

By this time Wilfrid's eyes were somewhat glazed, and all hopes of conversational car-pronking were lying *stukkend* as well.

Had the hitchhiker seen his mother in jail? Yes, and she had recently had a breast removed because of carcinoma.

By now desperate to find a topic unconnected with dire tragedy, Wilfrid asked the chap what he did for a living. He replied that he was a prison warder, but that he had doubts about his future as such because he had allowed a prisoner in his custody to 'ontsnap' [escape] and although the 'ontsnapte' [escapee] was recaptured the prison service did not relish 'ontsnappable' warders.

The unfortunate fellow got off at Paarl, declaring that he was looking forward to his first sight of Table Mountain.

Wilfrid drove off, and one gets the impression he had a genuine apprehension that if his hitchhiker got close enough to Table Mountain for a good view of it, with his kind of luck that seemingly stable berg might crumble into a heap on top of him.

In setting forth here the account of this unhappy man's misfortunes, one hopes that his plights are not relished upon their own merits, but in the absence of Herman Charles Bosman and his raconteur, Oom Schalk Lourens, it seemed necessary to place this extraordinary story on record – if only as a caution to new car owners in search of hitchhiking car-connoisseurs.

CHAPTER 15

APARTHEID'S DIRTY DEALINGS

Two apparently divergent trials of the 1980s
in which Wilfrid gained insight into
the underhand dealings and dirty tricks
of the apartheid government

'Your subsequent conviction, torture and ten years'
imprisonment constitute a case of severe ill-treatment
and a travesty of justice.'

– TRC COMMISSIONER YASMIN SOOKA

Wilfrid's involvement in politically related trials and inquests in the 1970s took its toll on him in a number of ways, not least of which was that he was not always available to take on the more lucrative commercial briefs. In effect he was punished financially for taking the moral high ground in his political work. Having assumed that he would be acting in the Bethal treason trial for most of 1978, he found himself stranded after the early termination of his brief and for the balance of the year little work of substance came his way. Early in 1979 he made the difficult decision to leave the Bar and joined the firm of attorneys of Buirski, Herbstein & Ipp (incorporating Frank Fabian) to do articles of clerkship and focus on criminal work. But after a few months he reached the conclusion that he should rather return to the world of law he knew. He was then readmitted to the Bar in November and reapplied for silk in February the following year.

The return to the Bar and his reacclimatisation were made easier in that he could take up his old room at Huguenot Chambers and immediately had the comfort of familiar surroundings. He spent the greater part of 1980 working on his next book, *Alcohol, Drugs and Road Traffic*, which he co-authored with TG Schwär and LS Smith, professors of forensic medicine at Stellenbosch and UCT respectively. The *South African Medical Journal* described it as 'the standard and definitive reference book on the subject'. In these years he also acted as an external examiner at UCT and UWC and was kept busy and stimulated by the writing of further legal books, among them his magnum opus, *Motor Law*. This grew out of a thesis for which he was awarded his second doctorate, an LLD, at UCT in December 1987.

In the 1980s the apartheid system began to unravel. Internationally, South Africa had become isolated and was treated as a pariah state because of its policy of apartheid and the brutality with which it was enforced. In response a number of countries, in line with resolutions of the United Nations, applied economic sanctions, banning the sale of oil and arms to the country, two commodities that were the lifeblood of the apartheid state. At home, the simmering unrest that had started with the Soweto uprising erupted into a full-blown civil revolt in the mid-1980s, to which the government responded by declaring a state of emergency and sending troops into the townships in an effort to quell the disturbances.

Under siege and under threat, the state now turned to covert operations to ensure its survival. To circumvent the sanctions on oil and arms, it engaged in underhand dealings to purchase these essential supplies. At home, to circumvent the constraints of the justice system and the vestiges of the rule of law, it increasingly resorted to extra-judicial means of dealing with its opponents. In both cases, the operations were mostly kept secret, entangled as they were in a murky world of corruption, torture and murder. But occasionally the lid was lifted on what was happening unbeknown to the South African public, particularly when related matters came before the courts. Wilfrid was prominently involved in two of these cases in the 1980s.

*

The procurement of crude oil in defiance of sanctions was one of the most closely guarded secrets of apartheid South Africa. Until the late 1970s the oil embargo had been only a minor irritant to the South African government as it could source oil from Iran. But with the fall of the Shah in February 1979, the need to access new sources became urgent. The government's oil procurement agency, the Strategic Fuel Fund (SFF) in collaboration with the parastatal SASOL, the synthetic oil manufacturer, resorted to using middlemen and 'door openers' to obtain oil for the country. The costs and dangers of this became evident when the SFF and SASOL were involved in the largest swindle in maritime history, which was related to the sinking of the *Salem* off the Senegalese coast.

The oil tanker *Salem* had sailed from Kuwait on 30 November 1979 loaded with 194,000 tons of light crude destined for Genoa. But under the new name *Lema*, she altered her course and arrived off Durban on 27 December, where she discharged 173,000 tons of her cargo. The SSF/SASOL paid $43 million to the traders from whom they had bought the oil. To maintain the impression that she was still fully laden, the *Lema* then took on almost the same amount of seawater and sailed from Durban on 2 January 1980. On 17 January 1980 she radioed that she was in distress off the Senegalese coast where she quickly sank, leaving almost no trace.

The circumstances of the mysterious sinking caused questions to be asked in public. Eventually, the Deputy Minister of Trade and Industry, Dr Schalk van der Merwe, admitted on 2 February 1980 that the oil had in fact been purchased on SASOL's behalf by Shell International.[1] In the meantime, an insurance claim of US$56.3 million had been made for the loss of the cargo by the cargo's owners, Shell; but not too long afterwards the insurance underwriters Lloyd's repudiated the claim. Shell then lodged an interdict to seize the oil, which the SSF/SASOL were holding in their tanks. Eventually the matter was settled in private by the parties, who split the loss 50/50.

The deals to procure oil involved the payment of substantial commissions to the middlemen involved. By 1984 it was estimated that the government was spending $450 million a year in paying commissions to keep the oil flowing. Despite draconian legislation to suppress the reporting of stories related to the procurement of oil, journalists were not deterred from investigating such matters and publishing what they could. On 10 December 1983 *The Citizen* first announced to its readers that a multimillion-rand claim against SASOL was being brought by 'an international consortium of businessmen represented by a leading London lawyer'. On 2 March 1984 the *Financial Mail* wrote of an innocuously named case, *M. Sillier and Others* vs *Sasol Ltd and Other*, which was due to begin in the Witwatersrand Supreme Court on 12 March. Interestingly, the SFF/SASOL were already in court supporting their prized oil procurer, 'Dottore' Marino Chiavelli – who was alleged to earn $7.5 million a month for his trouble – in his long-running court battle with an erstwhile business partner who was claiming $90 million in commissions owed.[2]

The SFF/SASOL were slow to acknowledge the claim against them that *The Citizen* had referred to. But details soon came to the fore that the case was being brought by Maurice Sillier, a consulting lawyer from Britain, Ezra Nonoo, a Middle Eastern businessman, and Trade and Technology (Holding) Ltd. They were represented by Advocates Sydney Kentridge, Sam Cohen and Peter Solomon. The defendants were SASOL, the SFF and the honorary consul for Peru in Cape Town, Helge Storch-Nielsen, with Fanie Cillers SC appearing for SFF/SASOL and Wilfrid for Storch-Nielsen. To add to the phalanx of advocates already involved, the minister of minerals and energy affairs also appointed a legal representative to hold a watching brief over proceedings.

At the time it was speculated that the claim involved some R270 million for unpaid commissions,[3] which was then one of the largest civil claims in South African legal history. To add to the veil of secrecy, the legal teams had to sign undertakings that they would not reveal any details of the claim; and on commencement of the trial Judge DA Melamet ruled that the matter would be heard in camera.

While there is much information in Wilfrid's file about the case, it cannot be written about here as the matter is still *sub judice*. That 90 court days were spent and that Wilfrid's files on the case weigh more than 30 kilograms says something about the extent and complexity of the trial. A report published by the

Shipping Research Bureau in 1995[4] sheds some light on what transpired. The Danish-born Storch-Nielsen had worked as a trade commissioner in Tehran for about ten years, during which time he built up a network of business contacts in the Middle East. Shortly after the fall of the Shah in February 1979, he approached the SFF/SASOL to offer his services to procure crude oil through his sources. In order to keep the identities of seller and buyer secret, the deal would be channelled through his two foreign-based companies, Semafor (registered in Panama) and Hestonie (registered in Switzerland). Through his extensive contacts, Storch-Nielsen was then introduced to Maurice Sillier, who was a legal consultant in Bahrain. Sillier in time introduced him to Ezra Nonoo who, though fronting as a banker, was essentially a 'door opener' supposedly with contacts in the oil-rich Sultanate of Oman.[5] Officially, the Sultanate at that time had a strict embargo against the supply of oil to South Africa.

After a number of trips to the Middle East, it appears that Sillier and Nonoo had not fully delivered on their promises, but in May 1979 Storch-Nielsen managed to meet a close confidant of the Sultan, Dr Omar Zawawi, in Muscat. With Zawawi's assistance a deal with Semafor was finalised on 12 June 1979 for a three-year contract for the supply of 44 million barrels of oil to the SFF/SASOL. The price of the oil included a 'special surcharge' of $4.50 per barrel. The first consignment sailed on 13 October, followed by two more shipments in November and December. But in January 1980, after failing to make a further delivery, the Semafor–Hestonie contract was cancelled and the Dutch oil trader John Deuss, in apparent collusion with the Sultanate and the SFF/SASOL, took up the role of supplying Omani crude oil to South Africa, together with 'Dottore' Marino Chiavelli. This breach of contract is said to have cost South African taxpayers $3.25 million.[6]

Despite the length of time in court (including five months of evidence and one month for arguments), the high-powered legal teams, the millions of rands in legal costs and the countless reams of paper that were expended on the case, when the doors were opened to the public on 20 November, Judge Melamet gave those present short shrift. He merely informed them that the claim against the SSF, SASOL and Storch-Nielsen had been dismissed with costs. His 'public' judgment was a mere five pages and, he ruled, it could not be published. (The actual judgment of Case 7216/82 runs to 196 pages.) But, whatever the details of the trial and the judgment may have been, Wilfrid had won his case: though it had been a frustrating and often tedious war of attrition, it was a pleasing outcome for him.

*

Wilfrid's last criminal case at the Bar was one of the most violent of his career. It was also one in which the hidden agenda of the apartheid government only became known long afterwards.

On 23 June 1986 Johannesburg newspapers carried the story of the triple murder of Alfons Talpa, his attractive daughter Pam Phakos and his son-in-law Costa in his luxury home in the upmarket suburb of Klippoortjie, Germiston. Speculation initially was that the murders were related to Costa Phakos's business activities. Soon afterwards two men, Dimitrios 'Jimmy' Skoularikis and Freddie Brenner, who both lived a three-minute drive from the scene, were arrested. Brenner, a business associate of Skoularikis, was in hospital being treated for wounds caused by a bullet with an odd trajectory: it had entered the left side of his chest, travelled through his body and finally lodged near his left elbow. The bullet was removed and given to the police for their ballistic experts to analyse.

Two months later Skoularikis and Brenner, though still not formally charged, were remanded in custody and a court date was set for February 1987. The police were, they said, still investigating leads to establish a motive for the slayings. They had determined from ballistic examinations that four handguns had been involved in the crime. Despite searching the homes of Skoularikis and Brenner, the police had not yet found the firearms.

The crime scene had all the signs of a desperate gun fight. All three victims had been shot first at close range, and then stabbed, with further evidence that they had been subject to a vicious and brutal assault. Talpa's hands were handcuffed behind his back and his mouth covered with masking tape prior to being murdered with a single shot to the head. He had seven lacerations and had been stabbed twice in the chest. Mrs Phakos had been shot six times in rapid succession and stabbed five times, while her husband had three stab wounds in the chest and had died from two shots to the head. There were bullet casings on the floor and blood in various amounts from the front entrance to the upstairs bathroom, where Talpa's body lay.

While the police never found a motive for the murders, they accumulated considerable circumstantial evidence at the scene that tied the crime to Skoularikis and Brenner. Then in January 1987 there was a breakthrough in the investigation when a Solomon Nkosi was arrested for unlawful possession of a firearm that was found to be one used in the murder. Nkosi led the police to a spot down a dirt road near Rand Airport. The previous year, he told the police, he had found a partly burnt bag or briefcase that contained five fire-damaged firearms, some handcuffs and two 'jungle' knives. The location was an easy ten-minute drive from Skoularikis's home. On examining the scene the police found some exploded bullets, two sections of the grip of a revolver and some partly burnt-out masking tape similar to that which had been used to cover Talpa's mouth. The police eventually recovered four of the five firearms: two were found to be licensed to Skoularikis and Brenner, a third to Phakos and a fourth to Skoularikis's father. Although it was possible to fire shots from the recovered firearms, their neglected state and the fire damage made it impossible to confirm whether they had been used in the killings.

At the trial Wilfrid represented Skoularikis and was assisted by Advocate AP Bruwer and the experienced attorney Jeff Matthee of an old Boksburg firm of attorneys, Malherbe, Rigg & Ranwell. Wilfrid's defence was difficult as he was faced with damning circumstantial evidence, including a roll of masking tape found in the bathroom with his client's fingerprint on it. He was perplexed that the police had still not found a motive for the murders after months of invetigation. His primary objective became, therefore, one of keeping Skoularikis from a death sentence: this he could only do by finding mitigating circumstances.

The State was represented by no less than the Attorney General Klaus von Lieres und Wilkau SC. He called a number of witnesses whose testimony built an invincible case against Skoularikis. Apart from the roll of masking tape with Skoularikis's fingerprint on it that the police found in the bathroom where Talpa was shot, there were two cartridge cases found in an ashtray in his bedroom. An eyewitness also testified that Skoularikis had been in possession of the firearms a few hours before the murders – the same firearms that were found near Rand Airport. As for Brenner, his blood-stained palm print had been found on the bathroom door of the Talpa house, which placed him at the scene of the crime.

When it came to the defence, Skoularikis refused to take the witness stand. However, his co-accused, Brenner, a big man at two metres tall and weighing 96 kg, came forward and told the court his version of what had happened on the afternoon of the murder. Hesitant, ill at ease and evasive, Brenner did not present himself as a good witness and endeavoured to deflect his involvement in the murders. He remembered entering the scene of the murder, going upstairs and finding Mr and Mrs Phakos's bodies on the landing. Hearing a noise, he turned while drawing his firearm and then was shot. On recovering consciousness, he went to the bathroom to drink some water and there found the third body.

This, he told the court, accounted for his palm print being on the bathroom door. His next recollection was of being outside the house in the passenger seat of his car. Skoularikis, a much smaller and slighter man, was next to him and told him that he had carried him out of the house. They then drove to Brenner's house a short distance away, where Skoularikis took off his clothes in the bathroom. He could offer no explanation about where he had put them as the ambulance attendants who arrived after being called testified that when they collected him at his house he was only in his underpants and there was no sign of his clothes. He could also offer no explanation about how his firearm was later found in the veld near the Rand Airport. At one point he told the court that he and Skoularikis had discussed the case in prison, but when asked by Von Lieres what his co-accused's version of events was in those conversations, he asked for time to think about his answer. After an adjournment he retook the stand and said he had decided not to answer the question.

Acting on Skoularikis's instructions, Wilfrid could not cross-examine Brenner.

In his closing argument to the court, Wilfrid made a lengthy submission. While the State had proved that Skoularikis had been at the murder scene, he said, it had not proved that he had murdered anybody. The fingerprint on the roll of tape, which the defence had challenged during the trial, proved that he was party to manhandling Talpa upstairs and into the bathroom where the latter was gagged and handcuffed. This, Wilfrid said, showed that there was no intention to kill. The killing only took place after something happened and there was a shootout on the landing. As to the evidence that his client had fired a pistol, he admitted that Skoularikis might have done so, but there was no proof that he had caused the death of anyone. In conclusion, he argued that the horror of the murders should not be allowed to cloud the objectivity of the court in determining where the responsibility for the murders lay.

On 23 February Judge HP van Dyk, who had been sitting with two assessors, gave a detailed summation of all the evidence and then focused on the facts he and his assessors found to have been proven. With no eyewitnesses to the murders, all the evidence was circumstantial but, he said, it conclusively pointed to Skoularikis and Brenner acting in concert with each other and showed that they intended to kill. As for Brenner, Judge Van Dyk found that he had not taken the court fully into his confidence, that he was an unimpressive witness and that his evidence was so improbable as to border on the ridiculous. The court could therefore only conclude that Skoularikis and Brenner, and no one else, had committed the three murders.

In the legal system at the time, where there were no extenuating circumstances in a murder trial, the death penalty was automatic. It was therefore crucial for Wilfrid to argue in extenuation of sentence if he was to keep Skoularikis off death row. After the judge had found his client guilty, Wilfrid met with Skoularikis and explained that an obligation now rested on him to bring forward evidence to satisfy the court that there were extenuating circumstances. He also underlined that unless he testified to the court, it could find that there were no extenuating circumstances. Skoularikis told him that he did not wish to testify.

The following morning when Wilfrid arrived at the court, he had a great surprise. His client informed him that he was innocent and now wished to address the court. As the State and defence cases had been concluded the previous day, Wilfrid could only address the court on the situation that now presented itself to him. He had no idea what exactly his client wished to say but there were now apparently a great many things on his mind. This was an unusual situation and one not provided for in the Criminal Code. But after Wilfrid addressed the court, the judge agreed that Skoularikis could be sworn in and allowed to make his statement from the witness box.

What followed dumbfounded all present. Skoularikis launched

into an attack on the court's findings and the conclusions it had reached on the basis of the evidence presented by the State. Von Lieres immediately objected that Skoularikis should have challenged the State's version before closing his case. Given the seriousness of the matter, the judge allowed Skoularikis to continue and for over an hour he attacked each of the more than twenty State witnesses and alleged they were either mistaken or had lied outright. Only Ioannis Phakos, father of Costa, he said, had attempted to tell the truth. He argued that the case against him and Brenner had been prejudiced by police involvement as Brenner was being blackmailed by certain policemen and the police had planted evidence. He also alleged that he had been the victim of unfair treatment by the police. After he finished, Von Lieres once again objected to his statement and pointed out that the State was unable to cross-examine him on the matters he now alleged. Judge Van Dyk agreed and ruled that Skoularikis's statement was out of order, being irrelevant to the matter of extenuating circumstances, and ordered that it be struck from the record. As for Brenner, he chose not to introduce evidence in extenuation and neither called witnesses nor gave evidence himself.

Judge Van Dyk, finding that there were no extenuating circumstances, sentenced the two men to death. He did, however, give them leave to appeal. The case was heard by Appeal Judge JW Smalberger, who in his judgment said this: 'What precisely happened there we do not know, but the evidence, coupled with the first appellant's [Skoularikis's] failure to testify to rebut the strong prima facie case against him, can lead in my view to only one conclusion, viz that the first appellant was party to the killing of the three deceased.' A further appeal to reopen the case was also dismissed, and the two men were sent to jail to await their execution.

In 1989 the family submitted a 6,000-page petition to State President FW de Klerk, which was by all accounts ignored.

Then suddenly in September of that year, the two accused were reprieved from their death sentences. This precluded any further chance of having the case reopened. Although the issue disappeared from public interest, Skoularikis's sister lobbied various organisations behind the scenes, including Lawyers for Human Rights and the International Commission of Jurists, for almost a decade. A further submission was also made to the new Minister of Justice, Dullah Omar, at the end of 1994 when the country was now a democracy under President Mandela.

*

Wilfrid was always puzzled by this trial and the bizarre antics of his client. His file had little in it besides the appeal document, the findings of which were damning. In researching further information I found a small article dated 30 January 1990 from the *Weekend Argus* at the Institute of Contemporary History at the University of the Orange Free State. The article was titled 'Release of two convicts demanded' and told of a protest by the South African Prisoners Organisation for Human Rights outside the Transitional Executive Buildings in Andries Street, Pretoria. It seemed motivation to pursue other information avenues and an application to the Truth and Reconciliation Commission finally brought light to the benighted case.

The Skoularikis family had, it turned out, made a submission to the TRC on 14 November 1996. At first sight it did not seem to fall within the ambit of the TRC's scope and work, but as the case officer investigated further and read through the supporting documentation, it became clear that the case had indeed an extraordinary political aspect, involving the Civil Cooperation Bureau. The CCB had been a secret security operation under the command of the South African Defence Force, which mainly targeted civilians regarded as a threat to the apartheid state. The Skoularikis case was then referred to the TRC's investigative unit. Eventually, the unit obtained a statement from a CCB operative, Frederick Alec Harding, in which he admitted to the murder of Alfons Talpa and Pam and Costa Phakos.

From Harding's statement, it seems that Talpa was the real target of the shooting; the other members of the family were not meant to be there. Harding alleged that Talpa had been involved with some kind of covert funding of the ANC or its allies or the Committee of Ten, a prominent progressive civic organisation in Soweto. The involvement of Skoularikis and Brenner was unforeseen but with the assistance of the Murder and Robbery Squad, using fabricated evidence of the crime scene, the security forces were able to 'kill two birds with one stone', as Skoularikis was also thought to be involved in covert support for the ANC and the Skoularikis family were identified as communists. Skoularikis was also believed to be involved with the KGB. Before he was imprisoned, he was subjected to electric shock torture, suffocated and had his body held out of a moving car with his head touching the road in an effort to force him to confess to the murder of Talpa and the Phakoses. Harding confirmed that Brenner has been an informer for another CCB operative, possibly Bram Cilliers, who had approached Brenner to spy on Skoularikis. When Brenner failed to co-operate, he was shot by unknown assailants.

The TRC accepted that the evidence presented to them overwhelmingly confirmed that both Skoularikis and Brenner had been framed for the triple murder of Talpa and the Phakoses. Commissioner Yasmin Sooka wrote to Skoularikis on 19 November 1999, saying, 'your subsequent conviction, torture and ten years' imprisonment constitute a case of severe ill-treatment and a travesty of justice'.

All these startling revelations finally made clear what had been so puzzling and inexplicable to Wilfrid when he defended Skoularikis in court. The hidden hand of the State had at last been exposed.

NOTES:

[1] *International Maritime Fraud* by Eric Ellen and Donald Campbell (London, Sweet and Maxwell, 1981)

[2] *The Citizen*, 10 December 1983

[3] *Sunday Express*, 4 March 1984

[4] *Embargo: Apartheid's Oil Secrets Revealed* by Richard Hengeveld and Jaap Rodenburg (Amsterdam University Press, 1994) p. 184

[5] *The Observer*, 19 May 1985

[6] *Embargo: Apartheid's Oil Secrets Revealed* by Richard Hengeveld and Jaap Rodenburg (Amsterdam University Press, 1994) p. 284

CHAPTER 16

THE BENCH, THE DEATH PENALTY AND RETURN TO CAPE TOWN

Elevation to the Bench and time in the Eastern Cape

'I have never come across a person who was too bad to defend. I always remembered that the person in front of me was a human being and a product of society, a victim of circumstances over which he or she had no control.'

– WILFRID COOPER

Wilfrid's appointment to the Bench was long in coming. There is little doubt that his appearing at the inquests of anti-apartheid activists who had died while in detention and his repeated vociferous challenging of the State's version of events did him no favours; nor did his defence of those politically opposed to the government. Already in 1983 and 1985 Wilfrid had discussions with Judge President George Munnik about an acting appointment in South West Africa. Munnik had seen no reason for objections, but nothing ever came of it and others were appointed instead.

In October 1980 Kobie Coetsee was appointed minister of justice. Known for his progressive thinking, he became involved in the covert talks with the imprisoned Nelson Mandela that would ultimately lead to his release. Coetsee and Wilfrid met at a social occasion in 1988 and got on well. Coetsee appreciated the depth of Wilfrid's legal experience and knowledge, recognising that it was not only deserved but appropriate that he should be appointed to the Bench. As there were no vacancies in Cape Town, Coetsee appointed him from 1 August 1988 to an acting position in the Eastern Cape. On hearing the news, his colleague at the Cape Bar, Ian Farlam, wrote to him saying: 'I was extremely pleased to hear the news that a long-standing injustice is being put right. You will be pleased to know that the news was greeted with universal pleasure in the judges' tearoom in the OPD, Smuts JP[1] saying he had never been able to understand why you had for so long been passed over; not only are you, he said, a counsel of great ability, but a fine lawyer too.'

On 1 March 1989 his appointment was made permanent. At the time his friend, the attorney Fred Stander, expressed the view that 'We never thought you would glide from an acting position into a permanent appointment. We had, of course, no doubt what the eventual outcome would be but such a smooth transition was rather out of character with the rest of your career. Seriously, it was particularly for the way you handled the setbacks and difficulties which you had to face in that career and to some of which I was privy that we learnt to respect you. The fortitude, courage and industry which you have displayed throughout all the doubtful days constitute an inspiring example for us all. But there is one qualification which we are pleased to note: the success is not just yours alone, it is also Gertrude's. Her faith that you were destined for great things never wavered. To have married such a wife is the part of fortune that you did not forge yourself.'

While he relished being on the Bench, the period in the Eastern Cape was gruelling for Wilfrid, as he was away from his beloved Gertrude and Riverside. Not being particularly self-sufficient, he found it hard to fend for himself in his bachelor-like situation. He also had to make the transition from advocate to judge away from his supportive Cape Town colleagues. Moreover, many of the cases he heard were taxing, involving the violent slaying of people in the tumult of the Eastern Cape townships during the civil unrest of the 1980s.

In March 1989 he heard the case of two men, Nelson Nhinhi Boss and Mncedisi Boss, who in 1986, together with three accomplices, murdered an alleged AZAPO member, Themba Mtshiya, in KwaNobuhle township outside Uitenhage. Mtshiya had been kidnapped and his charred body was later found on the township's rubbish dump. As the two accused did not present evidence in extenuation of the circumstances of their crime, Wilfrid was faced with having to sentence the men to death. He came home for the weekend and agonised over the case. With regard to the three accomplices, there were extenuating circumstances and they received sentences of five years' imprisonment for the kidnapping and fifteen years for the murder. But the Bosses had not presented any extenuating circumstances and Wilfrid had no alternative but to deliver the death sentence.

Wilfrid had always been vigorously opposed to the death penalty. His view was that 'when you give the death penalty it is an admission of failure. You are a judicial killer.' This harked back to his underlying compassionate philosophy that 'I have never come across a person who was too bad to defend. I always remembered that the person in front of me was a human being and a product of society, a victim of circumstances over which he or she had no control. But I also believe the courts are there to maintain standards that lead to self-discipline in society.'[2]

On one visit home in October 1990 Wilfrid showed me police photographs from the trial over which he was then presiding: the victims had been incinerated with a 'necklace' – a tyre filled with petrol placed around the neck and then set alight. The two, Mzwandile Njokweni and Nkosiyabo Ndaliso, had been friends and comrades of four Queenstown Youth Organisation members who lived in Mlungisi township. They had been invited to play cards one Saturday afternoon, but after a while the group turned on them, suspecting that they were police informers. Njokweni and Ndaliso fled from the building into the street, where they were stoned and then necklaced, one while still alive. The picture of the charred human remains, the distorted horror captured in perpetuity, still haunts me and leads me to believe that Winnie Madikizela-Mandela either never saw the results of her exhortations or was impervious to such atrocity when she encouraged those gathered at Munsieville in April 1985 that 'with our boxes of matches and our necklaces we shall liberate this country'. Certainly, Wilfrid was at a loss as to how anyone could champion the killing of another human, let alone in such a horrendous manner, even if it were to fight for freedom from the yoke of apartheid. Throughout his career he saw the sheerest human brutality in his work, but it was a particularly heavy burden to bear as a judge, when the fate of the murderers lay in his hand.

In this case, while the accused showed no remorse in court and 'sought refuge in sullen silence' for the merciless killing of their friends, Wilfrid looked deep into the evidence. This revealed a hostile relationship between the police and the community of Mlungisi, which, coupled with the prevailing deprived socio-economic conditions, had created a volatile situation and a siege mentality. This mindset turned the slightest rumour of collaboration with the police into a conviction that the individuals were informers or '*impimpis*'. The crimes, Wilfrid ruled, had to be viewed in the context of this 'most regrettable atmosphere' in Mlungisi. 'The four accused were members of the deprived community and were subject to social pressures and caught up in escalating violence which led to the killings.'[3] He handed down effective sentences of four to twenty years' imprisonment.

These cases and the stress of being away from home took their toll on Wilfrid. In mid-1990 he wrote to Kobie Coetsee to say: 'I need hardly stress the effect of living alone in the Eastern Cape and being away from home most of the year has had on me as well as Gertrude, whose poor night vision has become a matter of particular concern to both of us.' Coetsee's understanding came to the fore again. Wilfrid was appointed to act in the Cape from 1 January 1991, with his permanent appointment effective from 1 March, and he returned to living below his beloved Table Mountain and Devil's Peak.

NOTES:

[1] FS Smuts, Judge President of the Orange Free State Provincial Division (OPD).

[2] *Cape Times*, 20 May 1996

[3] *Eastern Province Herald*, 20 October 1990

CHAPTER 17

EXPERIENCES IN THE PLATTELAND

Wilfrid's love of the platteland, nurtured in his childhood, which drew him to take up cases in small country towns

'The day we met in the hotel and wrote [the agreement], we planted a seed. The seed was not good seed. It was weed. But the doctor still harvested it, weed or not.'

– JOHANNES THERON

All his life Wilfrid retained a deep love for the South African *platteland*, which had first been implanted in him as a boy growing up in Klawer and Malmesbury. He had an affinity for country ways, for the wide, open spaces of the countryside; he felt at home here and most himself. Wilfrid seemed in his element in the countryside, where he enjoyed the conversation and camaraderie of the local farmers and townsfolk. Here he could relax, ignore the stresses of his profession and then return re-energised to his chambers in Cape Town. Not surprisingly, he always jumped at the chance to take up legal work in the small country towns of the Cape, which other advocates would readily turn down.

Upington was one of the places to which he regularly travelled for a variety of cases. Here he was often briefed by Piet Lange of the local firm Wahl, Lange & Carr. In one of his last trials there he defended a farmer from the Keimoes area, Johannes Theron, who had murdered Dr Andries Visser. The case, which was extensively covered by newspapers around the country, was dubbed the 'Sultana Murder'.

Theron, one of eight children, was born on his father's small farm – *Beeld* referred to it as *''n lappie aarde'* [a patch of ground] – called Malanshoek on the banks of the Orange River near Keimoes. He had worked as a labourer on the railways and for the Divisional Council until 1967, when he could afford to buy a section of the farm and in time the rest. Here he eked out a living growing sultana grapes, but went deeper and deeper into debt. In October 1980 he met Dr Andries Visser, a successful businessman with a doctorate in economics, who had been a senator and a member of the Economic Advisory Council, the Atomic Energy Board and the South African Wool Board. After a brief meeting, Visser agreed to assist Theron and take over his debt of about R52,000. Theron was awed by the benevolence shown by the great man. The day after they met he entered into an unusual agreement dictated by Visser and laboriously handwritten by Theron in the lounge of the Oranje Hotel. This stipulated that Theron would continue to work the land, for which he would be paid R250 per month, with the proceeds of the harvest going to Visser. The agreement also contained an 'option' for Visser to buy the farm.

Just under a year later, in September 1981, Visser informed Theron that he wished to take up the option on the farm. Theron, however, disputed this: in his understanding the farm had been collateral for a loan from Visser that he intended to pay back. The matter was taken to the Kimberley Supreme Court but Theron lost his action and he was ordered to cede the farm to Visser. This was the proverbial straw that broke the camel's back. The relationship between the two men soon deteriorated into a feud. On the night of 20 October, Theron drove to Malanshoek where Visser was staying to talk to him. A gunfight ensued in which Theron was wounded, while Visser was shot in the head with Theron's rifle and died.

When Theron came before the court on a charge of murder, local supporters packed the room, many of them having made a contribution to his defence costs. But the evidence against Theron was damning. In his final argument, Wilfrid submitted 'that Dr Visser never wanted a document drawn up with a lawyer. He was using his business know-how to cheat Mr Theron, a man of limited intelligence. The deception was a gradual process and once Mr Theron had come to the cruel realisation that he had lost his farm he became irrational and impulsive.' At the same time Wilfrid conceded that 'Mr Theron should have realised that there was a possibility of confrontation and shooting when he went to the house that night. He should be found guilty of culpable homicide with extenuating circumstances.'

But Judge Rudolf Erasmus and his two assessors did not interpret the evidence this way. He found that Theron had set out from Upington on the night of the murder and driven the forty kilometres with the intention of killing Visser. There were no extenuating circumstances. 'It was a night of horror, and if one looks at the photographs of the body of Dr Visser taken in the mortuary after the shooting one gets a clear idea of what happened in the farm house. One is left with abhorrence.' Theron was found guilty of murder and sentenced to death.

Before Judge Erasmus passed sentence he asked Theron, whose evidence during the trial had been full of religious overtones, if he had anything to say. 'The day we met in the hotel and wrote [the agreement] we planted a seed,' Theron told the court. 'The seed was not good seed. It was weed. But the doctor still harvested it, weed or not. That night [when the shooting occurred] there was Dr Visser, myself and the devil. God was at a distance.'

Wilfrid always put his all into his cases and the outcome of this trial left him despondent. He felt, as did the local community, that the sentence was out of proportion to what had transpired; that Judge Erasmus had, as Judge Beyers did with Marthinus Rossouw, technically abided by the law while not acknowledging the truth of Theron's circumstances. Wilfrid could relate to Theron: here was a man who had struggled all his life; his first two wives had both died after suffering asthma attacks, his farm had twice been devastated by floods, and during the trial he had lost his sister. Theron reminded him of some of the parents of the children he had played with in his youth in Klawer, poor whites who had likewise scratched a living from the harsh countryside of the Namaqualand. Wilfrid was firm in his contention that Visser had manipulated the situation and had taken advantage of this poor man of limited education to obtain his farm at below market value. This deprived Theron not only of his land but of the means to support his family and, more importantly, his dignity.

Wilfrid appealed against the judgment, offering a spirited argument in mitigation of Theron's death sentence, but it was to no avail. In February 1984 the Appeal Court Chief Justice PJ Rabie, sitting with Judges Joubert, Cillie, Smuts and Grosskopf, did not agree with the argument put forward by Wilfrid. Chief Justice Rabie found that Theron had set out from Upington on the night of the murder and driven the forty kilometres with the intention of killing Visser. There were no extenuating circumstances. 'It was a night of horror, and if one looks at the photographs of the body of Dr Visser taken in the mortuary after the shooting, one gets a clear idea of what happened in the farm house. One is left with abhorrence.'

The death sentence of the trial court was therefore upheld.

*

With Wilfrid's travels to Upington on business came excursions into the Kalahari with his friends Izak Strauss and Piet Lange. On his return home we children would be regaled with anecdotes of what had happened while he was away. He loved those trips, as they regularly involved hunting and, while never a particularly good shot – he used to say, '*Ek skiet swak maar ek jag lekker*' – he revelled in being out in the veld with his friends. The first or second evening after he arrived back home, there was a ritual cleaning of his rifle, a sporterised .303 Lee Enfield of First World War vintage. Later, a grateful client gave him a Sako .338 magnum rifle and eventually he bought on auction a beautiful double-barrel Greener shotgun. He guided me through the mechanics of cleaning the weapons, as well as the rules of safety before they were finally locked away to await their next call to duty. Every time I smell Young's 303 cleaning oil I have memories of these occasions. I also still have the brown Gladstone bag in which he kept his ammunition and ammunition belt.

While the cases he handled in the country were mostly of a serious nature, there were lighter moments. In *Bar, Bench and Bullshifters* Gerald Friedman and Jeremy Gauntlett relate the story about a damages case in the Worcester circuit court in which a motorist had driven into a herd of cattle, killing some of them, including a young bull weighing approximately 900lb (400kg).[1] Wilfrid appeared for the owner of the cattle, who was suing the driver. In cross-examination, he asked some questions.

Cooper: Did you see the cattle?
Driver: Yes.
Cooper: What did you do?
Driver: I reduced speed.
Cooper: A lot?
Driver: Oh yes, quite a lot.
Cooper: What speed do you think you were travelling at when you hit the cattle?
Driver: About 10 miles per hour.
Cooper: Can you explain then how, from the point of impact established by glass fragments, a 900-pound bull could have travelled a distance of 25 yards where it was found after the accident?
Driver: Well, the bull dropped onto my bonnet and I was so shocked that I accelerated and it travelled 25 yards on the bonnet until it fell off.

The presiding judge was the keen-witted Bobby Bloch, who quickly remarked, 'Oh, so you are a bullshifter as well.' Sadly, Wilfrid's files contain no further information on this case or on how the 'bullshifter' fared in the claim against him.

*

At the age of ten or eleven my interest in trout fishing, first fostered in the Liesbeek River, became intense and I would pester Wilfrid to take me to various rivers around the Western Cape. One of our regular haunts was Ceres, where I would fish the upper reaches of the Titus River, or the Dwars River, which runs through the town, for rainbow trout. We would also fish in farm dams for largemouth bass. Following an introduction to Malan Cilliers of the farm Forelle by Wilfrid's friend Paul van Zyl, an attorney in the village and later a senator, we got to know many of the farmers in the area. Over the years we spent numerous weekends enjoying their hospitality. Wilfrid developed a particularly strong friendship with the farm manager, Hannes 'Bal' Retief and his wife, Monika, on the farm Kweperfontein. It was there in the humble surroundings of their rather dilapidated dwelling that Wilfrid found he could be himself over a braai with a glass of inexpensive wine and lots of conversation. One of Wilfrid's weaknesses was *afval* (offal) and Monika would regularly prepare it for him, lightly curried. Away from the stresses and strains of his profession, Wilfrid would immerse himself in honest friendship. He would bring Bal a case of wine or a bottle of whisky and chocolates for Monika and we would return home with the car laden with vegetables and fruit. Wilfrid came close to tears when he learned of Bal's death in 1994.

Across the Ceres Valley, and at the opposite end of the social spectrum, was the smallholding Summer Haze belonging to friends of ours, Mike and Lynn Reid, which lay just outside Prince Alfred Hamlet. Mike was a businessman and Lynn an exceedingly glamorous and vivacious socialite from a wealthy background, who met Gertrude while she was in charge of the social pages for the *Cape Times*. Mike sometimes went to shoot Egyptian geese on the farm Houdenbek in the Kouebokkeveld area and, knowing Wilfrid's love for a shoot, he invited us on a number of outings there. On one occasion a bird Wilfrid hit landed some distance away from the bank of the dam where we were shooting and I had to strip down to play 'gun dog' and swim out to collect it. Luckily it was mid-December and the water was reasonably warm – unlike the occasion at Kweperfontein some years before when I had had to do the same thing in early

September with snow on the surrounding mountains.

In my travels with him in the *platteland*, I saw a side of Wilfrid that was not apparent in Cape Town. It struck me that he yearned to lead a simpler life among people with a sense of community, generosity, hospitality and warmth. I saw too how easily and fluently he communicated with country people in their own language and was amazed by his command of Afrikaans. His close friend, the writer Etienne van Heerden, who was Professor of Afrikaans at Rhodes University in Grahamstown while Wilfrid was on the Eastern Cape Bench, has said of him: 'It was clear that he worked hard, as the son of an engine driver on the *platteland*, to become a judge, a respected academic, and a great conversationalist. In many ways he would break the bounds of formality and snobbery, of language barriers and distance – and that was what I greatly liked about him. His world had little boundaries in that sense.'

NOTE:

[1] *Bar, Bench and Bullshifters, Cape Tales 1950–1990* by Gerald Friedman and Jeremy Gauntlett (comp.) (Cape Town, Syberink, 2013)

CHAPTER 18

THE FINAL YEARS AND WILFRID'S TREASURE

Return to Cape Town and the end
of a distinguished legal career

'Allow me … to convey to you the State's appreciation for
the valuable services you have rendered as a member of the
Bench … Your services have contributed to maintaining its
traditionally high standard of integrity and impartiality.'

– DULLAH OMAR

Both Wilfrid and Gertrude loved the eastern slopes of the mountain, particularly the forested areas between Kirstenbosch and Newlands under Devil's Peak. Wilfrid had got to know them well when he ran cross-country for his school and Gertrude when she would walk up to the tea room at Rhodes Memorial during her years at UCT. Throughout the year we would walk on the lower slopes in Newlands Forest, either as a family with the dogs or with friends, but always aware of the towering mountain rising behind. Wilfrid would also take off alone with the dogs on a Sunday morning and venture further up through Newlands Forest to the contour path, from where there were sweeping vistas across the Peninsula.

Wilfrid's return to Cape Town in 1991 was a great relief to the whole family. He took up his position at the Supreme Court and slowly settled down to a normal life. While he had been away in the Eastern Cape, Gertrude began to realise that their time at Riverside was coming to an end. She was then in her late sixties and maintaining a large garden; no matter how much she loved it, was starting to become too much for her. As the children had moved out and there were now just the two of them, they had to start planning for the future and move to a smaller and more manageable home. Wilfrid initially greeted the idea with great hostility but in time reconciled himself to the inevitable. Riverside was sold and they moved to Cabernet Circle in Constantia, where Gertrude created another wonderful home for the last years of their lives. The move could not have come at a more opportune time as, not too long after this, Wilfrid's health started to decline.

In his time on the Bench in the Cape, Wilfrid was kept busy with various criminal and civil trials. One was dubbed by the local press as 'The War of the Roses', being a prolonged squabble by two landowners about a house allegedly built in a nature reserve in contravention of an oral agreement. The case dragged on for weeks and, after an inspection *in loco*, Wilfrid came home and sagely remarked that, given the cumulative cost of the legal fees involved to the parties, the trial was no longer a question of who won but who did not lose.

In 1993 a young chartered accountant, Joel Miller, was involved in a motor accident that left him paralysed from the waist down. The claim by Miller against Santam insurance company came before Wilfrid. After a trial of three weeks he found for Miller and ordered that Santam pay him R6.75 million to cover all his future medical costs. Wilfrid was very emotional and wept when he described the great human tragedy that had occurred. Jeremy Gauntlett, who represented Miller, wrote to Wilfrid: 'We were all deeply moved by your words in court. Thank you for them, and your own role in making much possible for Joel.'

While on the Bench Wilfrid never lost his compassion towards those less fortunate in society. In the trial of 18-year-old Margaret Lesch of Elands Bay, who murdered her young baby, he showed his feeling for a penniless, exhausted and discouraged young woman who had been 'thrown away by her family'. Lesch told the court that the baby's father, Zilindile Kala, did not care for the baby and, with no support from her family, she had trouble looking after it. Wilfrid found the case tragic and sentenced her to three years, suspended for five years; he also ruled that she be placed under the supervision of a probation officer and report to the Elands Bay family planning clinic every six weeks. He told her: 'You are very young and scarcely a woman. I hope the rest of your life will be sweeter and that the next man in your life treats you with love and respect.'

*

A few years after his return to Cape Town, we started to notice that Wilfrid's ability to walk was deteriorating, writing was becoming more of a problem and he was not following conversations as easily. These symptoms were a cause of frustration to him. He went to see a highly regarded neurosurgeon and was diagnosed as having the onset of a form of hydrocephalus, in which there is too much cerebrospinal fluid pressing on the brain. In June 1997 a shunt was implanted to drain the excess fluid and it was hoped that this would improve his health. Unfortunately this did not happen and his gait continued to deteriorate. The walks through Constantia, which he used to enjoy, became shorter and eventually dwindled to nothing.

After much discussion with Gertrude, he reluctantly decided that there was no other option but to retire from the Bench. So in early December 1997 Wilfrid wrote to Dullah Omar, the Minister of Justice, to formally request that he might be discharged from service. Omar's reply was businesslike and confirmed that he should step down from 1 February 1998: 'Allow me, at the same time, to convey to you the State's appreciation for the valuable services you have rendered as a member of the Bench in the Republic. The Judiciary is a source of pride to all South Africans. Your services have contributed to maintaining its traditionally high standard of integrity and impartiality.'

The last judgment that Wilfrid worked on was an appeal from the Magistrate's Court against a conviction for the attempted theft of a bicycle at his old university residence, Dagbreek. The matter was close to his heart as in his first year, when he was once late for a lecture, he noticed a woman's bicycle standing unattended. As there was no owner in sight, he decided to borrow it and pedalled off furiously, reaching the lecture just in time. Afterwards he found that the bicycle was still standing outside the lecture room and, with no owner in sight, he continued to use it for about a week. Then one morning a young woman student approached him and said, '*Meneer, kan ek my fiets terug kry?* [Sir, can I have my bicycle back?]' With equal courtesy he returned it to her and had to be content with walking to and from lectures once again.

*

After her own retirement from the *Cape Times*, Gertrude had been working part-time for a PR company run by a friend. She stayed there for ten years, sharing her extensive skills with a younger generation who fondly, and much to the annoyance of Wilfrid, called her Gertie. It was a life she relished, but in 1998, as Wilfrid's health declined, she selflessly stopped so that she could be at home with him.

She was exceedingly fit and healthy all her life and it therefore was a shock to all when in June 2001 she was found to have lung cancer, which had already spread into many parts of her body. Ironically, the type of cancer she was diagnosed with is associated with smoking. As she was a committed non-smoker all her life, this could have only come from the *Cape Times* newsroom where the journos of the time were incessant smokers. After getting over the initial blow, in her inimitable style she threw herself into the last lap of her life, tying up her affairs to ensure that we children would not be burdened with them after her death. This determination in fact resulted in her earlier demise. One afternoon when in the loft above the garage, sorting through old clothes to give to charity, she fell through the ceiling and cracked her pelvis and a vertebra. She was taken to Constantiaberg Medi-Clinic, where she stayed for a night or two, but despite being in great pain, she discharged herself and came home to the sanctuary of Cabernet Circle. The end came a few weeks later, on the evening of 17 April 2002.

My sister Susan had made the trip out from Ottawa, and she had helped look after our mother for a number of days without a break. On Gertrude's urging, she agreed to take the night off so that I could take her to Harbour House in Kalk Bay for a meal. It was a lovely evening at one of my mother's favourite places and we walked to the end of the pier and enjoyed the stars, the lights around False Bay and the gentle swell against the breakwater wall. When we came home we found Wilfrid lying on his side in the bedroom facing away from Gertrude, unmoving. I have never been sure if he was fully cognitive of what had just happened or whether he had retreated even further within himself so as to protect himself from the reality that his beloved 'Skattie' – his treasure – was now gone.

Wilfrid's own end came two years later: he died on the morning of 4 March 2004 after suffering a fatal heart attack. The Tiger had come to rest at the age of 77.

As is the tradition when a judge dies, his legal colleagues gathered a week later at the Cape High Court to pay tribute to him. Susan and I were invited to attend and we met the Judge President, John Hlope, in his chambers before entering Court 1, where he acknowledged Wilfrid's accomplishments as an advocate, judge, writer and academic. Those who attended included retired Chief Justice Michael Corbett and former Cape Judge President Edwin 'Sharky' King, who had been his junior in the Rabkin trial, as well as many from the Bar. The Directorate of Public Prosecutions was represented by Advocate Billy Downer, who enlivened the otherwise sombre occasion by remembering Wilfrid for being the character he was and recalling that in afternoon sessions he sometimes dozed off on the Bench after a good lunch and had to be gently prompted back into action by his assessors.

We chose two places dear to my parents' hearts to commemorate their passing: Kirstenbosch Botanical Gardens, where they had been members for almost thirty years, for their memorial services and False Bay to scatter their ashes. For the latter ceremony we chose the concrete walkway between Bailey's Cottage and Muizenberg Corner, where we as children used to play and swim in the sea.

From time to time I go down there to walk along the path and enjoy the fresh breeze off the sea. I often reflect on my parents while I am there and take pride that I was their son and that

I had them as parents. I have wondered if they had conducted their lives differently, possibly taking an easier path by leaving South Africa, as many did at the time, where it would have taken them and the family. I am convinced, however, that they would not have had it any other way. Wilfrid, the Tiger, was born to enter the legal arena of South Africa at a time when his values regarding his fellow man and his skills as an advocate mattered in opposing the injustices of those years. Though it often seemed a Sisyphean task during the dark decades of apartheid, Wilfrid was one of the few who ensured that the voices of those who could not speak out were heard. When we children were young, he and Gertrude had debated whether or not to leave South Africa in search of greener pastures overseas, as many of their friends were doing. They chose not to because their love of South Africa, and specifically the Cape, was strong. They also believed they could make a difference in what was a bleak time.

Gertrude stood by Wilfrid's side over the decades and with her strengths bolstered his weaknesses. Together they left their mark in Cape Town and South Africa.

THE ENIGMA OF DEMITRIO TSAFENDAS

Notes on the sanity of Verwoerd's assassin, after fifty years of hindsight and investigation

'A madman, or a man with a mission?'

– DAVID BERESFORD

While Wilfrid was satisfied with the outcome of the hearing into the sanity of Demitrio Tsafendas, it rankled him for the rest of his career that Judge Beyers had stopped him from cross-examining the State psychiatrist, Professor Van Wyk. Why had the man who at a preliminary meeting so confidently stated that he would prove Tsafendas was sane and fit to stand trial finally agreed with the defence's witnesses and their contrary view at the eleventh hour? Van Wyk was also the key State expert witness whose testimony had seen the Johannesburg station bomber, John Harris, found guilty and condemned to death. Did the State wish to send out a message that the wish to do away with Dr Verwoerd, 'the architect of apartheid', could only be the work of a lone madman and not have any real, rational, popular cause or foundation? Or was there even some other agenda?

Whether Tsafendas was mad when he committed the murder will perhaps never be known, but that he was no longer of sound mind at the end of his life is certainly true. Unlike the white, affluent David Pratt, who had tried to kill Verwoerd in 1960, Tsafendas was not committed to a mental hospital. Instead, after a brief time on Robben Island he was imprisoned in a cell in Section C – death row – of Pretoria Central Prison, where he remained until 1989. In isolating him so, the State was able to ensure he was virtually inaccessible to anyone outside the system. In November 1999 the journalist David Beresford wrote an article in the *Mail & Guardian* entitled 'The madness of Demitrio Tsafendas', in which he told of Tsafendas's abuse and suffering at the hands of his warders. They were alleged to have made a practice of urinating in his food and beating him up while he was restrained in a straitjacket. Tsafendas was also subjected to the weekly proceedings in death row when fellow prisoners went to the gallows: the singing, the crying and the thump as they took the drop. The sounds left Tsafendas, on occasion, 'like a dog howling its primordial fears at the moon'[1]. This account was largely borne out by Breyten Breytenbach, who was held in the same jail in the late 1970s. He also spoke of the abuse that the guards inflicted on Tsafendas as some form of 'ongoing sport' to torment him[2].

Interestingly, Tsafendas's incarceration in Pretoria Central was in conflict with the recommendations of the Van Wyk Commission, which was appointed to inquire into Verwoerd's death shortly after the assassination. The commission accepted that Tsafendas 'was not normally mental' and concluded: 'It is desirable that every person who requires treatment for a mental disorder should receive such treatment, and that every person who is a danger to others on account of some mental disorder should be detained in an institution where escape is impossible, and where the staff and other inmates can be afforded the necessary protection.'[3] The law also stated that state president's patients fell under the department of health and should only be kept in prison where the department did not have the appropriate facilities[4]. It was, however, only in 1994 that Tsafendas, at the age of 79, was finally sent to Sterkfontein Mental Hospital outside Krugersdorp. While still institutionalised, he was technically free after 31 years of being held at the State's pleasure.

Reports of Tsafendas's ill-treatment under the apartheid regime did surface from time to time, causing the government great embarrassment. In August 1976 an escaped prisoner, Brian Price, sold a story to *The Observer* in London in which he alleged that Tsafendas was 'treated with gross inhumanity and was a broken man'. Price added that he knew four other people living in England who could substantiate his story. To counter this, the government called in the services of the journalist and former BOSS agent, Gordon Winter, to write a series of three exclusive interview articles on Tsafendas. Interestingly these appeared in the state-owned newspaper *The Citizen* on 20, 21 and 22 October 1976, exactly ten years after Judge Beyers found Tsafendas to be insane. The photographs accompanying the articles showed a trim man – while only 58 he was noted to be 'extremely fit for his age' – talking to warders, polishing his shoes and enjoying a large private exercise area. Winter reported that Tsafendas had no complaints about his treatment and that he had regular visits by prison doctors and outside specialists, with 21 visits having been made in 1976 alone. He also noted that one of Pretoria's 'prominent medical men' had stated, 'The patient is well orientated, coherent, fit and in good spirits, but he continues to talk obsessively about the tapeworm inside him.'

Disingenuously, The Citizen editorial of 1 November 1976 noted that 'The Citizen is not a party to this dispute, nor has the one issue anything to do with the other. The Observer printed harsh allegations; The Citizen was able to refute them conclusively.' The newspaper also noted that Price was paid R300 by The Observer for his story – evidently he was desperate for money, having stowed away on the Windsor Castle to flee South Africa – which was most likely an attempt to cast aspersions on his claims.

Winter published a further article in The Citizen on 26 October 1976, an interview with the South African intelligence chief General HJ van den Bergh. Van den Bergh said that he had started 'quizzing' Tsafendas almost immediately after the murder of Dr Verwoerd. 'I sat talking to him the whole evening and right through the night,' he explained. 'I can tell you that no-one in South Africa history has ever been interrogated as much as Demitrios Tsafendas.' The next morning, Van den Bergh personally reported to Minister of Justice BJ Vorster that in his opinion Tsafendas was quite clearly mentally deranged. Van den Bergh 'continued his personal investigation and spent many days talking to Tsafendas,' according to Winter. 'All the findings confirmed that he was a totally irresponsible and demented man.'

What is the importance of Van den Bergh in this affair? Van den Bergh and Vorster had been members of the Ossewabrandwag together in the 1930s and '40s and were then members of the secret Afrikaner organisation, the Broerderbond. Van den Bergh was known to be a staunch supporter of Vorster and it is surmised by author Peter Lambley that he had been awaiting an opportunity to enable Vorster to seize power from Verwoerd. In his book The Psychology of Apartheid, published in 1980, Lambley wrote that his 'informants believe that Van den Berg let Tsafendas continue in his job in parliament, well aware of his demented plans, not in the firm hope that he would act but as one of several loose and vague possibilities and fantasies which Van den Bergh entertained ... On the other hand, there are people who believe that the whole thing was arranged from beginning to end by Vorster and Van den Bergh.'[5]

Much later, in an interview with Liza Key for her 1999 documentary, A Question of Madness: The Furiosus, Winter admits that he was tasked by General Van den Bergh to 'do a clean-up' after the appearance of the embrassing reports in The Observer of Tsafendas's mistreatment. Winter then makes an astonishing claim to Key: 'I don't believe that Tsafendas is mad. I believe that Tsafendas invented his madness in the form of a tapeworm because it is something you cannot prove.' Winter contends that Tsafendas had learned to 'play' the psychiatrists and tell them what they wanted to hear. Tsafendas had told him how, from his encounters overseas with numerous psychiatrists, he had learnt how to invent answers to their questions to fit into the psychiatric category they already felt he belonged to.

Winter was not alone in his views. Also in the Liza Key documentary, one of the defence witnesses in the Tsafendas hearing, Pat O'Ryan, explains that when the defence team came to interview him before the trial they told him to emphasise the tapeworm in his testimony, as it would help to get Tsafendas free. This is in contradiction O'Ryan's testimony of 33 years before. In 1966 he told Judge Beyers that the police had instructed him to omit the worm from his statement. In his interview with Key, however, he ignores this and chooses rather to emphasise that when 'the three gentlemen ... Cooper and them', came to interview him they told him, 'when you speak about it just mention the worm, and the worm, and the worm; just mention the worm'. They apparently then told him that by his emphasising the worm in his testimony they would be able to get Tsafendas free. Throughout the Key interview O'Ryan's wife Louisa sits next to him looking disconsolate. Possibly she recalled her husband's testimony better than he because the court record does not support this emphasis of the worm as related for the camera.

This view also has the support of the writer Terry Bell. In his book *Unfinished Business: South Africa, Apartheid and Truth*,[6] Bell sheds additional light on the matter of Tsafendas's sanity. After being arrested, he narrates, Tsafendas was interrogated at length by a number of high-ranking police officers, including General Van den Bergh.

Bell had sight, but for one night only, of the transcripts of the interrogation of Tsafendas, which have never been made public. These revealed that the story of Tsafendas's tapeworm and its central role in his life was largely a myth. There was only a single reference to the tapeworm in the transcripts and that was made in passing. The reason Tsafendas gave to Van den Bergh for his killing of Verwoerd was 'because I didn't agree with him'. It appears that Van den Bergh was 'more interested in knowing if Tsafendas had discussed the killing with anyone else' and whether Tsafendas knew that Verwoerd was going to make an important speech to Parliament on the afternoon he was killed. Had it been then that he decided to murder Verwoerd before he could deliver the speech?[7] Bell wrote further that in 1999 a 'senior detective from Europe' studied the transcripts and found 'that this was a very strange interrogation', which left more questions to be answered than before.

In fact, Bell's theory had already been adumbrated to some extent by the report of the Van Wyk Commission of inquiry into Verwoerd's assassination, which was published in December 1966. The report described Tsafendas as unscrupulous and crafty and claimed that his actions were born of 'a cunning plan to make use of his power to destroy the head of Government which he hated'. Although Tsafendas had stated to the Commission that he acted on impulse before the assault, the report concluded that this did not tally with the facts. From his statement to the Commission, it certainly appears that Tsafendas had been fixated on the idea of murdering Verwoerd for some time. He told the Commission, 'I was so disgusted with the racial policy that I went through with my plans to kill the Prime Minister.'[8]

Buried in Winter's third article in *The Citizen* of 1976 was this additional piece of revealing information: 'The best-kept secret in the amazing life of Dr Verwoerd's assassin, Demitrio Tsafendas, is the fact that he was once a card-carrying member of the South African Communist Party.' Winter reported Tsafendas as saying, 'I have always feared my membership of the CP would be twisted and distorted by people who wanted to believe I killed Dr Verwoerd for political reasons.'[9] The communist angle was then highlighted in the Van den Bergh interview under the banner 'Tsafendas was ineffective Red'. Here Van den Berg espoused that Tsafendas was a communist in Johannesburg in the late 1930s, though 'he was completely ineffective as a member'. His statement to the police in 1966, however, states that 'I am politically inclined but I do not belong to any political party. I like to read what goes on. I deny that I am a communist. I am a Christian and believe in the Bible.'[10]

In researching this book, I received corroboration for the view that Tsafendas was sane when he assassinated Verwoerd from Harris Dousemetzis, a Greek-born PhD candidate at the School of Government and International Affairs at Durham University in England. He has spent ten years researching the life of Demitrio Tsafendas and found conclusive evidence, he believes, that Tsafendas was not mad. From numerous interviews he has conducted on the matter, he discovered that Tsafendas learnt how to fool medical authorities by pretending he had a tapeworm while in an American institution. It appears he copied the ploy from a man by the name of Tom, a missionary/ preacher who also introduced him to a Christian sect. Having been found to be faking mental illness at one hospital, Tsafendas then used the tapeworm story at the next, most likely Grafton State Hospital in Massachusetts in 1946.

Dousemetzis also spoke to Tsafendas's stepsisters, who expressed surprise at the tapeworm story and denied it was true. The tapeworm, as Gordon Winter had explained to Liza Key, appears now to have been a ruse by Tsafendas used to great effect: it became the foundation upon which Wilfrid and his team built their defence of him. Tsafendas confided this to Pat O'Ryan and two priests, Fathers Minas and Ioanis, who visited him in prison and at Sterkfontein. Dousemetzis also mentioned that he had found that Tsafendas was more politically aware and active as a communist than had previously been known.

The revelations of Terry Bell, Gordon Winter, Liza Key and Harris Dousemetzis point to a different Tsafendas; not the man Wilfrid met in the Caledon Square Police Station, an inert shape on the floor of a cell who over a number of days told him a story of travelling the world and having been haunted by a tapeworm from age 16. Did Tsafendas create a myth around the tapeworm that my father then made use of to prevent him from being executed? Did he fool the team of eminent defence psychologists? Of this I cannot be sure, but I do know that Wilfrid would have leveraged any scrap of advantageous evidence and, using all his skills, would have mounted the best defence he could to save Tsafendas from the death penalty.

Of course, there are many who would refute the theory that Tsafendas avoided the gallows by playing the authorities for fools. One of those would surely be Henk van Woerden, who made a pilgrimage from his home in the Netherlands in 1997 to spend time with Tsafendas at Sterkfontein. The award-winning book *Een Mond Vol Glas*, emerged from their meetings over several days, catapulting Tsafendas back to the attention of the world. At their last meeting Tsafendas placed the blame for his predicament on the doctors who refused to operate on him and remove the creature. 'It will not die,' he lamented. 'I'm helpless against the Dragon-Tapeworm. I cannot do anything. But they won't investigate. Too difficult and very complicated. At night when I sleep I see orgies. All imaginations. Visions.'[11]

*

Demitrio Tsafendas died of pneumonia in the Sterkfontein Mental Hospital on 7 October 1999 at the age of 81, almost exactly 33 years after he was charged with the murder of Hendrik Verwoerd. Usually at the funeral of a person of political relevance in South Africa there are keynote addresses made by prominent speakers who give lengthy biographical details of the deceased. This was not the case with Tsafendas, and in fact every attempt was made by the government of the day – now led by the African National Congress, the party that had liberated South Africa from apartheid rule – to keep his death and funeral under wraps. On Saturday 10 October Tsafendas was buried in the Aghios Andreas (St Andrew's) Greek Orthodox Church in Krugersdorp. The service was conducted by Priest Dimitrios Zergitsis, though there were few mourners. While discouraged by officials, Pat and Louise O'Ryan flew up from Cape Town at a few hours' notice to attend; Aron Mabe of the PAC and Gagi Mohane of the ANC attended in their private capacity. Tsafendas's two sisters did not attend. Liza Key sent a large wreath of white lilies and ensured that a plaque went onto the coffin:

Dimitri Tsafendas 1918-1999
Displaced Person, Sailor, Christian, Communist, Liberation Fighter,
Political Prisoner, Hero
Remembered By His Friends [12]

The *Mail & Guardian* published what was probably the only obituary of him. It concluded as follows: 'Last Saturday he was buried quietly in Krugersdorp. Ten people, mostly pious members of the Greek community, were in attendance. The politicians, and the humble victims of apartheid for whom he had struck the most awesome blow in the fight for freedom, chose to stay away.'

So ended the life of Demitrio Tsafendas, incarcerated for longer than the longest of apartheid's political prisoners and probably under more inhumane conditions than any of them were forced to endure. Incarcerated without rights in a maximum security no-man's land, he was recognised not as a mental patient, as was the case with David Pratt; not as a political prisoner, as with those convicted at the Rivonia trial; and not as a criminal prisoner who would later be granted amnesty, such as Robert McBride, the Magoo's Bar bomber who killed three and wounded 69 in June 1986. His had been a life of torment and isolation: shunned by his family at an early age, rejected by societies across the world, imprisoned by the apartheid state for assassinating its icon, and ultimately forgotten in death.

*

In October 2013, almost on the 47th anniversary of the hearing into Tsafendas's sanity, an Eastern Cape MPL, Christian Martin, wrote to the National Heritage Council (NHC) requesting that the graves of Tsafendas and Verwoerd be declared heritage sites. 'Dimitri Tsafendas and Hendrik Verwoerd changed the course of post-war South African history more than any other, when Tsafendas stabbed to death the "architect of apartheid",' he wrote.[13] It was Martin's opinion that homage should be bestowed upon Tsafendas, a hero and martyr for the cause of the South African people.[14] The NHC rejected the request stating that 'it is important to realise that history and heritage are not the same thing'.

In life Tsafendas was seen as neither black nor white; Judge Beyers saw him as a 'meaningless creature'. He was not recognised as being a freedom fighter because his actions were deemed personal not political, and the court found him to be mad. Helen Suzman said of the murder of Verwoerd, 'I thought we were rid of one of the worst scourges we had.' She had no doubt that Verwoerd's death profoundly affected the course of South African history and set it on a path to democratic elections in 1994. But besides Martin's attempt to memorialise Tsafendas, there appears to have been little effort made by the current government to remember him, and the major post-apartheid histories of the ANC barely mention him in passing. Nelson Mandela's *Long Walk to Freedom* has only one reference to Tsafendas as 'the obscure white parliamentary messenger who stabbed Verwoerd to death, and we wondered at his motives'.[15] In the Thabo Mbeki-inspired *The Road to Democracy*, a history commissioned to address 'the paucity of historical records chronicling the arduous and complex road to South Africa's peaceful political settlement' there is scant reference to Tsafendas; it merely refers to Verwoerd's assassination by 'an official messenger, Dimitriou (sic) Tsafendas'.[16]

A review of the fate of Tsafendas does, to my mind, invite the question why it is that the actions of the slayer of the 'architect of apartheid', who was incarcerated for decades in a manner that can only be seen as a gross violation of human rights, were never investigated in detail by the Truth and Reconciliation Commission. Why was Tsafendas relegated to a mere contextual reference on Page 19 of Volume 3? Was it that the TRC took heed of Chief Justice MM Corbett's words: 'Tsafendas was brought to trial and on overwhelming medical evidence declared by the Court to be mentally disordered and therefore unfit to plead. The suggestion that the case should be "reviewed and investigated" is, with respect, pointless and absurd. To view him as a "victim of apartheid" is, in my opinion, bizarre.'[17] Did they wish to avoid having to investigate what is common currency that he was insane? Or was it that they wished to avoid a Gordian knot: that Verwoerd was possibly the victim of a political murder, the act being camouflaged by the plea – and convincing behaviour – of insanity?

In my research into my father's life, and particularly into this key individual in both his career and the historical trajectory of South Africa, I have found the contemporary perspective on Demitrio Tsafendas to be nothing less than an enigma. I was perplexed when I read in two works by an eminent history professor that his name was inscribed on The Wall of Names at Freedom Park outside Pretoria – and then found this to be apparently untrue. The Wall was erected under the presidency of Thabo Mbeki as a poignant tribute to the many lives lost in various global conflicts in which South Africans have fought, including the liberation struggle [18]; to me it would make sense to include Tsafendas in this roll call. When visiting The Wall prior to the publication of *Under Devil's Peak*, my wife and I spent more than an hour searching in vain for the name of Tsafendas. The chief curator of the park, Victor Netshiavha, confirmed his absence, though he couldn't immediately check his database due to a system failure. Several days later I received an email from the park's research manager, Tlou Makhura:

'Our records indicate that the name Dimitrio Tsafendas was submitted to Freedom Park, together with 44 others, on a list titled "Deaths in Pretoria Central Prison", [in] September 2011. The name, together with 44 others, was verified by the Names Verification Committee (NVC) at a workshop held on 28 September 2011. The NVC resolved that the name, together with 44 others, did not have enough biographical information to enable the process of verification and approval for inscription on the Wall of Names at Freedom Park. The entire list of 45 names, including the name of Dimitrio Tsafendas, was deferred to subsequent names verification workshops, with the proviso that further research to provide fuller biographies of the 45 names be conducted before the re-submission of the list.'

So it seems there are others who consider it appropriate that the name of Verwoerd's assassin take its place, carved in stone, alongside those of Steve Biko, Mapetla Mohapi, Imam Haron and the many others who gave their lives in the low-intensity war that was the struggle against apartheid. That he is considered someone who died 'in Pretoria Central Prison' when he in fact died while institutionalised at Sterkfontein Mental Hospital, and that the Names Verification Committee considers the biographical information available on him lacking, are two further curiosities to add to the enigmatic, history-changing life of Demitrio Tsafendas. Though his status in contemporary history remains in limbo, what is certain is that he assassinated the architect of apartheid, the only South African prime minister to have died in such a manner.

For the final words on the matter here, I defer to the acclaimed journalist David Beresford, who wrote extensively on Tsafendas and sadly died the month before the publication of this book:

'During that 1966 hearing on the sanity of Tsafendas there was a particularly piquant exchange between his counsel and Mr Justice Beyers. The Judge President asked: "Did the accused tell you that history will judge whether he was right in killing the deceased?" Dr Cooper SC replied: "I do remember him saying something to the effect that history will prove whether he is right, or wrong." A madman, or a man with a mission? Perhaps Mary Shelley came closest to summing up the life of Tsafendas, with the words she put in the mouth of Frankenstein's monster: "Am I to be thought the only criminal, when all humankind sinned against me?"[19]

NOTES:

[1] *The True Confessions of an Albino Terrorist* by Breyten Breytenbach (Taurus, Emmarentia, 1984), p. 209

[2] *A Question of Madness: The Furiosus*, Liza Key, South Africa (DVD, 1999)

[3] Report of the Commission of Enquiry into the Circumstances of the Death of the Late Dr the Honourable Hendrik Frensch Verwoerd, December 1966, RP 16/1976, Chapter 3, paragraph 2; Chapter 10, paragraph 20.

[4] Dissertation Zuleiga Adams (University of the Western Cape, 2011), p. 100

[5] *The Psychology of Apartheid* by Peter Lambley (The University of Georgia Press, Athens Georgia 1980), p. 237

[6] *Unfinished Business: South Africa, Apartheid and Truth* by Terry Bell (London, Verso, 2003), p. 57

[7] Verwoerd had met with Chief Leabua Jonathan, Prime Minister of Lesotho. This was the first time Verwoerd had met with the prime minister of an independent African state, so his report to the House was much anticipated. In his statement to the police Tsafendas said that the meeting with Chief Jonathan was a contributing factor in his decision to murder Verwoerd. It was also expected Verwoerd's address would expand on the policy of separate development.

[8] In Tsafendas's statement to the police at para 36 he stated that no one incited him to murder the prime minister but that he was 'dissatisfied about the existent racial laws in South Africa'. He was also frustrated that he 'was unable to mix with the class (financial) to which I belong'. He was classified as a white person and wanted, as he could not get himself a European wife, to marry a coloured woman, Helen Daniels. He applied for reclassification in 1965 and wanted a 'blank' identity card, which was given to him but was later taken back.

[9] *The Citizen*, 22 October 1976

[10] Paragraphs 33 and 44

[11] *Een Mond Vol Glas* was translated into English as *A Mouthful of Glass* by Dan Jacobs in 2000 and was awarded the prestigious Alan Paton Award, an annual prize for the best non-fiction book in South Africa, the following year. Two years later Van Woerden received the French Kellendonk Prize for his entire oeuvre. The quote is from *A Mouthful of Glass* by Henk Van Woerden, translated by Dan Jacobson (Jonathan Ball, 2000), p. 155.

[12] *A Mouthful of Glass* by Henk van Woerden (Jonathan Ball, 2000)

[13] www.timeslive.co.za/politics/2013/10/22/tsafendas-verwoerd-grave-requests-rejected

[14] www.iol.co.za/news/politics/make-verwoerd-grave-a-heritage-site-1595473

[15] *Long Walk to Freedom* by Nelson Mandela (MacDonald-Purnell 1994), p. 417. In fairness to Mandela, this is related when he was still labouring in the lime quarry on Robben Island when they heard of Verwoerd's death.

[16] *The Road to Democracy in South Africa*, Vol 1 (1960-1970), p. 43

[17] Chief Justice MM Corbett's letter to TRC dated 27 November 1997.

[18] Built at a cost of more than R700 million and opened on 27 April 2004 by President Thabo Mbeki, Freedom Park is situated on Salvokop, one of the two hills that guards the south-western approach to Pretoria. It is the most expensive of the Legacy Heritage projects championed by President Thabo Mbeki in terms of the National Heritage Resources Act No. 25 of 1999. According to its website www.freedompark.co.za, 'Freedom Park is a cultural institution housing a museum and a memorial dedicated to chronicling and honouring the many who contributed to South Africa's liberation ... The Wall of Names is a poignant tribute to the many lives lost in the numerous conflicts that have taken place on South African soil, from pre-colonial wars to the South African War (Anglo Boer War), World War I, World War II, and the liberation struggle. The 697m-long wall is inscribed with the names of those who played a role in these conflicts.' The wall is a contentious edifice; it includes the names of the Cuban soldiers who died in Angola during the Border War but not the nearly 2,000 members of the SADF who died during the same conflict; their names are recorded at the SADF Memorial Wall at Fort Klapperkop on the hill opposite Salvokop.

[19] 'The madness of Demitrio Tsafendas' by David Beresford *Mail & Guardian*, 30 October 1997

BIBLIOGRAPHY

BOOKS:

The Amazing Case of the Baron von Schauroth by Benjamin Bennett
(Howard Timmins, 1966)

Asking for Trouble by Donald Woods (Penguin, 1987)

Bar, Bench & Bullshifters by Gerald Friedman & Jeremy Gauntlet (SiberInk, 2013)

The Bethal Trial Story by Class of '76 (Class of '76, 2011)

Black South Africa and the Disinvestment Dilemma by Jack Brian Bloom
(Jonathan Ball Publishers, 1986)

Biko by Donald Woods (Paddington Press, 1978)

Biko: A Biography by Xolela Mangcu (Tafelberg, 2012)

Brushes with the Law by Marius Diemond (Human & Rousseau, 1995)

The Cape Times by Gerald Shaw (David Philip, 1999)

The Devils are Among Us by Denis Herbstein & John Enson (Zed Books Inc, 1989)

Eugene de Kock by Anemari Jansen (Tafelberg, 2015)

External Mission by Stephen Ellis (Jonathan Ball Publishers, 2012)

Historical Dictionary of Namibia by Victor Tonchi, William A Lindeke,
John H Grotpeter (Scarecrow Press, 2012)

A History of Resistance in Namibia by Peter H Katjavivi (African World Press, 1990)

Human Rights and the South African Legal Order by John Dugard (Princeton
University Press, 1978)

Inside Quatro by Paul Trewhela (Jacana, 2009)

International Maritime Fraud by Eric Ellen & Donald Campbell
(Sweet & Maxwell, 1981)

Justice Denied by David Klatzow (Zebra Press, 2014)

The Killing of the Imam by Barney Desai & Cardiff Marney (Imam Abdullah Haron
Education Trust, 1978)

The Last Afrikaner Leaders by Herman Giliomee (Tafelberg, 2012)

Law, Life & Laughter Encore by Ellison Kahn (Juta & Co, 1999)

A Mouthful of Glass by Henk van Woerden (Jonathan Ball Publishers, 1998)

Murder by Consent by Henry John May (Hutchinson of London, 1968)

My Times by David Bloomberg (Fernwood Press, 2007)

Namibia, the Violent Heritage by David Soggot (Rex Collings, 1986)

OB by George Cloete Visser (Cape & Transvaal Printers, 1976)

Political Trial: Gordian Knots in Law by Ron Christenson
(Tranaction Publishers, 1999)

The Psychology of Apartheid by Peter Lambley (University of Georgia Press, 1980)

Reconciliation Discourse: The Case of the Truth and Reconciliation Commission
by Annelies Verdoolaege (Benjamins Publishing Co, 2008)

The Road to Democracy Vol 1 and 2 by South African Democracy Education Trust
(Unisa Press, 2004)

South Africa's 'Border War': Contested Narratives and Conflitcing Memories
by Gary Baines (Bloomsbury, 2013)

Stephanie on Trial by Albie Sachs (Harwill Press, 1968)

The Super Afrikaners - Inside the Broederbond by Ivor Wilkins & Hans Strydom
(Jonathan Ball Publishers, 1978)

The True Confessions of an Albino Terrorist by Breyten Breytenbach (Taurus, 1984)

Unfinished Business: South Africa, Apartheid and Truth by Terry Bell (Verso, 2003)

Verwoerd is Dead by Jan Botha (Books of Africa, 1967)

The Villages of the Liesbeeck by Helen Robinson (Houghton House, 2011)

Was Justice Done? by Benjamin Bennett (Howard Timmins, 1975)

ARTICLES/ PAPERS:

'Amnesty International Briefing: Namibia' by Amnesty International (London, 1977)

'The Black Sash' (1970)

'Demitrios Tsafendas: Race, Madness and the Archive' by Zuleiga Adams
(University of Western Cape, 2011)

'Exile History: An Ethnography of the SWAPO Camps and the Namibian Nation'
by Christian A Williams (University of Michigan, 2009)

'Grim Nambian Portent' by Edward May (Lutheran World Ministries, 1975)

'Preliminary Notes of the Swakopmund Trial: The State vs Aaron Mushimba and
Five others' by Ralston Deffenbaugh Jr (Swakopmund, 1976)

'South African Medical Journal' (1977)

'A Study of Detention and Torture in South Africa' by Don Foster & Diane
Sandler (University of Cape Town, 1985)

'Testament of a Namibian Woman' by Rauna Nambinga (Episcopal Churchmen
for South Africa, 1981)

'Who Killed Clemens Kapuuo' by Jan-Bart Gewald (African Studies Centre, University of Leiden, 2004)

NEWSPAPERS:
The Cape Times, Cape Town
The Cape Argus, Cape Town
The Citizen, Johannesburg
Diamond Fields Adveritsing, Kimberley
Die Burger, Cape Town
Rapport, Johannesburg
The Sunday Times, Johannesburg
The Times, Johannesburg
The Windhoek Advertiser, Windhoek

WEBSITES:
African Activist Archive: www.africanactivist.msu.edu
All Africa: www.allafrica.com
The Archival Platform: www.archivalplatform.org
Bushwar Books: www.warbooks.co.za
Daily Maverick: www.dailymaverick.co.za
Department of Justice: www.justice.gov.za
Dispatch Live: www.dispatchlive.co.za
Famous South African Crimes: www.african-mystery.co.za
Ground Up: www.groundup.org.za
The Guardian: www.theguardian.com
Harfield Village: www.harfield-village.co.za
The Huffington Post: www.huffingtonpost.com
Independent: www.independent.co.uk
IOL: www.iol.co.za
LitNet: www.litnet.co.za
Magnus Gunther Collection: www.paton.ukzn.ac.za
Mail & Guardian: www.mg.co.za
The Namibian: www.namibian.com
Namrights: www.nshr.org.za

The New Statesman: www.newstatesman.com

The New York Times: www.nytimes.com

The O'Malley Archives: www.nelsonmandela.org

Politicsweb: www.politicsweb.co.za

South African History Online: www.sahistory.org.za

The South African Rock Encyclopedia: www.rock.co.za

Storm Chasing South Africa: www.stormchasing.co.za

SWAPO: www.swapoparty.org

Times Live: www.timeslive.co.za

Wikileaks: www.wikileaks.org

Wikipedia: www.wikipedia.org

Wikispooks: www.wikispooks.com

ACKNOWLEDGEMENTS

The Chinese philosopher Laozi said that a journey of a thousand miles begins with a single step, and on the journey you will encounter people who assist, inspire and direct you and who make it into the experience you will remember it to be. This certainly has been my experience in writing this book, and this is my attempt to acknowledge and thank all those who I have encountered along the way.

The first mention goes to Amanda Botha who provided the foreword and has been part of this project since she first assisted my father years ago. This is followed by author Penny Busetto who, over many cups of coffee, offered practical advice and guided me in what appeared at times to be an insurmountable task for an inexperienced writer. Once the words were pages and pages chapters, Daphne Endersby took on the task of reviewing what I had and turning it into a manuscript. Later Russell Martin used his well-honed editor's scalpel to shape the book itself.

In researching the many and varied aspects of my father's life, two people offered particular assistance and motivation for two key chapters: Harris Dousemetzis, who shared with me much information that immeasurably enhanced the chapters on Demitrio Tsafendas, and Colin du Preez who, despite poor health, was an invaluable source for the Swakopmund trial. Colin's efforts here encouraged me to ensure that this chapter was as accurate as it could be; his earlier efforts and sacrifices behind the scenes of the trial itself ensured that the defence won the day and justice was ultimately achieved.

I also thank Peter Pickup, friend and attorney of many years, who gave generously of his time to discuss, debate and offer his opinion on various legal aspects that arose.

There are many others who assisted in so many ways; to name a few: Karlien Breedt, Tamra Capstick-Dale, John Clayton,

Michaela Clayton, Ralston Deffenbaugh, Etienne du Plessis, Graham Freeling, Gerald Friedman, Pamela Lewin, Joanne McGilvray, Charlie Lewis, Celeste Munnitz, Victor Netshiavha, Hugh Rowles, Andre Sales, Farid Sayed, Oliver Trevor, Anthony Trew, Etienne van Heerden, Hesma van Tonder, Neil Veitch and Dillon Woods

This project would not have been possible without the assistance, advice and guidance of Tim Richman at Burnet Media, who I am sure still regrets offering an open invitation to Bishops old boys to approach him if they wanted to produce a book! Without Tim's patience and the diligence of his team – with a mention to Liz Sarant as well – this book would not have been produced.

Finally, thank you to my wife Maureen for her support, encouragement and patience over the past ten years through the ebbs and flows of the project.

INDEX

Haron, Abdullah
(see Haron, Imam
Abdullah)
Haron, Imam Abdullah
14, 135, 141, 142, 291,
296, *picture insert 1*
Harris, John 81, 82,
87, 95, 97, 107,
108, 280
Harwood KC, Attorney
General Ted 163, 220
Hattingh, Warrant
Officer GA 214, 216
Hawking, Dr RB 144
Helman, Dr Percy 140
Hengeveld, Richard 256
Henning, Dr PH 110
Henry, William 20
Hlope, Judge President
John 277
Hoffman, Jacob
'Kombuis' 43,
picture insert 1
Huis Dagbreek 30
Hurst, Professor LA 107
Inzadi, Angelo 171
Iten, Markus 173
Jacobson, Dan 293
Jennett, Justice 240
John Murray House 30
Joubert, Elsa 11, 72
Joyce, James 11, 16, 22,
29, 37, 74
Jubelin, Mr 154, 155
Kahn, EJ 'Jack' 116,
119, 296
Kala, Zilindile 274
Kallos, Mr A 111
Kebble, Brett 53, 54, 64
Kebble, Ingrid 54
Kemp, Robert 14, 226,

Kemp, Stephanie 77,
81- 88, 90, 92, 93, 94,
95, 97, 98, 138, 139,
227, *picture insert 1*
Kennedy, President John
F 100, 116, 127
Kennedy, Robert F 100
Kentridge, Advocate
Sydney 89, 98, 130, 246
Key, Liza 283, 284, 286,
287, 293
Kies, Ben 136, 154, 227,
picture insert 2
King, Judge President
Edwin 277
Klawer 19-25, 27, 31, 71,
236, 264, 266
Knobel, Dr Gideon 148
Kossew, Dr Ralph 117,
119
Kotze, ML 238
Kruger, Jimmy 134
Kuhn, JSP 137, 142
Kuny, Advocate Denis
213, 215, 216
Lamprecht, Brigadier
MC 227
Lange, Piet 264, 267
Larkin, Clare 39
Le Riche, Peter 55
Le Riche, Talita Cumi 55
Leftwich, Adrian 80-84,
86, 87, 89, 91-95, 97, 98
Lehnberg, Marlene 14,
157, 158, 160, 161,
163- 169, *picture insert 2*
Lesch, Margaret 274
Lewin, Hugh 50, 81, 301
Lourens, Oom Schalk 241
MacGregor, Dr James
'Jim' 105, 116, 120

MacLean, Alistair 74
Madiba (see Mandela,
Nelson)
Madikizela-Mandela,
Winnie 260
Madisha, Donald
Thabela 134
Mahomed SC, Ismail 165
Mail & Guardian 280,
288, 294, 298
Malan, Dr DF 41
Malmesbury 19, 23,
24, 26, 27, 59, 82,
238, 264
Mamasela, Joe 234
Mandela, Nelson
(Madiba) 79, 83, 88, 97,
128, 212, 222, 254, 258,
289, 294
Matthee, Attorney
Jeff 250
Matthews, Norman 43
May QC, Henry John 66
Mbeki, Govan 79
Mbeki, Thabo 289, 290,
294,
McBain, Ed 74
McGurk, Nigel 53
McSpadden, J Walker
155
Melamet, Judge DA 246,
248
Mendelow QC,
Aaron 63
Mene, Lawrence 230
Menssink, Willem 69
Miller, Joel 274
Mitchell, Michael
Lloyd 26
MK (see Umkhonto
we Sizwe)

WWW.BURNETMEDIA.CO.ZA